PORSCHE

Boxster & Cayman

THE 981 SERIES 2012 TO 2016

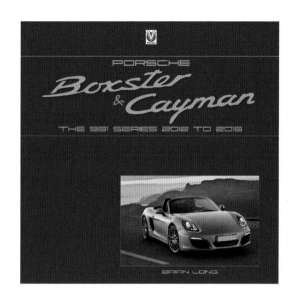

BRIAN LONG

More great books from Veloce

www.veloce.co.uk

First published in April 2023 by Veloce Publishing Limited, Veloce House, Parkway Farm Business Park, Middle Farm Way, Poundbury, Dorchester DT1 3AR, England. Tel +44 (0)1305 260068 / Fax 01305 250479 / e-mail info@veloce.co.uk / web www.veloce.co.uk or www.velocebooks.com.
ISBN: 978-1-787117-93-8; UPC: 6-36847-01793-4.

PORSCHE
Boxster
& Cayman
THE 981 SERIES 2012 TO 2016

BRIAN LONG

Contents

Introduction & Acknowledgements...5

Chapter 1 Boxster & Cayman heritage 7

Chapter 2 Birth of a new generation 20

Chapter 3 The new Cayman arrives 82

Chapter 4 Expanding the range...118

Chapter 5 End of the line..138

Appendix I Year-by-year range details 179

Appendix II Engine specifications 181

Appendix III Chassis numbers 183

Appendix IV Sales & production figures...185

Index 192

Introduction & Acknowledgements

Introduction

Strictly speaking, the Type 981 project spawned the third-generation Boxster and second-generation Cayman, although a few people class the face-lifts as another version, so there are some strange press releases out there, with plenty of articles to match in this copy-paste era we live in.

The first of the 981 breed was the 2.7-litre Boxster and 3.4-litre Boxster S, launched in the spring of 2012. The Cayman sister cars duly followed at the end of the year, with the same flat-six engines but a fraction more power, while the sportier GTS grade added to both

lines in 2014. Next up was the 3.8-litre Cayman GT4 and Boxster Spyder, but the release of the 'Black Edition' in 2015 signalled the traditional end of the line. Indeed, the first of the 718s that replaced these various models made its debut in the early part of 2016.

The 981 series models may not have stayed in the showrooms for long, but they certainly deserve their place in history, as, apart from being attractive to look at and good to drive, they were the last of the Boxster and Cayman lines to be fitted with a six-cylinder engine across the board – only a limited number of special-interest cars would come with a flat-six in the next generation.

Acknowledgements

The first Boxster title Veloce and I teamed up for was released in 2005. This was duly updated and released as a pure 986 series title a decade later, when the decision was made to produce a sister title on the 987s, including the Cayman – a car that I've always harboured a soft spot for. This volume on the 981s continues the series.

Help has come from many sources, as always, but I have to thank Jens Torner at Porsche first and foremost. As I've said before, I'm always grateful for his effort on my behalf, and proud to be able to call him a friend. Others that need to be mentioned are Dieter Gross at Porsche, Family Garage and K3 Works (now Nobel Co Limited) in Chiba, Kenichi Kobayashi at Miki Press, and the Japan Motor Industry Federation library in Tokyo.

I sincerely hope that you enjoy this book, produced during the COVID-19 era, making the endeavours of all those involved that much more admirable …

Brian Long
Chiba City, Japan

Chapter 1
Boxster & Cayman heritage

Before moving on to the main subject of this book – the 981 series models – it is worth taking a brief look at the birth and evolution of their predecessors to help put things into perspective. Here is the story of the 986 and 987 lines.

The Porsche Boxster's journey from concept car to production model was hardly plain sailing, coming in fits and starts, but once established, the open two-seater quickly became a highly-successful line for the Stuttgart manufacturer.

The first glimpse of the Boxster came in January 1993, when Porsche displayed a styling concept model on its stand at the Detroit Show. This move was made at a time when the Type 964 911 was about to give way to the 993 series, the 968 provided entry-level Porsche motoring, and the 928 was still the flagship Grand Tourer.

However, both the four-cylinder car and the big V8 were slated for the axe in the very near future, while the air-cooled 911 had just about reached the limit of its development.

As it happens, a small, lightweight two-seater had been looked into during the eighties, but lessons learnt from the 914 and 924 meant that any new car had to be 100 per cent Porsche if it was to gain universal approval from a finicky clientele. With exchange rates moving in the wrong direction, the strength of the Deutsch mark finally made the project unviable – to see any kind of profit would have meant a selling price far higher than the market would stand, which ultimately meant going upmarket, as luxury car buyers tend to have a more flexible budget.

Concept and reappraisal

It's fair to say that the Boxster concept had the press and public in raptures. When Dr Wendelin Wiedeking (Porsche's Chairman following the departure of Arno Bohn at the end of 1992), design chief Harm Lagaay, and Fred Schwab (PCNA's boss) pulled back the sheet covering the vehicle at the Detroit Show, there

Grant Larson with the 1993 Boxster concept car he designed, photographed at an event held at the Porsche Museum in Stuttgart.

was a resounding approval that seemed to go on for months. As is so often the case, this turned out to be both a blessing and a curse.

Naturally, the good publicity is always welcomed, but the production car would actually be quite different, not only in appearance, but size as well. Looked at logically the changes made a lot of sense, for the very survival of the company hung on the success of the mid-engined Boxster (given the Type 986 moniker) and the new water-cooled 911 (the rear-engined 996) that was waiting in the wings. As the only two vehicle lines that would carry the Porsche torch into the start of the 21st century, they had to be right technically, and also yield a decent profit to justify the expense of creating machines that would send the Stuttgart maker into what was basically uncharted territory.

With Wiedeking coming from a production background, his specialist knowledge was a great asset at this time, and he knew the only way to turn around recent losses was to become more efficient. Ease of construction and speeding up the build process would be one area to focus on, with cost reduction being another.

The use of shared components and common platforms (even the floorpan pressing alone) can save a fortune in development and tooling costs. As such, a large number of manufacturers have employed this money-saving technique from the very earliest days of the automotive industry. And then we come to Porsche, with the four- and eight-cylinder water-cooled cars of the 1980s sharing not much more than the badge on the nose, and the air-cooled 911 pretty much unique in every respect, as well as being incredibly labour-intensive to build.

If the 996 and 986 were to succeed they needed to share as many parts as possible, and this dictated the use of a slightly larger body. In the end, around 40 per cent of components were interchangeable, allowing Porsche to keep the price of the MR two-seater realistic, which was naturally a crucial part of the long-term business plan.

In reality, a lot of the fuss made in the press came about because the Boxster was actually larger all-round than the contemporary normally-aspirated 911, despite the latter being a 2+2! Of course, the planners had every right to expect that the cheaper car was the one that would garner volume sales, so the two-seater was launched a year ahead of the 996, otherwise this anomaly would not have come to light – the Type 996 911s were a fair bit longer, and duly shared a lot of the same nose structure.

Cutaway drawing of a 986 Boxster, showing the open two-seater's layout and packaging, with the flat-six mounted just behind the driver. Luggage space was provided in the tail (above the transmission) and ahead of the spare wheel up front.

The first generation

One has to remember that, during the Boxster's gestation period, thanks to the staggering success of the Mazda MX-5, there was something of an open car boom – the BMW Z-series and Mercedes-Benz SLK threatening to steal the Porsche's thunder. To maintain interest in the Stuttgart machine (Porsche's first 'middy' since the 914), the factory released some press material at the 1996 Geneva Show, and began placing adverts in newspapers and enthusiast publications.

These measures kept those sitting on the fence from falling into the BMW or Mercedes camps, for at least the styling and power-unit selection became clear. It was the final pricing, performance figures and driving feel that would be a deciding factor for many after that, so the stalling tactics were certainly helpful, making many wait for comparisons to emerge before placing their order for a German roadster.

The styling, as per the Detroit show car, drew heavily on the lines of the company's famous racers of the 1950s and 1960s, albeit to a lesser extent. Indeed, several magazines were quick to point out that lines on the showroom model were rather bland compared to the curves and latent aggression found in the concept. Nonetheless, it remained an open two-seater with a high-quality power-operated cloth top, with the mid-engined layout providing ample luggage space for weekend trips at both ends of the vehicle. The interior was modern, pointing the way forward for the 996 series, and far more ergonomic than the contemporary 993, if one ignores the myriad of small buttons on the centre console.

One of the first production cars on press photography duty.

Power was provided by the water-cooled M96/20 engine – a 2480cc version of the 3.4-litre flat-six destined to power the new Type 996 911s, and easily able to pass the noise and emission regulations that were starting to cause problems for the air-cooled units. The five-speed manual gearbox was based on VW-Audi parts, while the five-speed Tiptronic transmission was sourced from ZF. The front suspension was basically the same as that of the forthcoming 996 (duly launched at the 1997 Frankfurt Show), with coil springs over MacPherson struts, alloy lower control arms, and an anti-roll bar. The rear end was unique to the Boxster, but much the same as the front end, with the addition of track rods and a V-shaped metal brace bar. Steering was provided by a power-assisted rack, with braking via discs on all four corners; ABS was standard, along with 16in alloy wheels, although many opted for the 17in rims that were available as an extra.

When the Boxster finally made its official debut at the Paris Salon in October 1996, the flood of deposits picked up, to the point that more than 10,000 firm orders had been placed by the time deliveries began in early 1997. As well as an optional hardtop, there was a Classic Package and Sport Package available to transform the cockpit. In time, the option list would grow and grow, with things like body kits and new wheels added, meaning virtually every car leaving the line was a one-off.

The US market received the Boxster in January 1997, introduced at $39,980, with the same 204bhp (201bhp SAE) engine being employed. Other export markets followed the same pattern, although the popularity of the two-seater soon put a strain on the Stuttgart-Zuffenhausen production facilities. Working two shifts, six days a week (with a third shift in certain areas), simply couldn't keep pace with demand, especially with the new 911 coming online as well. With further expansion of the Porsche factory being out of the question, from September 1997 the majority of Boxster production was shipped out to Valmet Automotive in Finland, using replica lines and a selection of German staff members to ensure consistent quality, regardless of where the car was built.

Although the Porsche world was saddened by the death of Ferry Porsche, the company's founder, at the end of March 1998, he could rest in peace in the knowledge that the firm bearing his name was on the road to recovery with a completely new model range – one that was modern, appealing, and also profitable. A few days later, the last air-cooled 911 rolled off the line, bringing another era to an end.

More power

Rumours of a more powerful Boxster had been around ever since the car first broke cover, but, despite complaints from some quarters that a few extra horses wouldn't go amiss, sales were so strong, the addition of a hotter unit was deemed unnecessary until the autumn of 1999, when the Boxster line as a whole was overhauled.

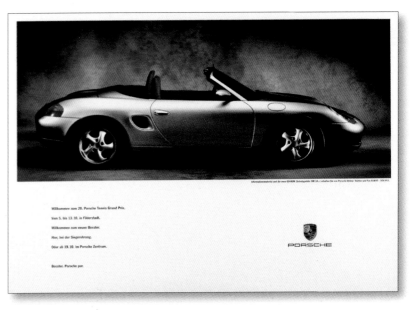

Domestic advertising from 1997.

An early car with the optional hardtop.

For the 2000 season, Porsche's engineers gave the two-seater a host of minor interior improvements to raise quality feel, and replaced the 2.5-litre six with a 2.7-litre version on the base car, giving buyers an extra 16bhp to play with. They also added a 3179cc version of the M96 unit to create the 252bhp Boxster S, which came with a six-speed manual or five-speed Tiptronic gearbox, uprated brakes, and a larger 17in wheel and tyre combination as standard.

While a lot of activity surrounded the launch of the new Cayenne SUV, the Boxster was not allowed to fade into the background. Indeed, for the 2003 Model Year, an updated version of the Variocam system was added to the engine specification, providing the 2.7-litre engine with 228bhp, and the 3.2-litre lump with 260bhp. The upgrade was accompanied by new wheel designs on the Boxster S, while both cars received fresh front and rear bumper mouldings, revised lighting units, and new intake grilles aft of the doors. There were also a few interior modifications, and the inclusion of a glass screen in the hood, complete with a heater element.

Valmet built its 100,000th Boxster at the end of August 2003, but time was running out for the first-generation cars. The model went out with a bang, thanks to a limited edition designed to celebrate the 50th anniversary of the 550 Spyder, but not long after, at the 2004 Paris Salon, the 987 series Boxster was destined to make its debut alongside the latest incarnation of the 911. In all, 164,874

Announced at the 1999 Frankfurt Show, the Boxster S was readily distinguished from its lesser brethren by the more aggressive air intake arrangement up front, the twin exhausts (still exiting in the centre of the valance), and different badging at the back.

Type 986 Boxsters were built, with 109,213 of them being produced in Finland.

The second generation

Announced at the end of 2004, the second-generation Boxster (Type 987) followed Porsche's usual policy of placing measured evolution ahead of radical revisions. As such, it took a dedicated follower of Stuttgart lore to realise they were looking at something quite new. The other interesting development was the concurrent creation of a fresh mid-engined coupé line based on the latest Boxster, but more on that later.

While the final rubber stamp was down to head of styling

A face-lifted version of the Boxster S from the 2003 season, with a base version in the background fitted with a hardtop.

One of the last 2.7-litre Type 986 Boxsters photographed in a garage at the R&D centre in Weissach.

Harm Lagaay, the job of overseeing the 987's revamp was given to Grant Larson, the ex-Audi man who was responsible for designing the Detroit Show concept as well as playing a leading role in the final shape of the production version of the original Boxster. In reality, there were few people better qualified for the exercise, especially considering the brief called for only minor revisions aimed at making the existing lines tauter and more masculine – after all, there is little point in changing what was obviously a successful formula.

The headlights were the biggest distinguishing feature, the 987 losing the signature 'runny egg' units in favour of more rounded projection beam headlights separated from the other lights, which were duly integrated into the stronger air dam design. Around the sides there were heavier wheelarch flares (to allow for a bigger standard wheel and tyre combination) and a larger intake grille aft of the doors, while the main change at the back came via the design of the rear combination lamps and a redesigned pop-up spoiler.

The exterior changes may have been subtle, but one didn't need to be a Porsche expert to spot the revisions made to the interior. While the concept was clearly carried over, with a T-shaped dashboard and hefty transmission tunnel, the rounded edges of the original cars gave way to altogether sharper lines in almost all of the design elements. In step with the modern era, and actually well ahead of it in this case, safety was also improved, with no less than six airbags incorporated into the cockpit. Another sign of the times was a new option called the Sport Chrono Package – a gadget to enhance engine performance and tighten the suspension settings at the push of a button, with a dash-mounted stopwatch showing the world it was fitted.

The layout and powertrain components were basically carried over from the 986. This meant the continued use of 2.7- and 3.2-litre M96 flat-sixes placed longitudinally behind the seats, and a transmission unit tacked onto the back. Thanks to a series of small revisions power was up, though, quoted at 240bhp DIN for the 2687cc unit and 280bhp for the 3179cc one. The base car came with an improved 5MT, while the S grade had a Getrag six-speed manual gearbox; both models could be specified with a five-speed Tiptronic S transmission for those who preferred two-pedal driving.

The Type 987 Boxster S at speed. The new car was still instantly recognisable as a Boxster, but had obviously bulked up its muscles during its transformation into the second-generation model.

The chassis components were also familiar – the all-round independent suspension being a polished version of that used on the 986 models. However, Porsche Stability Management (PSM) was now a standard fitment, helping to maintain traction and stability, with a PASM active suspension available as an option. The ABS braking system was suitably uprated, with the ceramic disc setup (PCCB) available as an option on the S grade. The base Boxster now came on 17in rims, with the S riding on 18in rubber.

The 987 Boxster duly made its debut in September

Tail of an early 2.7-litre Type 987 Boxster.

2004 at the Paris Salon, with the Exclusive catalogue augmenting an already extensive option list. Although domestic prices started at €43,068 for the home market, very few Boxsters – if any – would have left showrooms at that amount!

As with the 986 Boxster, many of the new cars were ultimately built by Valmet in Finland, as the level of demand for the latest 997-type 911 was restricting production space in Stuttgart. Other than the availability of yet more options, though, things went quiet on the Boxster front for a while, as the 2005 Frankfurt Show witnessed the debut of an all-new Porsche.

Along came a Cayman …

With the 987 Boxster safely delivered to the marketplace, it was time to launch the sister model – the Cayman coupé. At €58,529, the Cayman S was the first of this shapely line, employing 51 per cent of its parts from the 911, and another 29 per cent sourced from the contemporary Boxster. The other 20 per cent was largely made up of the parts that gave the tin-top model its unique appearance, including a fresh front air dam, a new roof structure with the glass and rear hatch incorporated into it, revised rear wing panels, a redesigned rear

bumper assembly (and spoiler unit above it), and a new 18in alloy wheel design.

The M97/21 engine employed in the Cayman S featured Porsche's Variocam Plus mechanism, endowing the 3387cc flat-six with 295bhp – an incredible amount for a normally-aspirated lump of such a relatively small displacement. Anyway, the power-unit was hooked up to either a 6MT or Tiptronic S gearbox, the shift sitting in a cockpit that was ultimately very similar to that of the new Boxsters.

With Porsche and Volkswagen company politics never far from the media's gaze, at least enthusiasts were able to rejoice in the arrival of the base Cayman in time for the 2007 season, powered by a 2.7-litre version of the M97 lump, and delivering a healthy 245bhp and 201lbft of torque. It was offered with a five-speed manual gearbox or the Tiptronic S unit, and rode on 17in rubber.

The Boxsters duly adopted the more powerful M97 power-units for the 2007 MY, while later in the year, Porsche released the Cayman S-based 'Porsche Design Edition 1' model. This was followed soon after by the Boxster RS60 Spyder, with the Americans also getting a 'Limited Edition' convertible, setting the tone for the future, with short run specials helping to boost sales. Indeed, some of the last 987.1

The striking lines of the new Cayman S (rear view overleaf).

Interior of an early Cayman S, which was much the same as that of the contemporary Boxsters. The more shapely shroud over the instrument binnacle was a feature on the closed cars only, though.

On the styling front, the face-lifted 987 models were given new headlights, a fresh front bumper assembly (with different intakes and grilles), revised rear LED light units, diffuser sections in the rear apron, and new alloy wheels. Inside, the steering wheel designs were modernised, as were the HVAC controls, and the optional PCM unit was vastly improved.

Another Boxster model was introduced at the 2009 Los Angeles Show – the Spyder. This fifth 987 variant ditched the power hood in favour of a two-piece manually-operated one, sitting low down on shorter side windows to hook into a brand new aluminium rear lid that featured dual cowls, aping those of earlier Porsche sports racers. Other weight-saving measures and the 320bhp engine from the Cayman S ensured that this was a pretty rapid machine, by any standards. Indeed, official figures stated it would dismiss the 0-60 dash in under five seconds, while the top speed was put in the region of 165mph (264km/h).

The Cayman range received another grade after this, with the lightweight Cayman R taking a bow in November 2010 to become a sixth catalogue model in the 987 line-up. This had a 330bhp version of the 3.4-litre flat-six, and, combined with a 1295kg (2849lb) kerb weight, made it quicker than even the Boxster Spyder.

The 2.7-litre Cayman arrived in time for the 2007 season, thus completing the basic Type 987 four-car line-up

cars were the 500-off 'Porsche Design Edition 2' based on the Boxster S, and the Cayman S Sport, limited to 700 vehicles.

A 987 swansong

The 997 had been given a face-lift in the summer of 2008, with a new line of MA1 six-cylinder engines and exotic transmission options. Not surprisingly, these latest drivetrains found another application in the updated 987.2 Boxster and Cayman models, which duly made their debut at the 2008 Los Angeles Show.

Base models went up to 2892cc, and developed 255bhp in the Boxster or 265bhp for the Cayman. With regard to the S grades, these now came with a 3436cc displacement, and punched out 310bhp in the open car, or 320bhp in the Cayman. A six-speed manual gearbox was made standard across the board, with a light and responsive seven-speed PDK unit replacing the Tiptronic S option.

The Boxster RS60 Spyder pictured with its namesake from a rather different era ...

One of the face-lifted Boxsters, this being a 2.9-litre car.

companies, like Mazda, for instance, set a specific target of X amount of previous sales (the X being 70 per cent in Mazda's case). If this can be achieved, a newcomer is allowed to hit the market, and if not, it's back to the drawing board to try something different.

Bearing this in mind, the 79,039 Type 987 Boxsters built may only represent about half of the number recorded against the 986 version (164,874 units in total), but add in more than 60,000 Caymans (with many of those moved being conquest sales), and Porsche's investment in the mid-engined line would certainly appear to have been well judged. Take the blip in global sales

The 'Black Edition' limited run models brought the series to a stylish end. But was the 987 range a success? Most manufacturers are resigned to a new generation not performing as well in the showrooms as its immediate predecessor – it's taken as read. Indeed, some caused by the Lehman Shock into account as well, and one can safely say that the Boxster and Cayman pairing was a success story, more than worthy of a place alongside the legendary 911, the Panamera, and the Cayenne SUV ...

The face-lifted Cayman models that were introduced at the 2008 LA Show. The red car is a 2.9-litre, while the green vehicle is an S grade machine.

The impressive lines of the Boxster Spyder, with its dual cowls on its rear lid resembling those of the racers of yore, or the short-lived Carrera GT supercar for that matter, which was sold in limited numbers until production came to an end in May 2006.

A Cayman R about to find a new home ...

Chapter 2

Birth of a new generation

"**Better than its predecessor in almost every way, [the new Boxster] is an astonishingly well-rounded sports car. More refined than before, but just as focused.**" – *Autocar*, **March 2012.**

The launch of the 981 series gave us the third-generation Boxster initially, which would duly go on to provide the basis for the second-generation Cayman, just as it had spawned the original coupé during the 987 series run. This chapter, therefore, looks at the creation of the new line via the open car, and follows the Boxster's first steps into the marketplace …

The third-generation Boxster at the time of its launch, featuring contemporary Porsche design language and a whole host of technical innovations.

The concept

The open car boom had just about finished, with the Honda S2000 and Toyota MR-S (aka MR2) falling by the wayside without replacements being fielded. BMW Z4 sales that had peaked at 20,000 units a year in the States were now hovering at around one-tenth that number, and Alfa Romeo gave up on the affordable Spider in favour of an upmarket mid-engined version and a Mazda MX-5-based Fiat in the future. While said Mazda was still selling well enough in NC guise, and old favourites like the Mercedes SL and SLK were proudly hanging on, the fact is that a stylish vehicle having a rag-top was no longer enough to guarantee sales – a car had to offer something special in terms of appeal, and with Porsche, that meant a superior driving experience.

There are many ways one can create a driver's machine, but when most of the elements are already in place, one of the few avenues of development left open to the engineers is cutting excess bulk. It has to be said, though, reducing weight from one generation to the next is never easy nowadays, with evolving safety requirements calling for extra this and extra that on a regular basis. Adding power is a quick way to overcome this, but more horses means uprating drivetrain components, braking systems and so on, so the advantage is far from clear-cut in the balance. Customers, too, have become used to convenience features that used to be options (or even deemed unnecessary in pure driving machines), all of which add bulk, and without doing something significant to cut weight in other areas, before you know it, there's a lot of extra poundage to carry around – poundage that works against good fuel economy and emissions, which is another thing to factor in, as a 'green' image is a must for any modern company.

Porsche had another part of this difficult conundrum to consider, and that was keeping the policy of progressive styling. As such, there was no possibility of taking a clean piece of paper to solve the problem, as Tadashi Nakagawa did with the Toyota MR-S, for example, for continuity was a trait associated with the Stuttgart maker, with the instantly recognisable silhouette of the 911 being a case in point.

Broadly speaking, it wasn't only open cars, but sports cars in general that were falling on hard times in the post-Lehman Shock era. If one looks at US sales during the spring of 2011, for instance, the Panamera outsold the 911 range, while the 911 easily outsold the Boxster and Cayman combined. More telling, though, the Cayenne SUV accounted for more sales than all three RR and MR sports car lines put together.

It was against this difficult background that Jan Roth, in his role as Project Manager, and the team gathered behind him, had to come up with something desirable that would reverse current trends, and help keep open cars in the spotlight ...

Heavily involved with the 987 series, Jan Roth was appointed Project Manager for the mid-engined sports car line-up. Having joined Porsche in October 1996, his work on the 981 Boxsters and Caymans was obviously appreciated, as he was selected to stay in this position for the 718 project later on.

Exterior styling

While Michael Mauer, in his role as head of styling at Porsche since the summer of 2004, was the man responsible for giving the final nod on the styling, it was Hugh Robinson that did the design work that was ultimately carried forward to production status. Educated in Industrial Design at Coventry University (still known as the Lanchester Polytechnic in his days there, named in honour of the exceptional engineer Frederick W Lanchester, and not far from where the author was born, as it happens), Robinson spent most of his early career within the General Motors empire before moving to Porsche in April 1999. As a team leader, he has already left quite a mark on the products from the famous Stuttgart firm, with the 981 Cayman exterior also being credited to him.

As with the styling changes that transformed the original 986 model into the 987 series, those that gave birth to the Type 981

Weight reduction measures

One of the key factors in the creation of a fast, good handling car is low weight. Engineers have known this since the dawn of motoring, drilling chassis rails and honing individual parts to rid them of excess poundage, while the birth of the Silver Arrows didn't come about thanks to a colour co-ordination specialist – Alfred Neubauer, who was running the Mercedes-Benz racing team in the 1930s, stripped the cars of their traditional white paint in order to save a kilo or two! A lower kerb weight can also help improve fuel efficiency, and that's an increasingly important thing to consider, too, in this modern era.

One could opt for an aluminium body, but a monocoque shell using this material throughout tends to be expensive – fine for certain machines that are less price sensitive, and more suited to closed vehicles if truth be told. Instead, Porsche decided to go down a sensible path of using super high-strength steel for much of the A-post area and the structure aft of the B-post, including the rear bulkhead and roll-over hoops. Strengthening pieces were added into the windscreen pillars, as well as the sills, with multi-phase steel added on the inner side of the rocker panels and ultra-high strength alloyed steel (22MnB5) on the outside. Multi-phase steel was also used for the door beams required for side impact regulations, while all other components (up to 46 per cent of the body, including the doors and front and rear lids), were executed in aluminium.

While super high-strength steel is self-explanatory, the term multi-phase steel deserves a few lines. This exceptionally strong material is usually formed via the heating and controlled cooling of TRIP-assisted (Transformation Induced Plasticity) steels in order to fine-tune the metal's microstructure. A

fairly new innovation, multi-phase steel offers excellent crash energy absorption, reasonable cost, and is markedly easy to work with. Meanwhile, boron-alloyed 22MnB5 steel offered exceptional forming accuracy combined with the ability to downguage yet retain the strength associated with more conventional HSLA grades, thus saving weight. This, combined with its high resistance to flexing and fatigue damage, made it an ideal option for parts that bore a lot of stress.

Using the latest CAD/CAM techniques to balance strength versus material usage and aid the placement of structural parts, the end result was a body-in-white that weighed significantly less than the all-steel 987 version. Crucially, it also displayed a 40 per cent increase in overall rigidity, which is ideal for accurate chassis component response, while the use of magnesium alloys in areas like the dash mounts and convertible hood frame ensured further weight reduction. Using this ultra-lightweight material in the hood also helped lower the vehicle's centre of gravity – another requirement in enhancing the handling of a top sports car, along with weight distribution, that generally has engineers trying to balance the car front and rear, and keep as much bulk as possible within the wheelbase. Generally is the operative word in Porsche's case, of course, for the company's 911 boldly breaks all the accepted rules of design!
The Boxster sports a 45:55 ratio.

The latest Boxster body, with light and dark blue shaded areas showing aluminium-based structures, green depicting high-tensile steel, yellow multiphase steel areas, and red boron-alloyed steel. Although the new Boxster was heavier than a 987.1 version in completed form, significantly, it was around 25kg (55lb) lighter than a 987.2 equivalent.

Boxster were subtle – very subtle, in fact. On saying that, there was still a clear generation gap if one was able to put a 987.2 Boxster and the newcomer side-by-side, with a number of details combining to deliver an altogether sharper impression.

Ultimately, the first chapter shows us that during the Boxster's evolution thus far, it had steadily evolved into a more and more sporting machine with each and every face-lift and/or upgrade applied to it. This development direction was continued for the 981, with more aggressive lines being adopted, further distancing the car from the 'cute' form of the original model launched in the 1990s.

Starting at the front of the vehicle, the headlights were the main feature, with similar units to those of the late 987 models giving the Boxster a quite different character to the 991-type 911 that would make its debut a few months before the new Boxster. Porsche had learned its lessons well, for the criticism levelled at the company regarding the similarity between the 986 Boxster and contemporary 911 (996) would never be repeated – the rounder headlights of the latest 911 Carrera would see to that.

Compared with the 987.2, the new lights were actually deeper, going into the area that sat alongside the leading edge of the 'bonnet' shutline, rather like those of the Panamera, with their less rounded corners being one of the key factors in obtaining that sharper look we mentioned earlier. It was a well executed balancing act, giving the 981 a fresh appearance whilst still continuing the DNA of the 987, and at the same time putting distance between the open car and its more expensive 911 brethren.

Looking at the car in detail, there were many changes to point out on the standard showroom models. The three openings in the front air dam were a styling item that was taken for granted now, with all Porsches from

As head of styling, it was Michael Mauer (seen here) who ultimately gave the rubber stamp on the 981's design work.

Design sketches by Hugh Robinson, with the 981's lines clearly showing through.

Head-on view of a Boxster S with stock headlights and bodywork features, such as the black slats on the outer air dam vents (they were painted in body colour on the smaller-engined cars).

987.2 Cayman than the outgoing Boxster one, with the central 'vent' being broader at the top than the bottom on the latest machines. As had been the case with certain 987s in the past, the central vent on virtually all 981 Boxsters (and lower-powered versions of the contemporary 911s, for that matter) was nothing more than a black blanking piece, hence the use of inverted commas around the vent. Much of this can be explained away by the fact that the third radiator that used to be a feature on S models was no longer deemed necessary for most applications, with only the extreme weather of the Middle East calling for one as a rule of thumb, and even then, just on the PDK-equipped machines as standard.

As such, it is only the pair of vents that do anything on the vast majority of vehicles, directing cooling air to the radiator positioned ahead of each front wheel. With the central 'vent' now effectively turned upside down, the design of those to the side of it could be simplified, again following Cayman practice, but with the driving light (doubling as a foglight and DRL unit) being similar to that of the outgoing Boxster, albeit narrower and independent of the grille of the 981, at least visually – it actually sat in the same plastic moulding that carried the two vertical slats that dressed the vent.

These slats were either black or painted in body colour. According to the parts book, strict Boxsters (or base cars, if you like) had black blades, while the S had colour-keyed ones. However, it simply doesn't stack up in real life – the first catalogue from November 2011 shows the opposite to be true (in words and pictures), and the Boxster S in the Porsche Museum also has black slats. Other catalogues from export markets and later price lists from Germany confirm things, stating that base models had painted blades (except those with black coachwork), while the S and black cars had black versions. This, therefore, is the definitive answer for the start of production, but, as we shall see, it would not remain this way forever, although the parts book is still not right even then!

the time carrying a variation on the same theme – even the Cayenne had them, albeit with the grilles higher off the ground, in keeping with the vehicle's height and SUV status.

Interestingly, the new Boxster layout was more like that of the

This front three-quarter shot of the same car emphasises the stronger curves built into the new vehicle's winglines. Note also the NACA duct aft of the door, with the angle showing its functional positioning.

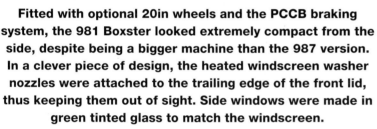

Fitted with optional 20in wheels and the PCCB braking system, the 981 Boxster looked extremely compact from the side, despite being a bigger machine than the 987 version. In a clever piece of design, the heated windscreen washer nozzles were attached to the trailing edge of the front lid, thus keeping them out of sight. Side windows were made in green tinted glass to match the windscreen.

Another profile shot, this one giving a clear view of the latest hood shape. Incidentally, lifting the door handle gave access to a keyhole, while an actual mechanical key was integrated into the transponder body, thus allowing owners to lock or unlock the car if the remote control unit's battery failed.

Incidentally, although the retaining frames that held the slats and LED-powered light unit (described by Porsche as an 'additional headlamp,' incidentally) were of the same design, the base models had a blanking piece behind them, partially shielding the radiator on standard cars. This may or may not matter to some folks, but in the future, when enthusiasts start restoring these cars as classics, these minor details will become increasingly significant.

Ultimately, with or without painted bits, the air intakes combined to give the new Boxster a far sportier look, aided by a more obvious and shapely lip spoiler arrangement and a slightly stronger fold line running off the upper edge of the driving light units. When fitted, the number plate sat above the dummy central vent, as was the norm, with a tow hook cover to the left of it if one was to view the vehicle head-on.

Moving back from the bumper assembly, although the 'bonnet' panel was a similar shape to that of the 987, the famous Porsche badge was now sunk into the front lid rather than sitting proud of it, as it had in the past. The wings either side of it had far crisper lines, giving the car a more chiselled look compared to earlier cars – an impression reinforced by the new headlight units.

The headlights used modern technology to provide a design that put real distance between the second- and third-generation Boxsters.

While the upper light (dipped beam) was in much the same location as it had been in the later 987s, the smaller one below it (high beam) was moved from its old inboard position to a new place underneath and slightly overlapping it. Meanwhile, the indicator unit was turned 90 degrees to take up an upright position on the inner face of the black-framed headlamp assembly. As before, twin-tube halogen lighting was the norm on base cars, although the more powerful Bi-Xenon version was now listed as standard on the S grade. There was an optional PDLS setup, too, readily identified by the washer nozzles ahead of the Bi-Xenon units, but more on that later.

If the changes made to the front of the car were extensive enough, there were a lot more surprises in store for those viewing the car in profile for the first time. These changes were an awful lot less subtle, but still aimed at continuing the evolutionary theme nonetheless.

The key factor in allowing so many styling changes was the decision to go with a 60mm (2.4in) longer wheelbase for the 981 series. This gave designers a great deal more artistic freedom in the update, as it was obvious that many new pressings would be required as a result of the increase. However, following the industry trend of adopting ever-larger wheel and tyre combinations, the overall impression was of a car that looked no bigger than its predecessor.

Starting with the nose and working our way back, the front

Leading dimensions

For reference, here are the leading dimensions of each Boxster generation.

For consistency, all numbers listed here relate to European-spec base models with a manual transmission, and the first of the breed.

	986 (EU)	987 (EU)	981 (EU)
Wheelbase	2415mm (95.1in)	2415mm (95.1in)	2475mm (97.4in)
Overall length	4315mm (169.9in)	4330mm (170.5in)	4375mm (172.2in)
Overall width	1780mm (70.1in)	1800mm (70.9in)	1800mm (70.9in)
Overall height	1290mm (50.8in)	1295mm (51.0in)	1282mm (50.5in)
Track (front)	1465mm (57.7in)	1490mm (58.7in)	1526mm (60.1in)
Track (rear)	1528mm (60.1in)	1535mm (60.4in)	1536mm (60.5in)
Weight (DIN)	1250kg (2750lb)	1295kg (2849lb)	1310kg (2882lb)

NB: The width quoted does not include door mirrors, and weights are German DIN figures, which tend to be on the light side compared with those posted in most other countries outside mainland Europe.

A Carrera GT on display at the San Jose International Auto Show in January 2006. This exotic model would disappear soon after, but many of its styling touches lived on in the 981 series models.

end was actually very similar to that of the last 987s in profile – the protruding front lip spoiler (integrated into the bumper moulding) and the visible parts of the headlights being almost the same. The grilles in the front of the air dam were different, of course, as were the lighting units within them; the repeater unit-cum-side marker was also changed to a sharper design, although its positioning (in the join between the front wing panel and bumper assembly) was familiar enough to Porsche fans.

In addition to a 27mm (1.1in) reduction in front overhang, careful inspection revealed a slightly stronger curve at the leading edge of the wings, and the fuel filler lid was rounder than before, albeit in the same place as it had always been on the Boxsters. For the record, the fuel tank capacity was 57 litres (12.5 imperial gallons) on the first 986, and enlarged to 64 litres (14.1 imperial gallons) for the 2000 Model Year. It was then retained on the 987s, and duly specified once again for the new cars.

The wheelarch shape was carried over – a flattened edge following the profile of the tyre most of the way around. The base Boxster now came with 18in rims as standard, their simple five-spoke design highlighting the lightweight sports concept. The S grade, meanwhile, employed 19in alloys, with the five spokes being wider and opened up in the middle to the extent that one could almost call the rim a ten-spoke design.

Rear three-quarter shot of the Boxster S, which came with a different exhaust system to the 2.7-litre model and an 'S' suffix added to the badge. The unusual ducktail spoiler arrangement shows up well from this angle, deploying automatically at speeds in excess of 75mph (120km/h), and lowering again once road speed dropped by a suitable margin.

Moving further back, a small fold running off the top edge of the wheelarch was allowed to develop into a stronger feature as it passed through the door, only to fade away again into the rear arch. Doubtless inspired by the Carrera GT, combined with a myriad of other detail changes, this was ultimately one of the main styling elements that separated the 981 series from its earlier brethren.

Whereas the 987.2 had a distinct step in the sill just below the door, the 981 had a more subtle one at the lowest point of the rocker panel, and a smaller piece on its trailing edge to deflect air around the rear tyres. The old 'step' was only allowed to return from around halfway beneath the door, and was then widened and curved upwards

Tail of the same reference vehicle, kept in the Porsche Museum collection. Please excuse the fact that the hood is up on most of these shots – the top is down on the vast majority of PR photos, so these actually provide a useful service.

to become integrated into the black side air intake pods, similar to the Carrera GT and the 2009 VW BlueSport and 2010 Porsche 918 Spyder concept cars that followed after its demise. To ensure a smooth transition, the trailing edge of the door panel was given a small kick at the bottom, helping it to blend in with the new lines.

While the general shape of the door was not all that different to earlier panels, the shoulder fold line flowing through the subtly revised and colour-keyed door handles was definitely new. Beginning at a point roughly in line with the new door mirrors (also body colour in the main, with folding versions available as an option), a stronger feature line combined with the one joining the wheelarches to create a ridge feeding the intake duct that ultimately balanced out the heavier shapes below. It expressed motion, even when the car was standing still …

There was another less obvious line near the top of the door, making the familiar curve of the rear wing appear longer and less of an afterthought. At its trailing edge, the combination lamps were given softer edges (something afforded by the upper plane no longer following the panel cut line) and a touch more bulk. While the rear bumper assembly and wheelarch profiles were generally similar in appearance to earlier cars, the LED light units were very distinctive with the central indicator rather cleverly formed to create the outer edges of a ducktail spoiler. Naturally, the self-framing lamp units were shaped in such a way as to allow all markets to be catered for, with the days of add-on bits to satisfy Federal regulations and so on long since passed.

Above the door, the screen angle appeared a touch steeper due to the front glass being moved forward around 100mm (3.9in) to become visibly deeper at its lowest point when combined with a similar A-post design. While the side window wasn't much different, the longer wheelbase allowed the designers to rework the convertible hood, though, with a more attractive top line and elongated tail. With the soft top being well lined and coming with a glass rear screen with heater elements, it was decided not to offer a hardtop for the 981. In reality, they're not the easiest things to put on and off without getting friends or a garage involved, and, as the author knows all too well, storing a hardtop can be a pain when it's not in use. With the latest hood being both weatherproof and refined (noise at cruising speeds was said to be cut from 75dB to 71dB), this move also gave the Cayman a clearer position.

Around the back, the initial impression was one of remarkable familiarity, but, once again, the detail work brought about some notable differences. With the convertible top up, it was obvious that the glass was taller and a fraction squarer in order to improve visibility. When the hood was dropped, the dark grey-coloured roll-over hoops appeared a little heavier than before, but they were basically the same shape, albeit placed further away from the seats in the newer model.

As at the front, the shoulders of the wings were squarer than before, and also more shapely as they merged into the engine cover profile. Like the doors, the rear lid was now formed with a subtle kick at the outer edges to blend in with the fenders, and was longer due to the elimination of the 'tonneau cover' panel that used to sit between the folded hood and rear compartment lid (moving upwards to allow the top to be erected), thus giving the car a more integrated look whilst lending a sense of volume at the same time.

The cut-out for the high-mounted rear brakelight was also stronger than before, playing host to a red LED unit. Aft of this, traditional 'Porsche' lettering from the sixties made a welcome comeback, placed above the model badge. Both the maker name and grade badges were given a chrome finish, regardless of the powerplant under the panel – the 'S' appendage was the only difference this time around for the bigger-engined variant, although buyers were able to have the car supplied without a model designation if they wished; the 'Porsche' lettering remained with the badge deletion option nonetheless.

The light units were very similar in shape at the top, but angled in an opposite direction on the inner edge, and flatter along the bottom, too – in fact, the combination lamp sat on a heavy ledge created by the rear bumper assembly, which was quite different to the small lip arrangement on the 987s. But it was the central nodule in the light that really set the 981 apart, extending to make up the ends of a rear spoiler.

This aerodynamic appendage was actually much like the Cayman one, as it appeared fixed, but an upper blade automatically rose from a base section on a pair of stilts when driving conditions demanded greater downforce. Interestingly, the base unit carried another LED cluster, with these looking after the reversing light and rear foglight functions.

Continuing down, the angle of the number plate housing was reversed, although similar in size to the 987.2 cut-out. This was the same shape for all markets, thus keeping production costs in check, as often manufacturers create a different bumper to suit local registration plates. Not surprisingly, the number plate was lit from above (using LED lighting), while a tow hook cover sat to the right of it. The only difference was in North American-spec cars, which employed a trick registration plate frame, with its raised edges doing away with the need for the hefty buffers used in the past on US models.

The stock diffuser was now a full-width insert, finished in black in standard guise, and comprising an upper frame and a single lower blade that resembled a wing on each side of a central moulding. The latter dressing piece played host to the car's tailpipes – dual round exhausts on the S, and a single oblong pipe on the base model, as before.

With extensive underfloor panels to back up the slippery shape of the body, and a whole host of small details, the new Boxster was quoted as having a drag coefficient of Cd 0.30 – an average of the original 987 figures, and well ahead of contemporaries like the Mazda MX-5, for instance.

And that completes the body, although we're far from finished in reality, as the list of options was extensive, to say the least, giving owners the ability to create something quite unique. We'll look at these options at the end of the chapter, thus giving us a firm foundation on which to build.

The interior

As with the exterior, there was a familiar air to the cockpit. Sure enough, the concept was the same, with the pair of seats separated by a centre console sprouting from a T-shaped dashboard, but careful analysis of the design revealed a very comprehensive overhaul of the interior.

Starting with the fascia panel, while the general profile and layout of the top roll was retained (with a cut-out for the instrument binnacle, along with a gentle slope on the vent plane, framed by a vast expense

beyond it and a metallic band below), the vents themselves were now squared off rather than round in shape, extending back to visually break up the upper surface of the dash.

Also, the Sport Chrono dial (when fitted) sat lower and looked an awful lot more integrated than before. Previously giving an impression of being something of an afterthought, if anything, the reverse was true this time around, implying that Porsche expected more and more people to take up this optional extra.

The idea of three main round gauges was carried over, albeit with a modern twist, as was a three-spoke steering wheel with controls placed around it. The glovebox was in its usual place, forming the lower section of the fascia on the passenger side, while the centre console that made up the tail in the T-shape was another design element that was brought out for service once again. For the 981, though, inspired by the Carrera GT interior, everything looked sharper and more cohesive, helped by the use of a standard audio unit and an electronic handbrake that did away with the traditional lever.

Shapely seats with their backs against the rear bulkhead were an obvious part of the equation, given the sporting nature of the machine and its mid-engined (MR) layout, while the door panels were redesigned to bring the releases, switches and other door furniture closer to hand. For those who deemed it necessary, there was also

Interior of the 2012 Model Year Boxster S in the Porsche Museum, which has black leather trim, a SportDesign steering wheel, and a PDK transmission. The stylists did a remarkable job of adding a higher level of perceived quality to the cockpit's design.

a windblocker, as before, that sat behind the seats to help reduce draughts.

Upholstery came in vinyl (or leatherette, if you prefer) with matching Alcantara seat inlays as standard in Europe, with leather as an alternative, available in various trim levels to suit personal preferences and/or budget requirements. The guide in the sidebar covers all of the coachwork and trim options available initially,

The early seat options, with the standard chairs (top left), P04 Sports Seats Plus (top right), P06 Power Sports Seats (lower left), and P07 Adaptive Sports Seats Plus, giving buyers plenty of choice. Even so, these would soon be augmented by yet another variant, with separate heating and ventilation packages also to be considered.

Boxster Colour & Trim Guide

These colour variations were listed from the start of 981 Boxster production until June 2013.

Solid coachwork colours
Black (041 Schwarz), Carrara White (B9A Carraraweiss), Guards Red (80K Indischrot), and Racing Yellow (1S1 Racinggelb). Carrara White replaced by White (C9A Weiss) from July 2012.

Metallic coachwork colours
Basalt Black (C9Z Basaltschwarz) Metallic, Agate Grey (M7S Achatgrau) Metallic, Platinum Silver (M7T Platinsilber) Metallic, Dark Blue (M5X Dunkelblau) Metallic, Aqua Blue (M5R Aquablau) Metallic, Mahogany (M8Y Mahogani) Metallic, and Anthracite Brown (M8S Anthrazitbraun) Metallic. Also, Amaranth Red (8L1 Amaranthrot) Metallic available from July 2012 onwards.

Special coachwork colours
GT Silver (M7Z GT-silber) Metallic, Lime Gold (5P1 Limegold) Metallic, and Cognac (M8Z Cognac) Metallic. Emerald Green (2G6 Smaragdgrün) Metallic available from July 2012 onwards. A 'colour to sample' option was also available.

Hood (convertible top) colours
Black, Blue, Red, and Brown.

Leatherette/Vinyl trim
Black, Platinum Grey, Yachting Blue, and Luxor Beige. Carpeting and floor mats came in matching hues, with the headlining in black.

Leather trim
Black, Platinum Grey, Yachting Blue, and Luxor Beige. Carpeting and floor mats came in matching hues, with the roof liner in black on all but the Luxor Beige option (this came with a beige headlining).

Regular two-tone leather trim
Agate Grey with Lime Gold, and Agate Grey with Pebble Grey. Also, Agate Grey with Amber Orange from July 2012 onwards. Carpeting and floor mats came in Agate Grey, with the roof liner in black.

Special leather colours and natural leather trim
Agate Grey, Carrera Red, Espresso, and Agate Grey with Pebble Grey. Carpeting and floor mats came in matching hues (Pebble Grey on the two-tone option), with the roof liner in black. A 'colour to sample' option was also available.

Cockpit details of a domestic manual Boxster S equipped with numerous options, including the SportDesign steering wheel and Sport Chrono package. Incidentally, the tunnel badge always carried the same script, regardless of grade, but the start-up icon in the TFT screen was model-specific, as was the colouring on the tachometer (being a lighter shade on the S) and the speedo markings, which were calibrated to 280km/h on 2.7-litre cars and 300km/h on the S, or the equivalent in miles per hour.

with notes on late arrivals and early replacements contained within; Carrera Red and Espresso are 'natural' leather shades, incidentally.

Looking at each component area in detail from a domestic market driver's point of view, the regular seats had power backrest control,

but fore/aft and height adjustment was done manually via a hook at the front and a lever next to the backrest button low down on the outer side of the seat base. Like the optional seats, with their deeper bolsters and extended power adjustment features, they came with an

Interior of a 3.4-litre car with a PDK transmission and Sport Chrono setup. The TFT screen display to the right of the tachometer is wrong in this car, but there are often minor discrepancies in the early PR photography, often having to be done months before the launch, and sometimes with one car having to masquerade as another.

integrated headrest, and a facility to fold the backrest forward, giving access to a coat hook. The basic seats had Alcantara inlays on vinyl for most markets, with different trim levels, seat heating and ventilation available. When fitted, the switches for the latter pair of options were located just ahead of the gearlever, with three settings available on each.

As mentioned earlier, the other seats came with either a more bucket-like profile and the same adjustment setup as the regular seats, or more power controls combined with either of the two bolster design variations; with these, buttons (in the same place as the backrest one and height lever on the more basic variations) controlled all adjustment, including bolster inflation on the top option. Incidentally, seatbelt receivers were an integral part of the seat, with the other two seatbelt anchor points being at the top and bottom of the B-post.

Vaguely similar to the stock 987.2 item from 2010 onwards, the standard 981 three-spoke steering wheel came with a leather rim, a round airbag housing and flat lower edge (something that was all the rage in sporting circles), and was adjustable for height and reach. One could also opt for a multi-function wheel, which was much the same but with buttons on the upper spokes for onboard computer, audio and telephone functions. In either case, vehicles with the PDK transmission had small shifters on the upper spokes, while the colouring (and that of the column) matched the main interior shade. The optional SportDesign wheel was also similar, but with alloy-type spokes, and came equipped with beefier shift paddles and a mode indicator on cars with a PDK gearbox.

Aft of the steering wheel, the upper left-hand column stalk looked after the indicators, main beam and parking light selection, as well as voice command activation when fitted, while the right-hand one opposite had the various wiper settings and screen washer activation on it, along with headlight washers if specified. Interestingly, a lower right-hand stalk controlled the menu and other features associated with the right-hand dial in the main instrument pack, although it wasn't fitted if the car had a multi-function steering wheel. Some cars had a fourth stalk, below the indicators, for the cruise control, known as Tempostat in Porsche lingo. Manual or power steering column adjustment controls were found on the lower part of the column surround.

Beyond this was the instrument pod, with a separate shroud curving over the three main gauges. In keeping with sports car tradition, these had black bezels, angled to keep out stray reflections. For some reason, Porsche's designers decided to give the tachometer on the S grade a subtly silvered dial face, but otherwise black dials were the norm.

There was a large 9000rpm central tachometer, with a slightly smaller speedometer to the left (calibrated to either 280/300km/h or 175/190mph depending on the market), along with a dash light rheostat. A digital speedo was added at the base of the tachometer to back-up the analogue version to the side, while PDK-equipped machines had a gear indicator above this. Off to the right of the instrument binnacle was a TFT colour screen, framed to match the size and appearance of the traditional speedo opposite. The TFT screen displayed fuel level, engine oil and coolant temperatures, time, outside temperature, onboard computer data, et cetera. Indeed, it gave virtually all information beyond the road speed, engine speed,

odometer readings, and gear position on PDK cars (explaining why so many pages are dedicated to it in the owner's manual), although warning lights were clustered pretty much everywhere within the gauge pack.

The instrument binnacle sat in a full-width fascia, with a vent at each end and two in the middle. The pair on the driver's side framed the gauge pack, while the opposite pair framed the passenger-side airbag. The vents were extended deep into the top roll, with a thumbwheel in the centre to control airflow volume, and moveable slats at the front. These slats were housed in a bright surround to match other areas of the interior, with the Sport Chrono dial also having this finish on its bezel, although the dial face was black. When fitted, the Sport Chrono dial sat between the two central vents with the hazard warning light and door lock switches above it, while cars without this option had the two switches only, placed lower down in a less ornate cut-out.

Moving further down, the fascia was dressed with a band in the same material as the air vent frames. Split in the middle to make way for the centre console (the 987 trim strip was full width), it was made of what Porsche called 'Galvanosilber,' and it looked a lot like aluminium alloy trim. It was also used for the frame that formed a surround for the transmission gate and switchgear aft of it, and the door and glovebox handles; some cars also sported a matching insert just below the door cappings. Interestingly, the larger piece on the passenger side (directly above the lockable glovebox containing an airbag kill switch and USB/audio AUX port with a 12V socket) opened to reveal two pop-out cupholders, which solved one of the great design problems of the modern era – how to incorporate the wretched things without creating an eyesore.

On the driver's side, close to the door, the dashboard dressing piece played host to the main light switch (now with an automatic setting on the headlights) and ignition barrel. In a new arrangement, the huge transponder key body locked into the barrel to become the starter switch. The key continued to carry the remote control central locking functions on it (including electronic releases for the two luggage compartments), and contained an integrated immobiliser, which was duly hooked into the alarm system when fitted. Also new was the electronic handbrake, with the small lever-type switch associated with it placed below the light switch.

Down in the driver's-side footwell was the expected pedal set, of course, complete with a footrest to match off to the left. Fuse boxes were located in both footwells, incidentally, while the passenger was given a map net and another 12V socket on the transmission tunnel to make up for the lack of pedals to play with. One should also be aware of the petrol filler cover release in the door jamb closest to the lid.

The centre console was dominated by the standard CDR31

audio system, which included a CD/radio unit and a seven-inch touchscreen that could be used for all manner of functions. The optional PCM unit, with easier access to more advanced features, looked surprisingly similar in its latest guise, and both came with four speakers (two in the corners of the dash top roll and two in the doors). Audio upgrades included a CD-changer and enhanced sound systems, but the head units continued to look much the same nonetheless.

Between the AV head unit and gearbox was a band of buttons and levers controlling the air-conditioning system. This was fitted as standard, complete with a stepless fan, defrost and circulating air functions, and an active charcoal filter. A dual-zone version was also available, with the fan control moving to the centre of the bank of switches in this case, while the smaller buttons that used to be there were moved up alongside the digital HVAC display.

Moving further back, there was the leather-trimmed gearshift, and aft of this, another bank of switches, arranged in three vertical rows within the same 'Galvanosilber' frame. The central row was a constant, being the power hood controls (a single button for opening the roof, and another for closing it, with all other operations, such as undoing clamps and so on, no longer being necessary), although those to the left and right of it depended on what options were fitted. Buttons that were always there covered the manual deployment of the rear spoiler, one to turn the PSM traction control system off, and a switch to shut off the automatic engine stop feature, which was useful in the fight against emissions but could be tiresome at times. There was also a 'Sport' button that changed the engine mapping and throttle response for those wanting to enjoy an open road.

Different switches with options could include Sport Chrono-associated items, like the 'Sport Plus' button, and the PASM active suspension mode switch, and later, an exhaust sound switch. Aft of these was a small oddments tray that could be converted via the

smoker's package into a covered ashtray and lighter, while the central armrest (covered in leather on the S) acted as a lid for another storage compartment, the latter containing yet another 12V power socket.

The door furniture was definitely more stylish than that of the earlier Boxsters. The 'Galvanosilber' door releases were lower down than before, making them less of a stretch to get to, while the door handles were incorporated into the angled switch panel, with leather trim on the latter to add a sense of luxury, duly extended to the door armrests on the S as well. The driver had power window and power mirror controls within the switch panel (both standard on the 981s, with integral heater elements on the mirrors), and occasionally a set of seat position memory buttons above these, while the passenger had to make do with a single window lift. Below the door handle was a speaker enclosure and storage bin, while a second storage bin was located underneath the door armrest and above the courtesy light that warned oncoming traffic that the door was ajar.

More switches were contained in the upper console that played host to the rearview mirror, but only really for the LED interior lighting and HomeLink buttons, whenever the latter was fitted, as well as a parking sensor kill switch and a warning lamp to say the passenger-side airbag had been disabled. Both sunvisors came with an illuminated courtesy mirror, incidentally.

Finishing the cockpit area, there were black treadplates with a metal model-specific logo insert. There were also front and rear luggage compartment lid releases via switches in the driver's-side sill, handed for lhd and rhd cars. It seems odd, and was perhaps a

A shot used in the Tequipment catalogue to show the plastic box to line the main part of the front luggage compartment, although it also serves as a useful reference picture: more space was available at the back of the vehicle. Screenwash (blue) and brake fluid filler lids can be seen close to the bulkhead.

Safety

The strength of the bodyshell played a key role in the safety of passengers, with front and rear crumple zones built into the design, and door beams to reduce cockpit intrusion from a side impact. In a roll-over situation, a combination of specially selected steels ensured the windscreen frame would create a safety cell up front, while the hoops behind the seats (made from a composite of aluminium alloy and steel) did the same job at the rear of the vehicle.

Numerous areas within the cockpit were padded to reduce injury, and naturally the seatbelts used all the latest technology available, such as pre-tensioners and force limiters. In more serious collisions, folks could rely on full-size dual airbags up front, and Porsche's POSIP side impact system, which incorporated a small airbag in the outer side-frame of each seat and a larger curtain one in the door cappings that deployed upwards in order to protect an occupant's head.

Accident avoidance is by far the best policy, of course. Lighter weight meant that the car was endowed with a nimble chassis, and combined with superb brakes (with an ABS and EBD system as standard), electronic traction and stability aids, decent lights and the power to make a positive move, Porsche made sure that drivers were given the foremost chance of going down this more desirable route long before other safety features needed to be called upon.

In addition to the car's nimble reactions and strong body, safety was enhanced via an array of airbags and door beams, with electronics then adding another layer of driver protection.

sign of the times, but these were the only releases – in contrast to the 914 of yore, there was no access to the engine compartment on any of the Boxsters without a lot of work, and one could only learn to appreciate the longer service schedules introduced on the modern Porsche range.

Naturally, this arrangement was pleasing from an aesthetic point of view, too, although owners were restricted to the absolute minimum of maintenance, with fillers for the engine oil and water in the rear trunk (now separated and relocated to the upper corners of the trunk), and windscreen washer and brake fluid at the front. Adventurous types could also access the tools neatly hidden in the sides of the front luggage compartment, although they were few and far between

as there was no spare wheel (a tyre sealant was supplied instead in order to save space and weight, with a compressor situated next to the battery underneath the cover that dressed the area between the trunk and front bulkhead); a warning triangle was added in countries that required them, such as Germany.

Luggage capacity was unchanged regardless of whether the hood was up or down (unlike some trick convertibles that put styling ahead of practicality), with 150 litres (5.3 cubic feet) of space available at the front, and a further 130/4.6 in the rear compartment – more than adequate for the majority of weekend tourers, especially with fitted luggage or squashy bags, and exactly the same as that quoted for the previous generation of Boxster models.

The drivetrain

Initially breaking cover in the 1960s, Porsche's trademark flat-six engine had gone through numerous stages of evolution by the time the 981 project came into being, morphing from an air-cooled unit to a water-cooled one, and adopting new technology to improve performance and economy at every opportunity. First seen in the 987.2 generations of the Boxster and Cayman (and 997.2 version of the 911), the latest incarnation of the boxer engine was known as the MA series.

These early applications called for 2.9- and 3.4-litre versions of the MA1, with a six-speed manual gearbox specified across the board, and, at last, the option of the race-inspired and long-awaited double-clutch PDK transmission, which replaced the Tiptronic S gearbox on the spec sheets.

The design of these normally-aspirated all-alloy water-cooled 24v engines was completely overhauled, with significantly less moving parts

The internal workings of the award-winning MA1 engine.

compared to their predecessors (including the dismissal of the IMS shaft, which had been known to cause problems in service on early M96 units), and seven per cent less rotational mass for quicker response to the electronic throttle. New, stiffer cylinder blocks were prepared, with a different bore and stroke relationship, and the lubrication system was changed with an oil scavenge system that included four pick-up points and the use of an electronically-controlled oil pump, hooked into the ECU to react to loading better, thus improving oil consumption and giving a slight power gain into the bargain.

At the top end, direct fuel-injection was employed for the first time within the Boxster and Cayman lines. Combined with a higher compression ratio, the DFI system boosted power, and also reduced fuel consumption and emissions compared to earlier port injection setups thanks to the use of leaner air/fuel mixtures. This naturally led to the adoption of a new air filter housing and intake manifolds, but there were also lighter tappets for the double overhead camshafts on each bank, as well as a new water pump and a new exhaust system. As before, individual coils were adopted for the sparkplugs, which

sat between the four valves in the middle of the combustion chamber roof.

Ultimately, both sixes were about 5kg (11lb) lighter than before, more refined, and capable of delivering better mid-range punch thanks to a resonance-effect intake manifold arrangement (further refined via the addition of a switchable valve in the S) and the innovative Variocam Plus variable valve timing mechanism. In addition, the engine height was reduced, lowering the car's centre of gravity, and it was quieter, too – a point not always appreciated by petrolheads, but the flat-six still sounded nice approaching the red-line, and an optional sports exhaust was duly made available in any case; that sounded real sweet!

For the 981, while the 3.4-litre capacity was retained for the S grade, it was decided that the base car should use a smaller 2.7-litre lump, reverting back to the early days of the 987 series. This gave a stronger defining line between the two models, and also helped Porsche in the fight against emissions through lower fuel consumption. Ultimately, a higher compression ratio on the strict Boxster (upped to the same value as that specified for the S model) and tuning tweaks via the Siemens SDI 9 black box used on the 981 machines allowed an on-paper gain in power anyway, thus creating a win-win situation on all fronts.

Looking in more detail, the 2.7-litre MA1/22 unit kept the 89mm bore of the old 2.9-litre engine and combined it with a shorter 72.5mm stroke to give a cubic capacity of 2706cc. With a 12.5:1 c/r, it produced 265bhp DIN at 6700rpm and 206lbft of torque at 4500rpm when used in the Boxster. While the torque figure may have been a fraction less than the previous model (down 8lbft, or four per cent), it should be noted that the torque curve was flat until 6500rpm, and power had increased by 10bhp – together, these things more than made up for the loss, and a specific output of 98bhp per litre was outstanding for a road car from any era, let alone one having to push its 'green' credentials, which it did through delivering significantly better fuel economy figures than those posted by the old 2.9-litre engine.

Meanwhile, the 3.4-litre MA1/23 powerplant kept its 97mm bore and 77.5mm stroke, thus resulting in a 3436cc displacement. Sporting the same 12.5:1 compression ratio as before, power increased by 5bhp, nonetheless, compared to the old Boxster S, now being quoted at 315bhp DIN at 6700rpm (both Boxster models red-lined at 7600rpm, by the way), whilst peak torque was basically unchanged at 266lbft, developed from 4500rpm and continuing all the way out to 5800rpm. At 92bhp/litre, the specific output may not have been as eye-watering as that posted by the 2.7-litre engine, but it was still impressive, and better than the 90 quoted for the 987.2 Boxster S whichever way one looks at it – add in the 14.9 per cent improvement in fuel consumption, and it was all the more remarkable. As with the strict Boxster, the 'Sport' button on the centre console gave more dynamic engine response, while the Sport Chrono package took things a stage further, typically cutting 0-60 times by 0.2 seconds.

Integrated dry sump lubrication helped with packaging, eliminating the need for an external oil tank, and better thermal management translated into quicker warming up times to improve economy. An interesting development was the intelligent electrical system recuperation setup, that focused battery recharging windows on braking periods, thus reducing engine loads when power was called for, while at the other end of the scale, an auto stop feature shut down the power-unit when certain situations arose (such as sitting at traffic lights) in order to save fuel, automatically starting it again as soon as the driver was ready to move off, either by putting the vehicle back in gear on manual vehicles, or releasing the brake on PDK-equipped machines.

Incidentally, air was drawn into the power-unit on the nearside only on the 987, with an extractor fan on the opposite side to aid engine bay cooling. With the 981, air was pulled in from either side of the boxer six, with a housing fixed to the back of both side intake vents with an attachment point for the engine's air cleaner duct (that also carries the cone-shaped air filter element) and a smaller fan on each.

As noted earlier, a six-speed manual gearbox was now considered standard on mid-engined models, while the Tiptronic option had been superseded by the sportier seven-speed PDK transmission on the later cars, bringing with it a lot of advantages. Developed in conjunction with ZF, it was not only more compact and 10kg (22lb) lighter, with no transmission oil cooler necessary, it offered far quicker changes (up to 60 per cent faster), and adaptive programming

A dressed 3.4-litre Boxster S engine.

The Boxster S six (Type MA1/23) seen from above and ready for installation, complete with its PDK transmission and exhaust system, which came with twin pipes on the 3.4-litre cars. Note the new air intake arrangement, and the oil and water filler tubes next to it.

via eight sensors and a powerful computer, combining to give better acceleration and greater fuel efficiency.

Left to its own devices, when hooked into the Sport Chrono package system, the PDK gearbox gave sportier reactions in 'D' whenever the 'Sport' or 'Sport Plus' mode was activated. In addition to its fully automatic mode for those who disliked manual cars, or did a lot of town driving, it had a manual shift mode, like the old Tiptronic gearbox. As far as Porsche was

Another engine was considered for the 981 line, as it happens – a CI unit. The diesel Boxster ultimately came about as a result of the Volkswagen BlueSport concept shown at the 2009 Detroit Show, which was well-received. Component sharing was a must to keep costs in check, so the V6 TDI vehicle was investigated at Porsche, along with an Audi version. This is a 2012 Boxster, but it was not released for public sale at the time, and the 'Dieselgate' scandal that would unfold over the next few years put a stop to the idea once and for all. One should also remember the electric Boxster running around Stuttgart in 2011, pointing to an additional line of powertrain research ...

concerned, it offered "the driving comfort of a converter automatic transmission with the dynamic gearshift of a sequential racing gearbox."

Autocar summed up PDK thus:

"Put simply, PDK consists of a conventional manual gearbox and a hydraulic system divided into two separate transmission units, with the odd gears and reverse on one shaft and the even ratios on another. Each set of gears is accessed via its own separate wet clutch. Via a number of valves, the hydraulic unit masterminds both clutches, with each ratio being pre-selected as one clutch opens and another closes as the driver changes up or down the gearbox.

"From behind the wheel it just feels like each gearchange occurs super-smoothly and very quickly, up or down the 'box. That's because the gears are, in effect, already meshed when you shift gear, and on the way up this means power from the engine never needs to be interrupted. Sounds complex, and is complex, but in practice it works quite beautifully."

The design was duly polished over the years, so that by the time it was ready to go into the 981 it featured better cooling, and electronics saw to it that even faster shifts could be obtained. At the same time,

a coasting feature helped enhance fuel economy by a significant amount.

The PDK selector, with a lock in the upper part of the head, looked and worked much like a traditional automatic transmission if one left it in 'Drive,' reacting to driver input to give either quicker response or rapid shifts to higher ratios to save fuel. Moving the lever across to the left allowed manual changes, with up and down shifts executed by the gearlever or buttons/paddles on the steering wheel.

Although the base car employed the CG2/05 unit and the S the CG2/25, both Boxsters ultimately used the same PDK ratios, with 3.91 on first, 2.29 on second, 1.65 on third, 1.30 on fourth, 1.08 on fifth, 0.88 on sixth, and 0.62 on seventh. Combined with a 3.25:1 final-drive, this translated into a 0-60 time of 5.7 seconds on the 2.7-litre model, and 5.0 on the standard S, ie without the Sport Chrono package. Top speeds were quoted at 163mph (262km/h) and 173mph (277km/h), respectively.

As for the Getrag 6MT gearbox, this came with a four-plane layout, with first through sixth in a traditional double-H pattern, and reverse up and to the left, opposite first gear. Hooked up to a 240mm (9.4in) diameter dry-plate clutch on a dual-mass flywheel, internal ratios were 3.67, 2.05, 1.46, 1.13, 0.97 and 0.84 on the G81/00 unit used on the 2.7-litre machine, and 3.31, 1.95, 1.41, 1.13, 0.95 and 0.81 on the G81/20 gearbox employed by the S grade. Both manual models had a 3.89:1 final-drive, which made them 0.1 seconds slower in the 0-60 dash (0.3 if the Sport Chrono package was fitted), although both could boast a tiny advantage in the top speed stakes, being some 30kg (66lb) lighter than their PDK equivalents.

Not surprisingly, given the MR layout of the 981 series (mid-engine, rear-wheel drive), power was taken from the side of the transmission (or transaxle, to be totally correct in this case) to the back wheels via traditional CV-jointed driveshafts.

Incidentally, a mechanical limited-slip differential was included in the optional PTV

Cutaway drawing of the revolutionary PDK transmission.

Dynamic transmission mounts, which came as part of the Sport Chrono package, and helped remove vibration and unwanted movement from the drivetrain.

involved, which is another plus point to be considered, of course.

Anyway, this electro-mechanical system employed an electric motor attached to the rack, using sensors to gather information on driver input and data from the road wheels in order to judge the amount of assistance necessary (with variable ratios ranging between 16.5:1 and 12.4:1) according to the calculations made by the black box's software. As such, it was programmed to give a more agile response at higher speeds, and greater assistance at lower speeds. An optional Power Steering Plus setup brought a speed-sensitive element into the equation, which was particularly useful for urbanites constantly having to make parking manoeuvres.

As was becoming the norm in the modern era, the catalogue wasn't much use when it came to describing the make-up of the all-round independent suspension – more space was dedicated to gadgets, and marketing types deemed that all one needed to know was that the car did indeed have one. In this case, the 981 was fitted with a lightweight suspension, no less!

As we stated at the start of this section, it was similar to previous Porsche sports car designs, with wider tracks to help minimise roll (and bring the wheels flusher to the body sides to deliver a sportier impression whilst the car was stationary), geometry changes, and the honing of certain components to improve things further, such as the adoption of a new front crossmember structure to optimise location and enhance the precision of parts as they moved in reaction to driver input and road conditions.

The suspension system at the front-end consisted of a modified MacPherson strut secured at the top and placed into a hub carrier, with a pair of lower links attached to the bottom of the strut to form a wishbone of sorts. This 'wishbone' was then bolted to the alloy

system, which we'll come to later, but was not deemed necessary for cars in standard trim.

Before leaving this section, one should also be aware of the dynamic gearbox mounts included in the Sport Chrono package, which used sensors to instruct the pair of active mounts to counter the inertia we encounter when driving. Their stiffness and damping could be controlled to suit tastes and conditions via the 'Sport' or 'Sport Plus' switches on the centre console, but ultimately they were a traction aid with the added bonus of being able to help cancel out drivetrain vibration.

Chassis details

Sharing many parts with the 911, the chassis components would have been familiar enough to any long-standing Boxster and Cayman enthusiasts, with, in the main, only minor tweaks being applied to existing designs. One of the biggest changes was in the power-assisted steering system, which went from traditional hydraulic assistance to electrical assistance (EPS).

Generally speaking, having vintage leanings, the author is no fan of these systems, but in the modern era, the fuel saving they provide by cutting out a drain on engine power is all too often given priority over ultimate steering feel and feedback. There's also less maintenance

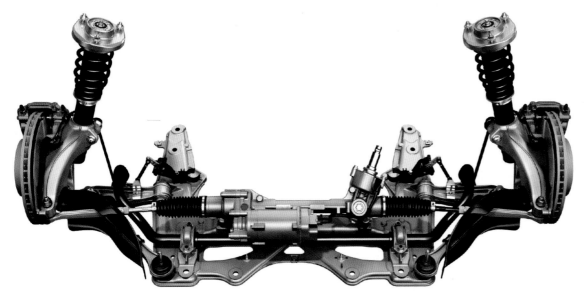

The front suspension, braking system, and EPS steering rack.

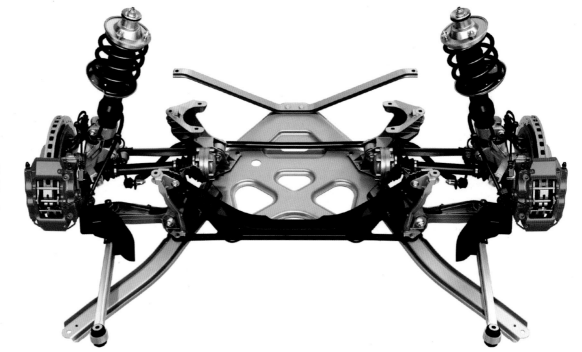

The rear suspension system, with the brakes and driveshafts also in place.

front subframe, which also carried the anti-roll bar mounts; as before, the sway bar and steering rack (with a two-piece steering column sprouting from it) were placed ahead of the front axle centreline, while dedicated spoilers helped guide air around the various arms.

The suspension at the back was much the same as before, and not dissimilar to that at the front in many respects, mounted on an elaborate subframe. The spring and damper unit bolted to the body at the top once more, and again sat in a hub carrier. This time, though, the latter was shaped so that the pair of lower links were widely spaced, with a trailing arm added for location; the anti-roll bar ran aft of the axle centreline in this case.

While the regular suspension used traditional gas-filled shocks, there was also the availability of the advanced PASM active suspension setup. Secured via option code 475, the PASM system had different electro-magnetically controlled dampers hooked up to a black box to provide an active suspension with 'Normal' and

The 18in alloy wheels fitted as standard to the strict Boxster (code 395).

The 'Boxster S' rims (code 400), as seen below, came as part of the package with the 3.4-litre car, and were available as an option on the 2.7-litre models.

'Sport' mode selection, giving the driver a choice in whether to go for ride comfort or a range of sportier settings. PASM lowered the car by 10mm (0.39in), while another option that became available later on (the more conventional X73 Sport suspension) lowered the vehicle by 20mm (0.79in) thanks to its stiffer springs, shocks and anti-roll bars.

As mentioned earlier, base cars now came with an 18in wheel and tyre combination, while the S had a 19in one. The 'Boxster' rim (code number 395) was a basic design with five very narrow spokes, while the standard 'Boxster S' aluminium alloy wheel (400) was more intricate, with stylists obviously gaining a lot of inspiration from the earlier 987.1 wheel designs. The 2.7-litre model came with 8J wheels shod with 235/45 ZR-rated rubber at the front, combined with 9J rims and 265/45 ZR18s at the rear; the 3.4-litre car employed 8J wheels and 235/40 ZR19s up front, and 9.5J rims with 265/40 tyres at the back. Not surprisingly, many owners opted to fit bigger wheels, with numerous options available, and the chance to change the 395 rim for the 400 one.

Braking was via discs all-round. All four were vented and cross-drilled, served by four-pot aluminium alloy monobloc calipers front and rear on both models. The base model came with 315mm (12.4in) diameter discs up front, which were 28mm (1.1in) thick, while the

Cutaway drawing of the Boxster S with a PDK gearbox, showing the location of all the key components that went together to make the latest Porsche convertible.

larger S version was the same thickness but 330mm (13.0in) across; both had the same 299mm (11.8in) x 20mm (0.8in) discs at the rear.

In addition to the disc size difference, the brake calipers were black on the strict Boxster, and painted red on the 3.4-litre models – one of the few reliable distinguishing features when looking at a vehicle from the side. Notwithstanding, some cars had yellow calipers, signifying the fitment of the optional PCCB braking system. This included 350mm (13.8in) diameter ceramic discs all-round, which weighed about half as much as regular rotors, along with six-pot front and four-pot rear calipers. Incidentally, calipers were always mounted at the trailing edge of the front discs and the leading edge at the rear, thus keeping as much weight as possible within the wheelbase in order to improve handling through a reduction in yaw moment.

In all cases, a four-channel anti-lock braking system via the Bosch ABS 9.0 setup ensured weight reduction and optimised brake force distribution (EBD), with servo-assistance taken as read. Further use of the latest electronic advances was evident in the adoption of

the electric parking brake (EPB) we mentioned in the interior section, which employed a dash-mounted switch to apply and release the handbrake rather than a traditional lever or pedal, although it also had an automatic deactivation setting that doubled as a hill-start assistance feature. In simple terms, the EPB worked via a small electric actuator motor attached to the rear brakes, with shoes employed to give a good handbrake, acting on the inner surface of the elongated rear brake disc centres.

The Porsche Stability Management system (PSM) was a standard fitment, using the electronics in the brakes to monitor the car's direction, speed, yaw velocity and lateral acceleration so that it could control extreme oversteer and understeer situations via selective braking on individual wheels (and cutting power if necessary) in order to rein in those that push a little too hard for their own good. The system included ABD and ASR functions, helping maintain traction and stability, as well as MSR throttle control, although it could be switched off when desired.

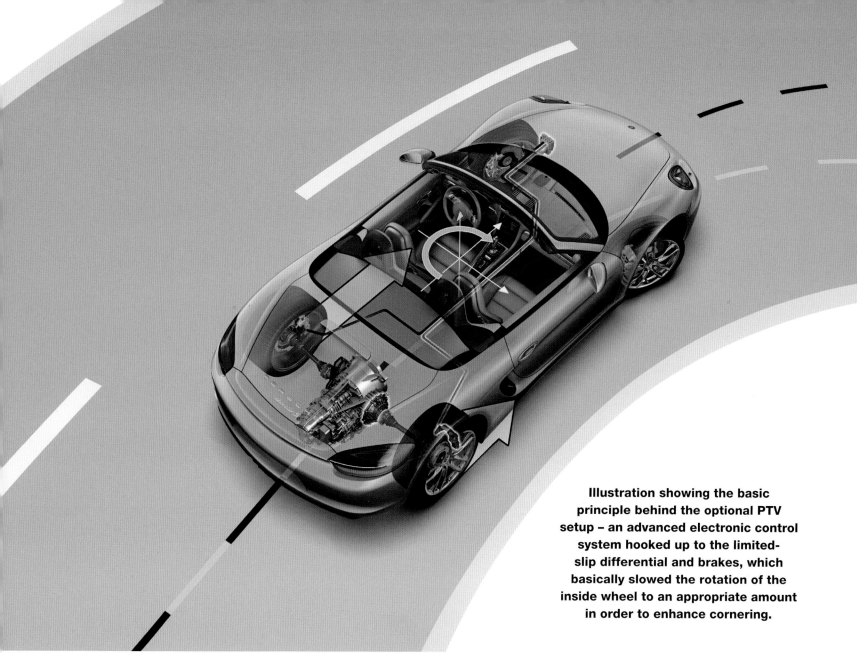

Illustration showing the basic principle behind the optional PTV setup – an advanced electronic control system hooked up to the limited-slip differential and brakes, which basically slowed the rotation of the inside wheel to an appropriate amount in order to enhance cornering.

Porsche Torque Vectoring (PTV) took things a stage further, working in tandem with the electronics of the PSM system and adding a limited-slip differential into the equation to further enhance stability during high-speed cornering and improve traction coming out of bends. Using the familiar 220 code that used to be assigned to an lsd only, for sure, one could reduce lap times if that way inclined, but the purity of direct car control was slowly being eroded with each and every 'advance' demanded by the newer generations. One cannot blame today's makers, of course, and sales of the Porsche brand have never been so high – it just seems that the Stuttgart company is catering for a rather different clientele to

the one that would have considered nothing but a Porsche only a couple of decades earlier.

Ready to roll

With limited factory space in Stuttgart, a large percentage of earlier Boxster and Cayman models had been assembled by Valmet in Finland in order to keep up with demand. However, this arrangement came to an end at the tail-end of the 987 run (the last car was built there in May 2011), with Magna Steyr of Austria being tipped to take over as early as 2008. Martin Winterkorn put a fly in the ointment, though, declaring that the old Karmann works in Osnabrück should be called upon

Politics

The new millennium was littered with politics in Stuttgart, all of which had a bearing on the 981's path of development, so it's worth a few lines here to set the scene.

Under the instructions of Porsche's boss at the time, Wendelin Wiedeking, Porsche had managed to gain a 42 per cent stake in Volkswagen by the autumn of 2008, and was poised for a takeover that had seemed all but impossible just a few years earlier. Then, things started to go dreadfully wrong. The financial crisis, caused largely by easy credit but symbolised by the Lehman Shock, sent shares crashing, and sales of luxury goods were put on hold – a situation that took a long time to turn around.

By mid-2009, Porsche was struggling to handle the debts it had chalked up in trying to take control of VW (Porsche Automobil Holding SE actually held 51 per cent of Volkswagen AG before proceedings on a fresh merger started). VW now had the upper hand, and Porsche was ultimately forced to become part of the Volkswagen Group, which by this time already included Audi, SEAT, Skoda, Bentley, Lamborghini, Bugatti, and the Scania AB commercial vehicle concern.

Wiedeking's incredibly bold plan had been scuppered, and, to keep the peace, he was dismissed in July, along with his finance man, Holger Haerter. This was probably the best move, as people had been starting to take sides since May, and the German press corps was having a field day.

Wiedeking's place as CEO of Porsche AG was immediately taken by Michael Macht, who'd been appointed head of production in mid-1998. Born in Stuttgart in 1960, Macht was to be assisted by Thomas Edig, while Wolfgang Leimgruber, a Porsche man since 1978, took over Macht's old job as production and logistics chief.

On the Porsche SE side, Martin Winterkorn (a respected VW man) was appointed CEO in September 2009, with Hans-Dieter Potsch as the new CFO. Following an injection of cash that secured ten per cent of Porsche SE ordinary shares by Qatar Holding LLC, and a separate investment that bought a large chunk of VW, Porsche would ultimately be merged into the Volkswagen Group.

Meanwhile, as the 981 was showing its head on the horizon, Macht moved up the Volkswagen corporate ladder, and Matthias Müller officially became the new Porsche Chairman from October 2010, only weeks after ItalDesign became yet another company to fall to VW. Interestingly, Müller had been in charge of product planning at Volkswagen before his move to Stuttgart, so it was a fair assumption that shared platforms and components would become more and more common as time rolled on.

Following on from an announcement that Porsche was investing €150 million in its R&D facilities (with a new design centre and wind-tunnel accounting for most of the budget), rumours were flying in the first weeks of 2011 regarding the development of a four-cylinder engine at Porsche, perhaps earmarked for the Boxster and Cayman, as well as the forthcoming baby SUV codenamed the Cajun, but ultimately christened the Macan.

Shortly after, Porsche appointed Wolfgang Hatz as the new head of the R&D section. Officially taking over from Wolfgang Dürheimer (who was given a fascinating new challenge in the Volkswagen-owned Bentley and Bugatti camps) in February 2011, Hatz had a career taking in spells at BMW, Opel, Fiat and Audi, as well as a four-year tenure at Porsche, working under Hans Mezger as a key member of staff on the V12 F1 engine project.

Ultimately, it was a busy 2011, witnessing the opening of a huge new paint shop in Stuttgart to coincide with the launch of the new 991-type 911, and a ground-breaking ceremony to expand production facilities at the Leipzig plant at the end of the year. With record sales and the new Macan waiting in the wings, it was perhaps ironic that in the summer of 2012 it was announced that Porsche Automobil Holding SE and Volkswagen AG would form an integrated automotive empire, with Porsche AG duly becoming part of the Volkswagen Group. Given the intertwined histories of these German giants, it could easily be said that what goes around, comes around …

instead as the outside contractor for the the 981, again augmenting Stuttgart production rather than taking its place completely.

This made a lot of sense, as the Osnabrück site had become part of the Volkswagen empire in November 2009 (Karmann having filed for bankruptcy a few months earlier), so this kept the money moving within the group rather than having to pay an outside supplier. There was also the historic link to conjure with, as Karmann had built quite a few bodies for the 356 and early 911s, as well as a significant number of 914s, of course.

With an extensive testing programme duly completed and everything else finally in place, the new Boxster went on sale in its native Germany on 1 February 2012, five weeks before its official

The new Boxster on display at the 2012 Geneva Show. *(Courtesy Norbert Aepli, Switzerland/Wikimedia Commons)*

launch at the 2012 Geneva Motor Show (which opened on the 8 March that year and ran for 11 days), and started filtering through to dealers from 14 April onwards.

The basic 2.7-litre model was priced at €48,291 including VAT (a standard rate of 19 per cent had been applied in Germany since 2007, and would continue that way for well over a decade), while the S commanded €59,120 – almost €30,000 less than the cheapest 911. These represented only a small increase on the RRP of the final 987.2 versions (the old Spyder was still listed, incidentally) given the level of standard equipment noted in the text, although very few vehicles would have left showrooms at those prices, as owners had plenty of temptations placed in front of them before signing off the papers at their dealership.

Ultimately, the days of a handful of options being a small footnote at the end of a catalogue were long gone. Now, one almost needed a separate publication to list them all, and a glance at an official contemporary price list hints that people tackling restorations in the future are going to be navigating their way through a minefield. Still, by taking things in chronological order and noting changes as they happened, we should be able to build up a clear picture of what was (and what wasn't) standard for any given year.

Paintwork and basic trim options have been covered earlier, but it's worth listing them again in order to make this section complete. As such, in addition to solid hues, we have metallic paint, shades termed as special colours, and the option of unique coachwork as per the customer's sample. One could also specify the roll-over hoops behind the seats in body colour (option 546), or with an Alu-Look finish (547).

Partial leather trim (946) included hide on the seat facings and upper side bolsters. Moving up to the leather package (980, and available in standard monotone or two-tone colour schemes) brought with it extra hide trim covering the instrument binnacle, the door

(Continues on page 50)

Some of the pictures released at the time of the Boxster's launch. The darker car is a 2.7-litre machine on 'Boxster S' wheels, while the lighter one is an S riding on 20in 'Carrera S' rims.

The optional 'Carrera S' alloy wheel design (code 423).

The 20in 'Carrera Classic' rims (code 427).

Several steering wheel upgrades were available, including these variations. From left to right we have the stock wheel on a 2.7-litre car for reference, then the multi-function version, and a SportDesign one with PDK shift paddles.

and central armrests, and the inner door handle, as well as the 946 upholstery specifications. Full leather trim cost twice as much, but, in addition to the 980 bundle, added hide pieces to the dashboard, centre console sides, door cappings and cards, and the lower bolsters on the seats. The latter option was listed for regular colours, special colours, two-tone schemes (970, although the grey/orange trim was not available until the summer of 2012), natural leather shades (998), and a colour matching a customer's sample.

Mechanical options included the seven-speed PDK transmission (option code 250), cruise control (454), the Sport Chrono package (639 if specified without the PCM setup, or 640 with it), the PCCB

brake upgrade (450), the PASM active suspension package (475), the PTV system (220), and speed-sensitive power steering (658).

Base car owners could have 19in 'Boxster S' alloy wheels fitted, while either Boxster could be shod with 'Carrera S' (423) or 'Carrera Classic' (427) rims. The latter pair, both sporting a ten-spoke design, had an 8J x 20 front and 9.5J x 20 rear combination, coming with 235/35 and 265/35 ZR-rated rubber, respectively. Coloured wheel centre crests (446), and a tyre pressure monitor (482) rounded things off in this area.

Upgrading the headlights was possible via option 603, which brought a Bi-Xenon setup complete with PDLS and a washer system,

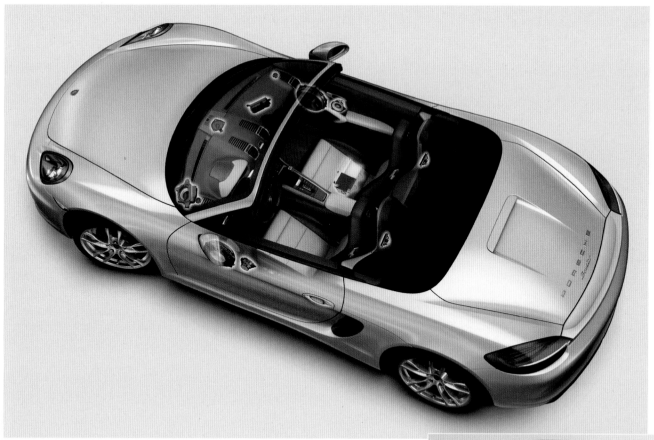

The Bose audio upgrade, available via option code 680.

The CD changer setup, seen here sitting above the dual-zone air-conditioning control panel.

with high-pressure nozzles ahead of the lamp units. PDLS was basically an evolution of the idea first seen on the innovative Citroën DS, with the main headlamps moving in relation to the steering angle to illuminate more of the road entering a turn. In addition, sensors controlled the range of the dipped beam in relation to speed, while turning on the rear foglight fine-tuned the headlight pattern to reduce reflection in poor conditions.

Other options included a windblocker (551), deletion of the model badge (code 498), a grey tinted band on the windscreen (567), automatic dimming interior and exterior mirrors combined with a rain sensor (P13), electrically-operated folding door mirrors with courtesy lighting (748), a parking assistant system using ultrasonic sensors hooked up to an audible warning and visual guidance setup (635 for the rear only, or code 636 for both the front and rear of the car), a HomeLink garage door opener (608), fire extinguisher (509), a PVTS tracking system (674), and an alarm with an interior monitor (534). By the way, Germany listed an alarm as standard on the S grade, so the 534 code was applied for the cockpit sensors only in that particular case.

Interior options were plentiful, to say the least. Dual-zone automatic air-conditioning (code 573) was joined by items like floor mats (810), a multi-function steering wheel (844), a SportDesign steering wheel (840, with shift paddles on the PDK version), steering wheel heating (345, with the switch located on the back of the lower spoke), the 630 lighting package (with additional LED lights overhead, in the door panels, footwells, and luggage compartments), childseat preparation (899), and a smoker's package (583). A variety of extended trim parts were also listed, mainly in the Exclusive catalogue, but most were not available until the spring, so we shall look at these items later.

Meanwhile, seating could be upgraded via the P04 option (Sports Seats Plus, with the same two-way – ie, backrest only – power adjustment as the standard seats, but with leather inserts, stronger side bolsters, and a silver-painted backrest shell), the P06 option known as Power Sports Seats (a leather-trimmed version of the regular seat with 14-way power adjustment and an advanced memory function linked to the steering column), or the P07 option (Adaptive Sports Seats Plus, which were shaped like the P04 model but built on the Power Sports Seats spec with additional adjustment on the side bolsters). Heating (342) was available for all seats, including the standard items, along with a ventilation package (541).

As for audio items, the P23 Porsche Communication Management (PCM) package was the main one, for although it had the same touchscreen size as the standard CD/radio unit, it contained a navigation system module and was easy to upgrade. For instance, option code 671 brought in voice control, 666 was a telephone module (669 being the cordless handset to go with it), 676 a TV tuner, and 641 an electronic logbook. Meanwhile, the Sound Package Plus took the speaker count up from four to seven (option code 490, available on standard audio and P23 setups), and the Bose surround sound system (680) took things a stage further with ten speakers and a stronger amplifier. A six-CD changer was listed for the standard stereo (692) and PCM unit (693), and there was also a mobile phone preparation service (619) for those without PCM.

Many of these items were available via the Tequipment catalogue, meaning dealers could add them at the time of purchase or as a retro-fit. Winter tyres on standard rims were a useful accessory for those wishing to keep a car for a decent length of time, although snowchains were also offered as an alternative. Locking wheel bolts, crested tyre valve caps, rubber floor mats, luggage compartment liners (a front one came first, with a rear version following in early 2013), childseats, car covers (indoor and outdoor types), cleaning materials and a dedicated 12V trickle charger covered all the practical angles of ownership.

Early press reception

Along with the Cayman, the Boxster had been a consistent entry in Car & Driver's '10 Best' listing, and winner of Automobile magazine's 'All-Star' award more times than any of their rivals wished to admit

to. The list of accolades is really quite impressive given the vehicle's market positioning. As such, it's fair to say that the 981 had a lot to live up to.

"Never before in the history of the Porsche Boxster has a change of generation been so comprehensive," said the gushing official press release issued in January 2012, but it was the view of the motoring press that would be the acid test.

Regarding the body, Autocar ran a piece in its 14 March 2012 edition, stating that the styling represented a real jump: "A combination of revised detailing, a more cab-forward silhouette, crisper swage lines, tauter and more structured surfacing, larger wheelarches, more distinctive air vents and a complex rear end with an automatic wing partly integrated into the taillights give the new Boxster a more individual appearance than at any time in the past … The only questionable styling feature is the ugly black plastic insert used in the side air vents."

The same article also said that "the newly designed cabin looks and feels much classier than before," and special attention was paid to the hood, which could be opened and closed at speeds of up to 31mph (50km/h) and all at the touch of a button, either on the centre console or the keyfob. The operation was remarkably fast, taking less than ten seconds to complete.

Summing up the S model, the British magazine concluded: "On first acquaintance, the new Boxster is nothing but brilliant – a car that is surely set to continue the success of the previous two generations."

In Germany, Auto Motor und Sport was full of praise for the new Boxster, which "combined comfort and dynamism" while "communicating everything necessary." Even the steering was given the nod, surprising the author, along with high marks for the performance, body rigidity, and build quality. About the only things the AMS testers were unhappy with was the air-conditioning, the clarity on certain instrument readouts, the big gap between sixth and top in the PDK transmission, and the cost of options.

Car & Driver on the other hand, did pick up on the steering: "The EPS requires less work than it did before, thanks to lighter weight. It's faithfully accurate, but at the same time it's less involving." Everything else got a thumbs up, though.

Greg Kable, writing for Autoweek, noted that "The engine in the Boxster S is as responsive and stirring as ever, equally at home crawling along in city traffic as it is chasing the 7700rpm red-line on the open road. While peak torque arrives 100rpm higher than with the old S's engine, there is now a generally stronger feel through the mid-range, whatever the chosen gear."

At the other end of the driving equation: "The standard steel brakes are on the money. They're nicely progressive, high on feel and full of strength when you really get on them hard." Indeed,

Kable was only really critical of the fiddly rocker switches for the PDK (recommending the optional paddle setup) and the view when reverse parking, which was not as clear as before due to the new body and rear hoop design.

Also present at the press launch in the south of France was Nic Cackett, who tried the 2.7-litre car. He noted that while it may have lacked the top-end punch of the larger-engined machine (on roads that would allow it to become apparent, of course), "like the S, its ride, refinement, enhanced appearance and dazzling chassis make it easily the finest roadster within the reach of modest money." The scene was well and truly set ...

Interior of an early 2.7-litre car with the standard steering wheel when teamed up with a PDK transmission. The two-tone leather trim was eye-catching, to say the least.

More options

From April 2012, one could ask for wheels to be painted with a satin platinum finish (option code XDH), a gloss black one (XDA) or colour-keyed to match the body (XD9), although XDA and XD9 actually appear to have been rolled out later than planned (along with CRX). The headlight washer nozzles that came with the PDLS lights could be painted in body colour (XUB), and sports tailpipes (XLS) were at last made available.

Two months later, a few more Exclusive options came online, including fully painted door mirrors (CNL), painted side intake surrounds (CAC), and a colour-keyed rear apron (CNG). Having wheels painted in a contrast colour (CRX) was another way of securing individuality, although there appears to be a delay on this option, while the 20in 'SportTechno' wheels (XRT) were definitely there now, with a five-spoke 8.5J rim fitted with 235/35 tyres at the front, combined with a 10J version at the back, which came shod with 265/35 rubber.

As for extended trim parts, most were listed in the initial price list (with numerous items also featured in the contemporary Tequipment catalogues), but were officially unavailable until either April or June, with white painted components in particular being delayed due to the change in exterior coachwork hues.

Notwithstanding, the interior package was available with a colour-coded painted finish (EER for the dashboard dressing piece and door capping insert at the same height, or XDM for the dash piece only, albeit changed to an EET code in 2013), with other painted parts including the dashboard air vent slats (CDN), the PCM unit (CUF), the centre console aft of the audio unit and ending at the point where central armrest begins (XYG), and the car key body (CWK, later changed to CPK). It was also possible to specify the Sport Chrono dial in beige (CZT), red (CGG), yellow (CGE) or white (CGJ).

The wood interior package used mahogany trim pieces, EEB being the dashboard, door capping trim and gearknob for manual cars, while EEC was the fascia sections and gearknob only; EED and EEF were the equivalent parts for cars with a PDK transmission. XHF was a multi-function steering wheel with a wooden rim to match, and XHG was the frame in the extension of the centre console.

The carbon interior package was much the same, with EEG being the same in make-up as the EEB wood equivalent, EEH corresponded to EEC, EEJ to EED, and EEK to EEF. XHL was a multi-function steering wheel with a carbonfibre rim, and XHM the part that trimmed the centre console aft of the HVAC and audio controls. It was a similar story with the brushed aluminium package, with EEL, EEM, EEN and EEP making up the gear selector and trim pieces, while XYE was the console section; XYA was a special alloy head for the PDK selector, and EFA was an aluminium alloy pedal set.

The interior package in leather saw the dash and door strip in hide that matched the interior (EEA), with XVP (later EES) being the dashboard dressing piece only option. The dashboard trim package (CZW) included the outer edges on both sides, the area butting up to the windscreen and speaker covers being trimmed, while CXM was the equivalent for the doors, albeit not dropping as low as the

An early Boxster S with a number of Exclusive paint options, including colour-keyed wheels, side intakes, door mirrors, rear apron, and headlight washer posts; the body-colour roll-over hoops were a regular option (code 546).

loudspeaker grille. The PCM unit and HVAC control panel had a leather trim option, too (code CUR), as did the console aft of that (XHB), the air vent surrounds on the fascia (CZV), the seatbelt receivers (CDT), fusebox lids (CUJ), and the rearview mirror (CVW).

Cars with the leather package or full leather upholstery could have the central armrest upgraded with a Porsche crest (XPT) or model designation script (XUV), while XSC was the code for a Porsche crest on the seat headrests.

Alcantara trim could be specified on the PDK selector (option CLH), although the gearknob for the manual transmission (CLB) took a little while to follow. The initial Exclusive catalogue listed a steering wheel in Alcantara (CLA), incidentally, but this failed to show up in price lists, so one has to assume it was thought of but ultimately not offered. Coloured seatbelts were another Exclusive option, coming in silver-grey (XSH), beige (XHP), red (XSX), yellow (XHN) or blue (XHR), while personalised floor mats with leather edging (CFX) and a leather key pouch (CPE) rounded things off for the time being.

Soon after, July brought with it a full sports exhaust system (XLF), to give a throatier sound that reminded enthusiasts of the Porsches of

Another S with Exclusive paint touches, but more importantly, being shod with 'SportTechno' alloys.

The Exclusive programme really did allow an owner to create exactly the vehicle they wanted ...

Porsche Exclusive

Creative freedom is another form of exclusivity.
With the range of options featured in this catalogue, you can make your Porsche even more special. Introducing Porsche Exclusive. Have your vehicle individually

and exclusively tailored to your wishes even before it leaves the factory. Aesthetically and technically, inside and outside, using fine materials and with customary Porsche quality.

Our overriding principle? That your car is uniquely handcrafted to your taste. You will find a wide range of design options in the separate Porsche Exclusive Boxster catalogue.

Either your Porsche Centre or the customer centre in Zuffenhausen (phone +49 (0) 711-25977) will be happy to answer any questions about Porsche Exclusive that you may have.

The new P03 bucket seat option.

the regular cruise control setup (454), it was not a substitute for an autonomous setup, but for those fond of gadgets ...

Finally, the P03 option, which was a lightweight leather-trimmed bucket seat with a carbonfibre shell, had been around for a while in the 987s and 997s, but was not listed for the new Boxster initially. The author has been unable to pin down exactly when it made the 981 catalogues, although it was in the first Cayman price list without any delays noted, so we can assume it was ready for 2013 season. Incidentally, heating was not available on the P03 seats until the autumn of 2013, and the ventilation package was simply not suitable; quoting option CMT, though, brought a painted finish to the seatbelt passages.

Like the P03 option, the coloured instrument faces appeared mysteriously. As with the Sport Chrono dial, four hues were available: Beige (XFL), red (XFG), yellow (XFR) and white (XFJ). The last oddities include an Alcantara-trimmed gearknob for manual cars (CLB), a SportDesign steering wheel in Alcantara (XLK, regardless of transmission), carbon treadplates (X69, or XXD when fitted with lighting, or CXE if lit and personalised), stainless steel treadplates with the same variations as the carbon ones (X70, XXB and CXC), a contrasting leather colour on the steering wheel rim, which could be specified using the Exclusive CLU code, a leather steering column surround (XNS), a leather main instrument surround (XNG), a leather back and base for the P07 seats (XWK), a powerful Burmester surround sound system (682) with 12 speakers, and an online services package (UN1), for those that just can't stay off the net. Again, though, the gaps would point to a 2013 Model Year introduction, with the treadplate options definitely coming online in November 2012.

Other European outlets

We had been in a 'world car spec' situation for some time at Porsche, with a domestic vehicle being almost identical to a French one or a Swiss one, for example, with the same grades available and the same options. Even advertising and other promotional material was shared across borders well beyond the EU, with only the language changing from the original scripted in Stuttgart to suit the local environment.

One of the few markets displaying major differences compared to the German models was the UK one, mainly due to the right-hand drive, but also the use of miles per hour for road markings – a 175mph clock was used on the strict Boxster, while the S inherited a 190mph one. Otherwise, except for the position of the main light switch, ignition barrel and handbrake (and the fitting of an alarm as standard on both grades), the specifications were basically the same.

Available from June 2012, so the chances of seeing a Carrara White car are remote to say the least, the strict Boxster was priced at

yore. Also, the Carrara White hue was replaced by plain old White on the colour charts (a purer shade), while Amaranth Red and Emerald Green joined the fray for the first time, along with a grey/orange two-tone interior choice.

One would have thought things would settle after this, but the options kept on coming. Introduced on the new 911 Carrera 4, an adaptive cruise control (ACC) system was announced for all Porsche models in the autumn of 2012. Using a radar mounted in the central 'intake' in the front air dam to sense closing speeds and the distance from the car ahead, it was hooked up to a Porsche Active Safe (PAS) system that adjusted the throttle position and applied the brakes if necessary in order to keep a reasonable gap between vehicles. Obtained via the 456 option code and costing five times more than

A manual UK-spec 2.7-litre Boxster enjoying the country roads of Britain – one of the world's best sports car environments once you can escape the crowds.

£37,589, while the Boxster S was listed at £45,384 – similar money to the AMG version of the Mercedes SLK and the big BMW Z4, with the 2.7-litre model competing nicely with machines like the Lotus Elise.

Autocar did a full test on a 3.4-litre car equipped with a PDK transmission, and liked the "benign, involving handling," as well as the everyday practicality and "formidable engine and gearbox" – the former sporting "flexibility, response and creamy smoothness" while the PDK was described as being "lightning fast." Comment was also passed on the steering ("no more to be feared here than it was with the 991 911") and the distinct lack of scuttle shake and chassis flex, while a test average of 25.2mpg was definitely something to be applauded.

However, Britain's usual blend of weather was apt to compromise grip, and the testers mentioned an "occasional gearbox shunt" that went against the general praise for smooth shifts. The coasting feature wasn't appreciated either, although the 'Sport' mode quickly disabled it.

There was also the issue of standard equipment, for while the basic price of the Boxster was reasonable enough, options were rather expensive, with £182 being asked for a windblocker for instance, while the cost of wheels and suchlike soon added telephone numbers to the invoice – PDK transmission adding £1922, over a grand for the Sport Chrono package, £971 for PASM and £890 for PTV. Still, this has always been the case with German cars for as long as time itself.

The rhd steering was something inherited by the good folks in the Antipodes, of course, due to their links with Britain. Australians preferred the metric system, though, so speedometers were marked up in kilometres per hour rather than miles per hour.

With sales starting in July 2012, the 6MT base car was listed at $107,000, with the S grade at $133,300; PDK transmission was a $5300 extra on both grades. However, prices were reduced slightly as the Aussies entered the 2013 season proper – enough to make the PDK option appear free compared to a few months earlier.

Another major market having right-hand drive as the norm is Japan, although, unlike Australia, left-hand drive is allowed, and indeed quite common on imported vehicles, being regarded amongst connoisseurs as something of a status symbol.

Gauges are calibrated in km/h, although given Japan's ridiculous speed limits (seemingly unchanged since the horseless carriage era in many areas), few owners would get to see the speedo needle sweep majestically much beyond its halfway point. Notwithstanding, the following for Porsches in Japan is very strong, and always has been.

Available in the Land of the Rising Sun from June 2012, the 2.7-litre car was priced at 5,840,000 yen in manual guise, or 6,310,000 yen if the PDK gearbox was specified. The S, meanwhile, was 7,270,000 yen with the 6MT setup, or 7,740,000 yen with the seven-speed PDK transmission. To put this into perspective, the cheapest 987 Cayman was just over 6,000,000 yen, while the Mercedes-Benz SLK line-up started at 5,250,000 yen; the two-litre Mazda MX-5 enjoyed a huge price advantage, of course, the NC3 RS coming in at 2,600,000 yen at the time.

Whilst in Asia, we should mention China, not least because by the time the 981 series came along, it had already become a very important market for the Stuttgart maker, moving up to be second in the league table of Porsche outlets. Unlike Japan, with a long history attached to the marque, this lhd country is a newcomer to the joys of Porsche motoring. But, as with parts of the Middle East, this is somewhere we will have to acknowledge as a major market sooner or later, assuming the current pace of growth keeps up.

The US market

Although the new Boxster had been announced at the beginning of 2012, as with most export markets, it wasn't until the start of summer that the first deliveries took place Stateside. The 2.7-litre model was priced at $49,500, incidentally, with the S put at $60,900, although a $950 delivery charge was quickly added to the invoice before any options were specified, and, as in Germany, there were plenty of those to choose from!

Despite the 'world car spec' scenario in place in virtually every corner of the globe, the front repeater (side marker) lenses were orange on US cars, and the American importers also had their own ideas on a few things – nothing dramatic, as most bits and pieces were the same, but enough to set the US Boxsters apart from their cousins abroad.

For sure, the left-hand drive was common enough, and the mph calibrations on the speedo were used in the UK as well, so they were not unique. However, the faux suede Alcantara insert was shunned in favour of ventilated vinyl on the basic seats, and cars with full leather were generally given a bright dressing strip underneath the door cappings.

Although the catalogue has areas where the specifications have been carried over from Germany instead of showing the true US

Opposite: A British rhd PDK-equipped Boxster S running on 'Carrera S' alloys. In addition to the conventional interior shot, we also have one of the rear luggage compartment seeing as we showed only the front one earlier in the chapter.

The 981 series was a runaway winner in the 'World Performance Car' category in the annual World Car Awards for 2013, the ceremony being held at the New York Show in March that year. Naturally, given the launch date of the new Cayman, it was the Boxster that was largely responsible for the accolade. Here, PCNA boss Detlev von Platen can be seen holding the WCA trophy next to a US-spec Boxster S, with the amber repeaters used in the States in clear view.

situation, we can safely say that a tyre pressure monitor was classed as standard, as was cruise control, steering wheel heating, an alarm, and the HomeLink garage door opener.

One could also buy bundle packages not listed elsewhere. These included an Infotainment Package, which included the PCM head unit with a navigation module, the Sound Package Plus speaker upgrade, and a SiriusXM satellite radio receiver; there was also a second option that replaced Sound Package Plus with the Bose setup.

Next up was the Convenience Package, with a windblocker, dual-zone AC and seat heating. This became the Premium Package when PDLS headlights, P06 seats and auto-dimming mirrors were added to the other three items. Alternatively, for $5265, one could change the P06 seats for the P07 version with an even higher level of power adjustment.

A press launch is always a good indication of what's on offer, but in places like America, with rather different road conditions to those of Europe, as well as different expectations from customers, it's the domestic journalists that can sway a decision on potential purchases.

Judging by the *Car & Driver* report from Don Sherman, there was no need for the folks back in Stuttgart to worry: "Leaving well enough alone doesn't translate into German, especially the dialect spoken by Porsche engineers. Witness the new, judiciously polished Boxster, a machine that advances the modern sports car."

Commenting on the lack of scuttle shake and wind noise before clocking a 0-60 dash of 4.4 seconds and a standing-quarter time of 12.9 with a manual S, Sherman added: "So good is the new Boxster's driving experience that we forgot to mention how good it looks. It looks really good." Enough said.

Meanwhile, *Road & Track* observed: "The 2013 Boxster S is a sweet, viceless car, but the powertrain is the heart of the package, [creating] a yowl that had the locals peeking out their front doors, expecting something far more exotic." The scribe was happy with the ride, too, as well as the brakes and steering, and found the PDK was intuitive enough to be left in 'D' without the need to resort to manual shifts. Real-world fuel consumption was also mentioned, making those in the catalogue seem surprisingly realistic.

Esquire immediately named the new Boxster its '2012 Sports Car of the Year,' stating: "The Boxster is a near perfect sports car. It's fun, aggressive and sounds great. It serves as a thrilling reminder that cars still maintain the power to stimulate the imagination." A few weeks later, *Automobile* gave the newcomer its 'Design of the Year' award, and the silverware would keep on coming, especially after its tin-top cousin joined the ranks …

Selected pages from the first American catalogue. Although not identical to the ones released in Europe, official Porsche brochures (and adverts) were now near enough the same across the globe, with only languages changed to suit. (pages 60-81)

The New Boxster.

A higher form of intelligence.
A pure expression of independence.

Has it really been 15 years since the debut of the original Boxster? An instant design classic, a powerful mid-engined sports car, a purebred roadster. It was clear the Boxster did full justice to its predecessors in the Porsche lineage. As Porsche engineers planned the third-generation Boxster, the question was, how could it continue to do so in the future? How could the Boxster evolve into something even more evocative of the essence of Porsche performance? The answer was found where it always is at

Porsche: in the harmonious blending of style, functionality, and innovation. The new Boxster is nothing less than the total refinement of Porsche's belief of what a roadster should be, honed and sharpened to give it a completely new expression.

We achieved this with Intelligent Performance. With increased power that is delivered more efficiently. With innovative technologies, the strategic use of lightweight materials in its construction, and with an

exterior and interior design that puts aesthetically appealing lines and curves in all the right places.

More independent of spirit than ever before, the Boxster is now even more powerful, visceral, and intense.

Rarely has intelligence looked so sensuous.

Design.

Exterior
In elevating expectations of how the Boxster should perform, Porsche has once again succeeded in creating an icon of automotive design. It is a Porsche that continues to epitomize the feeling of power in

its most efficient form, of pleasure heightened by functional excellence. The vertical contour of the headlights was inherited from Porsche race cars of the 1960s and 1970s. The new Boxster may be infused with the genes of past generations, but it ushers in a new and forward-looking design ethos.

Large air intakes give the front a powerful appearance, while the side contour hints at the performance within. The long wheelbase and low, raked windshield are integral to forming the stretched, wedge-shaped silhouette. With the top up, this impression is reinforced by the extreme roofline.

Large wheels, up to 20 inches in size, emphasize the Boxster's wide track and help to achieve a completely new level of athletic performance.

The distinctive shoulder lines give further emphasis to the wheels,

which, in combination with the side air intakes and the mid-engine layout, are reminiscent of the 718 RS 60 Spyder, a lightweight mid-engined Porsche from the 1960s that achieved remarkable success in endurance racing and hill-climbing championships.

The precise lines are more sharply defined than on any previous Porsche design, and run elegantly across the fenders to the rear. It's an imposing look that makes the new Boxster unique among other Porsche models.

The exclusive door styling reflects more recent Porsche design developments. In typical Porsche fashion, it has a clear function. The dynamic contouring improves airflow to the side air intakes.

At the top, it leads into a precise longitudinal edge and, at the bottom, it is underlined by the sculpted door-entry guard. The exterior mirrors are mounted directly on the doors to enhance aerodynamic flow and reduce wind noise.

The rear spoiler is not only a visual treat, but also deploys automatically to reduce lift. Aerodynamics and aesthetics are combined to superb effect. Retracted, the spoiler separation edge makes a seamless transition to

the LED taillights. The narrow direction indicators appear to extend the rear spoiler further. Each taillight sweeps around the central brake light and accentuates the contours of the entire unit. For a striking effect, the reverse

Promise fulfilled.

Design.

Interior

The interior of the new Boxster delivers exactly what the exterior promises—a light, uncluttered, and defined design, existing to fulfill one single aim: the perfect drive.

The entire concept—from the power and contour to the driver's vision—are all drawn in the direction of travel. The Boxster driver's concentration is kept purely on the road, thanks to the intelligent operating concept and the logical arrangement of the controls. The elevated center console cocoons the driver and reduces the

distance from the steering wheel to the shift lever for fast and ergonomic gearshifts. It's just one of many ways that Porsche transfers its experience from the racetrack to the road.

The door styling is similarly dynamic. The door pulls mirror the lines of the center console and blend seamlessly into the overall design. The door storage compartments are sweeping and practical.

The athletic proportions of the new Boxster models make it possible to introduce a new interior architecture. The

driver's seating position is low, and from that vantage point, there is a feeling of space and light without compromising the authentic roadster experience.

Ready to assert your independence? You'll find the ignition located to the left of the steering column, reflecting Porsche's racing heritage. The three-spoke sport steering wheel fits perfectly in your hands. Facing the driver is a cluster of three large circular instruments. The instrument on the right is now a 4.6-inch TFT screen that shows information from the onboard computer or information from the audio system. An inconspicuous shroud shades the instruments for optimal visibility.

The steering wheel rim, shifter lever/gear selector, and door-pull inlays are finished in tactile leather. Silver-colored details add to the refined tone. These include the instrument cluster trim strip, the side and center air-vent surrounds, and the center console.

1 Boxster S with natural leather interior in Carrera Red, SportDesign steering wheel, and other optional equipment

and rear fog lights are arranged in the middle underneath the rear wing. It's a lighting concept without precedent, the result of Porsche's modern use of form. The diffuser with stainless steel tailpipe (dual-tube on the Boxster S) integrated

into the center adds the finishing touch to the powerfully designed rear end.

The new Boxster is clearly inspired by Porsche history. But it is not a mere exercise in retro styling. It is a

completely new interpretation of the mid-engine Porsche roadster, with a clear focus on what Porsche engineers believe the future of the roadster should be.

1

Once again, Porsche erases the line between you and the road.

Boxster.

Everything done to create the new Boxster has a sole purpose: to bring the driver closer to the road. Its 2.7-liter flat-six engine with Direct Fuel Injection (DFI) and VarioCam Plus produces 265 horsepower at 6700 rpm, with a maximum torque of 206 lb.-ft. available from 4500–6500 rpm.

The top track speed is 164 mph. With the precisely geared six-speed manual transmission fitted as standard, the Boxster accelerates from 0–60 mph in just 5.5 seconds. With the optional 7-speed Porsche Doppelkupplung (PDK) and the optional Sport Chrono Package including dynamic gearbox mounts, this time is cut to 5.2 seconds.

Power is transmitted to the road by 18-inch Boxster wheels. Their distinctive five-spoke design affords an unobstructed glimpse of the braking system's black, four-piston, aluminum monobloc fixed calipers. The optional Porsche Ceramic Composite Brakes (PCCB) provide motorsport braking performance.

The slats on the front air intakes a painted to match the exterior colo unmistakable Porsche sound is em via a central exhaust tip in brushed stainless steel.

The engine is in the middle. But everything else is in the extreme.

Boxster S.

The engine is in the middle. But everything else is in the extreme. The Boxster S is an even more vehement interpretation of the Porsche roadster. It has been engineered to provide an immediate, intense experience.

Producing 315 horsepower at 6700 rpm, and a maximum torque of 266 lb.-ft. at 4500–5800 rpm, the 3.4-liter flat-six engine with DFI and VarioCam Plus delivers an added 50 horsepower and 50 lb.-ft. of torque more than the engine in the Boxster. The sprint from 0–60 mph is completed in just 4.8 seconds, and a top track speed of 173 mph can be achieved.

Yet even this exceptional level of dynamic performance can be further enhanced. With the optional Porsche Doppelkupplung (PDK) transmission and the optional Sport Chrono Package, the new Boxster S is capable of a 0–60 sprint in a mere 4.5 seconds.

Optional Porsche Torque Vectoring (PTV) offers increased agility and driving pleasure at the same time as improving traction and handling.

Extra horsepower demands extra stopping power. The front brake discs are 0.59 of an inch larger in diameter than those on the Boxster, and the brake calipers are finished in red.

19-inch Boxster S light-alloy wheels with a double-spoke design create an exceptionally powerful presence. The slats on the front air intakes are finished in black. The Boxster S comes with Bi-Xenon™ headlights as standard. The centrally positioned dual-tube twin tailpipe in brushed stainless steel sounds as impressive as it looks.

In the interior of the Boxster S, the door panel armrests and the storage compartment lid in the center console are additionally upholstered in leather. The rev counter has an aluminum-colored dial face.

**The mid-engine belongs at Porsche.
And it belongs in the Boxster.**

Boxer engines.

Porsche first explored the mid-mounted engine in the 1950s, in sports cars such as the 550 Spyder. The advantages were obvious. The concentration of mass close to the center of the vehicle and the low center of gravity heightened the car's cornering dynamics. At the same time, evenly distributing the engine's weight between the front and rear axles created handling characteristics that were equally well-balanced. The driver of a mid-engine Porsche could wring satisfaction from every corner.

Porsche's mid-engined design proved to be a key factor in countless racing victories. On some of the world's most famous racing circuits, Porsche drivers often found they could out-corner their heavier, more powerful competition. In the 1960s, the 718 RS 60 Spyder solidified the reputation of Porsche's mid-engined race cars as "giant killers," with numerous wins in hill-climbing and endurance events.

For us, there are many reasons to remain faithful to the mid-mounted engine concept, to keep transferring performance from the racetrack

to the road, and to continue to combine tradition with innovation. How do we do it? Through Intelligent Performance, our commitment to high power with comparatively low fuel consumption and emissions figures.

With this aim, we developed two compact and lightweight boxer engines able to deliver high levels of power and efficiency simultaneously. Both engines are equipped with efficient technologies as standard, including VarioCam Plus, Direct Fuel Injection (DFI), Auto Start Stop, electrical system recuperation, and enhanced thermal management.

What else could we have given the mid-mounted engine? An even more agile response. One press of the Sport button on the center console makes engine performance even more dynamic for driving pleasure at the limits of performance. Let's take a look in more detail.

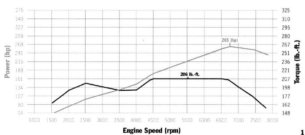

1 Power output and torque chart for the Boxster
2 Power output and torque chart for the Boxster S
3 Boxster S engine

2.7-Liter Engine

The Boxster model is equipped with a 2.7-liter flat-six engine with Direct Fuel Injection (DFI) and VarioCam Plus. It generates 265 horsepower at 6700 rpm. A maximum torque of 206 lb.-ft. is available over a broad engine-speed range from 4500–6500 rpm.

3.4-Liter Engine

The Boxster S is powered by a 3.4-liter flat-six engine with Direct Fuel Injection (DFI) and VarioCam Plus. It develops 315 horsepower at 6700 rpm and a maximum torque of 266 lb.-ft. is produced between 4500 and 5800 rpm.

Direct Fuel Injection (DFI)

Direct Fuel Injection (DFI) is featured as standard in both Boxster engines. Multi-hole injectors deliver fuel directly into the combustion chamber with millisecond precision. The injection pattern has been optimized for torque, power output, fuel consumption, and emissions.

With direct injection, the engine management system regulates injection timing individually for each cylinder, as well as the injection rate for each cylinder bank. This optimizes the combustion process and enhances fuel economy. Depending on the engine operating conditions, multiple fuel injections can take place on each operating cycle. This allows the catalytic converter to reach normal operating temperature sooner after a cold start and to achieve a higher maximum torque. DFI improves the internal cooling of the combustion chamber by having the mixture prepared directly in the cylinder. This allows for a higher compression ratio, which helps to deliver higher power output at the same time as enhanced engine efficiency. Injection is regulated by the electronic engine management system, and each stereo lambda sensor monitors emissions.

VarioCam Plus

VarioCam Plus is a two-in-one engine concept for adjusting the intake camshafts and switching the lift of the intake valves.

The system first differentiates between driver inputs that typify normal, everyday driving and those inputs that demand maximum performance. The electronic engine management system then imperceptibly adapts valve operation to the prevailing conditions.

The result? Instant acceleration and extremely smooth running.

Integrated Dry-Sump Lubrication

Integrated dry-sump lubrication ensures a reliable supply of oil even when a performance driving style is adopted and the vehicle is experiencing powerful lateral acceleration. It also has additional cooling functions.

The oil tank is located in the engine, eliminating the need for an external oil tank, and saving both space and weight.

To help reduce power losses and incre[ase] efficiency, an electronically controlled oil pump supplies the lubricating point[s] inside the engine when required. This results in an optimal supply of oil, lowe[r] fuel consumption, and reduced emissio[ns]

Thermal Management

The Boxster models feature a new version of thermal management to reduce friction losses that arise during the warm-up phase.

Thanks to the selective control strategy and on-demand, gradual activation of the various cooling circuits, the engine and gearbox warm up to normal operating temperature more rapidly. The consequent reduction in friction also contributes to reducing fuel consumption* and CO_2 emissions. During performance driving, thermal management also acts to reduce temperatures so that a high level of performance is maintained.

A cross-flow cooling system supplies each engine cylinder uniformly with coolant, which helps to protect the valves against thermal overload and premature wear. Keeping each cylinder cool improves combustion and keeps emissions, fuel consumption, and noise comparatively low.

Exhaust System

In the new Boxster models, each cylinder bank has its own stainless steel exhaust tract. Downstream of their respective rear silencer, the tracts converge into a connecting tube and a single (Boxster) or twin (Boxster S) tailpipe. The stereo lambda control circuitry monitors each cylinder bank separately. For each exhaust tract, four corresponding oxygen sensors regulate the composition of the exhaust gas and monitor the performance of the catalytic converters. Having separate tracts means that the exhaust gas can flow more freely. The resulting reduction in pressure loss has a positive impact on power output, torque, and the unmistakable engine sound.

Available as an option for the new Boxster models is the sport exhaust system, including Sport tailpipe. It produces an even more resonant Porsche sound.

Sport Button

Select the Sport mode by pressing the Sport button on the center console. Throttle response becomes even more direct, the rev limiter is adjusted to a harder setting, and engine dynamics are tuned for performance driving. The Auto Start Stop function is also deactivated. Coasting mode is also deactivated automatically.

With the optional Porsche Doppelkupplung (PDK) transmission, the shift points are reconfigured to operate at higher engine speeds. Shift times are reduced and gearshifts become firmer and more immediate, while throttle-blip downshifts are accompanied by an emotive engine sound.

Auto Start Stop Function

This fuel-saving innovation is designed primarily for use in congested traffic. The Auto Start Stop function switches off the engine when you stop, select Neutral, and release the clutch pedal. In cars with Porsche Doppelkupplung (PDK), it is simply a case of applying and holding the brake.

All audio and communication systems remain switched on, as does the air-conditioning system. The engine will restart as soon as you operate the clutch or, in cars with PDK, release the brake. The Auto Start Stop function can be deactivated and reactivated using a separate button on the center console. The function may be deactivated automatically under particular circumstances, such as when the Sport button is selected or there is low battery charge.

*Note: Please see fuel economy estimates on page 108.

Electrical System Recuperation

For enhanced efficiency, the new Boxster models are equipped with intelligent electrical system recuperation. The vehicle battery is recharged by the generator, predominantly under braking. Thanks to this selective recharging, when you require full driving power, the maximum possible output can be directed straight to the road.

1 Boxster tailpipe
2 Boxster S twin tailpipe
3 Sport button
4 Auto Start Stop button

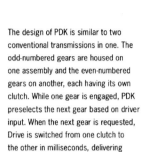

4

Act or relax as you please.

Transmission.

1 Gearshift for six-speed manual gearbox
2 PDK gear selector
3 PDK gearshift switches on multifunction
  steering wheel
4 Porsche Doppelkupplung (PDK)
  Half gearbox 1: gears 1, 3, 5, 7, R
  Half gearbox 2: gears 2, 4, 6

Six-Speed Manual Gearbox

The new Boxster models come standard with a lightweight six-speed manual transmission. Gearshifts are smooth and optimally adapted to the respective engine map. Shifting is short and sporty and the gear lever is easy to operate, enabling a rapid gearshift action and providing a truly engaging driving experience. The upshift indicator located in the central circular instrument helps you to maximize fuel efficiency.

The elevated center console gives you an authentic sports car feel. It positions the gear lever close to the steering wheel, which enables you to change gear as fast and as ergonomically as possible.

Porsche Doppelkupplung (PDK)

Available as an option for the new Boxster models is a completely re-tuned 7-speed Porsche Doppelkupplung (PDK), featuring both manual and automatic modes.

PDK offers extremely fast gear changes with no interruption in the flow of power, improved acceleration over the manual gearbox, very short response times, reduced fuel consumption, and a distinct increase in comfort.

In total, PDK has seven forward gears at its disposal. Gears 1 to 6 have a sport ratio, and top speed is reached in 6th gear. The 7th gear ratio is longer and keeps engine speed low to improve ride comfort and reduce fuel consumption at higher speeds.

The design of PDK is similar to two conventional transmissions in one. The odd-numbered gears are housed on one assembly and the even-numbered gears on another, each having its own clutch. While one gear is engaged, PDK preselects the next gear based on driver input. When the next gear is requested, Drive is switched from one clutch to the other in milliseconds, delivering gear changes with no loss of power.

With the Sport button selected, the full advantages of the new version of PDK are brought into play: a more immediate response to throttle inputs; even shorter shift times; and swift, throttle-blip downshifts on overrun and when braking. Even the sound you hear from the exhaust is altered to elicit a more visceral response.

With the optional Sport Chrono Package, PDK is enhanced by the Launch Control and motorsport-derived gearshift strategy functions, for even faster and firmer gear changes and the best possible performance, thanks to a boost in torque during upshift phases. Overrun downshifts provide extremely sporty braking and acceleration for added excitement.

Coasting

A coasting function within the Porsche Doppelkupplung (PDK) helps save even more fuel when the situation allows. The engine is decoupled from the transmission to prevent deceleration caused by engine braking. So the vehicle's momentum is allowed to carry it for longer distances, conserving fuel.

As you ease off the accelerator pedal, PDK deselects the current gear automatically and you begin to coast in Neutral until you have reached your desired speed. As soon as you operate the accelerator or brake pedal, PDK re-engages the appropriate gear within fractions of a second. The process is smooth and seamless, thanks to the extremely fast clutch.

Another way to reduce fuel consumption is to activate the coasting function on downhill gradients that are gentle enough for you to maintain a constant speed. Efficient on long uninterrupted drives such as an interstate journey, PDK remains ready to respond as swiftly and precisely as you would expect.

In short, driving in coasting mode increases fuel efficiency without any need for compromise in comfort or performance.

Self-control is a sign of intelligence.

Chassis.

The chassis of the new Boxster models is the ideal match for the more powerful engines. Axle components are now made predominantly of lightweight aluminum. Keeping the weight of the vehicle and its unsprung masses low reduces fuel consumption,* improves comfort, and increases agility.

The wheelbase has been extended by 2.3 inches (60 mm) compared with the previous model. The wide track provides additional stability and enhanced comfort. The new independent suspension features lightweight spring-strut axles with longitudinal and transverse links and, at the front, cross members that have been refined for optimal control. As a result, each wheel

moves precisely to help ensure excellent directional stability and superior handling.

What does this mean for the driver? The sophisticated engineering of chassis, combined with the mid-engine layout, translates intelligent design into dynamic performance. Body roll and pitch have been practically eliminated to offer a level of agility that turns each corner into an incomparable experience.

Porsche Active Suspension Management (PASM)
The optional PASM brings a remarkable level of intelligence to how the Boxster reacts to the road. An electronic suspension control system, PASM actively and continuously regulates the damping force for each wheel according to the road

conditions and driving style. In addition, PASM lowers the suspension by 10 mm.

The driver can select between two different modes: "Normal," which is a blend of performance and comfort, and "Sport," where the setup is much firmer. Depending on the mode selected, PASM can be both sportier and more comfortable than the standard chassis. The PASM control unit evaluates the driving conditions and modifies the damping force of the shock absorber on each of the wheels in accordance with the selected mode.

Sensors record the body movements that accompany powerful acceleration, braking, or uneven road surfaces. This enables an intelligent response

for the selected mode, optimizing contact between each individual tire and the road and reducing pitch.

In Sport mode, the suspension is set to a harder damper rating. On uneven roads, PASM immediately switches to a softer rating, thereby improving contact between the tires and the road. When the road surface improves, PASM automatically reverts to the original, harder rating. If Normal mode is selected and the driver's style becomes more assertive, PASM switches to a harder rating to increase driving stability and road safety.

The results are tangible: increased driving stability, enhanced driving pleasure, and improved performance.

Steering
The Boxster models now employ a new electromechanical steering system. Unlike a conventional hydraulically assisted steering system that draws engine power continuously, the electric motor in the

new electromechanical system uses energy only when the steering wheel is actually turned. Fuel consumption is reduced, and the absence of hydraulic fluid reduces the need for servicing.

The new steering system even improves the steering feel. Its variable-steering ratio provides precise and direct feedback for more agile response at higher speeds, while at the same time achieving a high level of comfort and steering ease at

low speeds. Power Steering Plus, the optional speed-sensitive power-steering system, further minimizes steering effort during maneuvering and parking.

1 Front axle of the Boxster S
2 Rear axle of the Boxster S

Wheels

The standard wheels on the new Boxster models are now one inch larger in diameter compared with those of the previous models. Made from a lightweight alloy, the larger wheels reinforce the new design's imposing presence and further hone its performance edge.

The new Boxster is equipped with 18-inch wheels. Their minimalist five-spoke design is sporty and elegant in equal measure. Tire sizes are 235/45 ZR 18 and 265/45 ZR 18 at the front and rear respectively.

The Boxster S has 19-inch wheels with a dynamic dual-spoke design. The tire size at the front is 235/40 ZR 19 and 265/40 ZR 19 at the rear.

The larger rolling circumference improves comfort and performance. At the same time, the rolling resistance of the new generation of tires has been reduced, which, in turn, helps to reduce fuel consumption.

Wheels up to 20 inches are available as an option.

Tire Pressure Monitoring System (TPMS)

The standard Tire Pressure Monitoring System (TPMS) sends warnings to the onboard computer's display screen in the event of low tire pressure. The 4.6-inch TFT screen in the instrument cluster enables the driver to check the pressure in all four tires. The system updates quickly and accurately after every engine start, tire pressure correction, or wheel change—for increased comfort and safety.

Brakes

Both models are equipped with four-piston, aluminum monobloc fixed calipers at the front and rear. This design means that not only are the brakes extremely resistant to deformation, but they are lightweight for a particularly fast and sensitive braking response.

The new generation of brake caliper at the front axle, combined with enlarged brake pads and the newly developed brake booster, has managed to improve braking and component stability even during continuous use. These

Porsche Ceramic Composite Brakes (PCCB)

The optional Porsche Ceramic Composite Brake (PCCB) system has long proven its worth in motorsports, fitted in cars that compete in demanding events such as the Porsche Mobil 1 Supercup.

The cross-drilled PCCB ceramic brake discs for the new Boxster have a diameter of 13.77 inches front and rear for even more formidable braking performance.

The use of six-piston, aluminum monobloc fixed brake calipers on the front axle and four-piston units at the rear—all finished in yellow—

ensures extremely high brake forces, which are exceptionally consistent.

PCCB enables shorter braking distances in tough road and race conditions. Excellent fade resistance ensures greater balance when slowing from racetrack speeds.

The ceramic brake discs are approximately 50 percent lighter than standard discs of similar design and size. This represents a major reduction in unsprung and rotating masses. The consequence of this extremely low weight is better roadholding and increased comfort, particularly on uneven roads, as well as enhanced fuel economy.

5

1 18-inch Boxster wheel
2 19-inch Boxster S wheel
3 Standard brake on the Boxster
4 Standard brake on the Boxster S
5 Porsche Ceramic Composite Brake (PCCB)

two characteristics have also been optimized by the newly developed brake ventilation system with a modified air spoiler at the front and rear axles.

The enhanced dynamics of the Boxster and Boxster S also demand appropriate brake discs. All Boxster brake discs are internally vented and cross-drilled for improved braking in wet conditions. On the Boxster S, the diameter of the front brake discs has been enlarged by 0.59 of an inch, to 12.99 inches. At the rear, the diameter is the same as on the Boxster—11.77 inches. The brake calipers on the Boxster and Boxster S are black and red respectively.

Please note that circuit racing, track-day use, and other forms of performance driving can significantly reduce the service life of even the most durable pads and discs. As with conventional high-performance braking systems, we recommend that all brake components be professionally inspected and replaced where necessary after every track event.

Electric Parking Brake
The electric parking brake, which can be activated and deactivated manually, is released automatically as you pull away with your seat belt fastened. A hill-hold function is integrated as standard for the manual gearbox and for PDK. It assists you in making a comfortable, smooth, and roll-free start on an incline.

Whenever you come to halt on an incline, this is detected automatically and the braking effect of the electric parking brake is supplemented by application of the wheel brakes. As long as a gear remains engaged, the brake pressure is maintained at all four wheels. To pull away, simply apply throttle (manual gearbox: Apply throttle and release the

clutch pedal). The wheel brakes are released as soon as sufficient starting torque is available, and the parking brake is released as the vehicle moves off.

Porsche Stability Management (PSM)

Enhanced Porsche Stability Management (PSM) is standard. This system uses sensors to continuously monitor the speed, yaw velocity, and lateral acceleration of the car. Using this information, PSM is able to calculate the actual direction of travel at any given moment. If the car begins to oversteer or understeer, PSM applies selective braking on individual wheels in order to help restore stability.

Under acceleration on wet or low-grip road surfaces, PSM improves traction—as well as agility and safety—using the Automatic Brake Differential (ABD) and Anti-Slip Regulation (ASR). Integrated ABS is designed to minimize braking distances.

If you prefer an even sportier drive, PSM can be switched off. For your safety, however, PSM remains set to intervene if the vehicle is braked and ABS assistance is required. ABS and ABD remain switched on at all times. Also included with PSM is Engine Drag Torque Control (EDC), precharging of the brake system, and Brake Assist. If you suddenly release the accelerator pedal, PSM automatically prepares for your next action: The braking system is precharged so that the brake pads are already in light contact with the brake discs. Maximum braking power is therefore achieved much sooner. Brake Assist detects a panic braking situation and generates the brake pressure required for maximum deceleration.

Dynamic Gearbox Mounts

Dynamic gearbox mounts are included as part of the optional Sport Chrono Package. They are designed to enhance both performance and comfort by controlling centrifugal forces.

The electronically controlled system minimizes the oscillations and vibrations of the entire drivetrain, especially the engine.

The gearbox is bolted to the body by two mounts. Like any mass, it obeys the law of inertia. This means that it will continue moving in a uniformly straight line unless some force causes it to change direction. Put more simply: When you are driving into a curve, the vehicle will follow your steering but, at first, the mass of the drivetrain will not. This means that the rear of the vehicle will ultimately be pushed outward as a result of the drivetrain's force of inertia.

Dynamic gearbox mounts minimize this effect. Steering angle and both longitudinal and lateral acceleration are constantly recorded by sensors. The stiffness and damping performance of the gearbox mounts adapt to changes in driving style and road surface conditions, which is achieved by use of a fluid with magnetic properties. This results in greater traction, perceptibly more stable handling under load-change conditions and in fast corners, and, in conjunction with the Launch Control function for example, extremely fast acceleration.

Using the Sport or Sport Plus button, you can switch the dynamic gearbox mou[nts] from Normal to Sport or Performance mode and intensify your driving pleas[ure].

Sport Chrono Package

Time is precious and every hundredth of a second counts. The optional Sport Chrono Package provides an even sportier tuning of throttle response and handling characteristics.

The package comprises dynamic transmission mounts, a performance display, a digital and analog stopwatch, and the Sport Plus button. When this is pressed, optional Porsche Active Suspension Management (PASM) offers more intensive roadholding, switching to Sport mode for firmer damping and more direct steering.

The trigger threshold for the Porsche Stability Management (PSM) system is raised. Agility is perceptibly enhanced when braking for corners with PSM, allowing even sportier braking and exit acceleration. For even greater dexterity,

PSM can be set to standby while the car is still in Sport Plus mode. For safety, it is set to intervene automatically only when ABS assistance is required.

In conjunction with the optional PDK, the Sport Chrono Package comes with two additional functions. The first is Launch Control, which is designed to optimize acceleration from a standing start.

The second function is a motorsport-derived gearshift strategy. Using this, Porsche Doppelkupplung (PDK) is geared up for the shortest possible shift times and optimal shift points, while torque boosts during gear changes provide the maximum acceleration available. This involving experience is further enhanced by overrun downshifts and the throttle-blip function for uncompromising driving pleasure.

An additional display in either the steering wheel or the instrument cluster indicates

the Sport or Sport Plus button—and, with PDK, Launch Control—has been activated. In conjunction with the optional Porsche Communication Management (PCM), a special display enables you to view, store, and evaluate lap times or other driving times. It shows the total driving time, lap distance, lap number, and lap times recorded so far.

1 Sport Chrono display on the PDK steering wheel
2 Sport Chrono stopwatch
3 Sport and Sport Plus buttons

44

injunction with the optional PCM, the ...e graphic on the TFT screen in ...ght-hand circular instrument enables ...o view the lateral and longitudinal ...s as they act on the vehicle.

1 Dynamic gearbox mounts

Porsche Torque Vectoring (PTV)

This optional system for increasing dynamic performance and stability varies the distribution of torque to the rear wheels and includes a mechanically locking rear differential.

When the car is driven assertively into a corner, moderate brake pressure is applied to the inside rear wheel.

Consequently, a greater amount of driving force is distributed to the outside rear wheel, inducing an additional rotational pulse (yaw movement) around the vehicle's vertical axis. This results in a direct and sporty steering action as the car enters the corner.

At low and medium vehicle speeds, PTV significantly increases agility and steering precision. At high speeds and when accelerating out of corners, the rear differential lock helps to ensure greater driving stability on a range of surface conditions, including wet and snow.

The results are remarkable stability, easier handling, and outstanding traction, as well as greater agility at speed with precise steering and stable load-transfer characteristics. What else? As ever, lots of excitement at every twist and turn.

Lights

Clear glass halogen headlights are fitted as standard on the Boxster. The Boxster S is equipped as standard with Bi-Xenon™ headlights. On both models, LED daytime running lights and position lights are housed in a separate auxiliary light unit above the outer air intakes. LEDs provide powerful illumination, respond extremely rapidly to driver input, offer a longer service life, and have an unmistakable appearance.

LED technology opens up entirely new possibilities for designers. Not only are LEDs capable of fulfilling all the functions of the imposing taillights and third brake light—they are integral to safety and create a look that is unmistakable, day and night.

Bi-Xenon™ Headlights Including Porsche Dynamic Light System (PDLS)

Why should independence be enjoyed only at night? The optional Porsche Dynamic Light System (PDLS)—which comprises Bi-Xenon™ headlights with halogen main-beam headlights, a headlight-cleaning system, and automatic dynamic range control—provides uniform illumination of the road, whether dipped or high beam is selected.

The dynamic cornering light function swivels the main headlights toward the inside of a curve, based on steering angle and road speed. Put simply, a greater part of the road ahead is illuminated the moment you enter a curve.

The system also includes a speed-sensitive headlight range control function. With adaptive light systems, it is possible for the maximum range of the dipped beams and their lighting power to be adjusted as a function of the speed of the vehicle. PDLS takes care of this automatically in two stages. Stage 1 is the basic position, optimized for driving at lower speeds such as in city traf[fic]. Stage 2 is designed for driving at higher speeds, such as when on the highway. Another function of PDLS i[s] the adverse weather function. Activ[e] when you switch on the rear fog ligh[t] it reduces the effect of reflection phenomena in poor visibility conditi[ons].

The foundation of Intelligent Performance.

Safety.

All of the performance goals of a Porsche are grounded in the belief that peace of mind is essential to driving pleasure. The active and passive safety concept of the new Boxster models is founded on a precisely engineered chassis and high-performance braking system. It also involves intelligent control systems such as Porsche Stability Management (PSM), and depends on an innovative body construction designed to keep your roadster stable without diminishing its agility.

Engineered Body Design

The bodyshell of the new Boxster models is based on an intelligent lightweight principle involving the composite construction of aluminum and steel. The use of dissimilar but precisely combined components makes it possible to utilize specific material properties exactly where they are needed. Not only does this provide a high level of safety for the driver, but it also offers a considerable weight saving compared with the bodyshell of the previous model. This is why the doors of both luggage compartment lids are made from lightweight aluminum.

The crumple zones in the front and rear aprons feature integral light-alloy bumpers, while impact absorbers offer additional safety. For the protection of occupants, energy-absorbing padding is used selectively in important areas within the passenger cell.

Fuel Economy and Recycling

Intelligent lightweight construction has been fundamental to the Porsche identity since 1948 for both technical and ecological reasons. This forms the basis for achieving efficient fuel consumption values in conjunction with outstanding performance.

On the technical side, various compo[nents] are made with a high proportion of aluminum, magnesium, plastics, and super high-strength sheet steel. The materials used have been selected f[or] their ability to withstand load, yet the[y] are considerably lighter than conver[...] steel. As a result, the bodyshell of t[he] new Boxster models has a light-alloy content of approximately 46 percen[t].

...matic Headlight Activation

...e new Boxster models, automatic ...light activation is available as ...dard. The system automatically ...ches between daytime running lights ...dipped beams, based on ambient ...ng conditions.

1 Night design, front
2 Night design, rear
3 Taillight
4 Brake light
5 Taillight and direction indicator

Live for the moment.
Plan for tomorrow.

Environment.

Every automotive manufacturer must ask itself what it has to offer in terms of reducing environmental impact. At Porsche, our answer has long been the same: Intelligent Performance—a combination of high power output and high efficiency.

In recent years, Porsche has managed to reduce fuel consumption across all model ranges by a double-digit* percentage compared with the respective previous model, even though performance has been increased in every generation. This is made possible by an efficient drive concept (e.g., Direct

Fuel Injection (DFI) and VarioCam Plus), lightweight construction, optimized aerodynamics, and low rolling resistance.

The environmental management team at the Porsche Development Center in Weissach aims to demonstrate a high level of environmental responsibility. Here, technological developments are carried out with environmental protection in mind.

The goal is to enhance performance— but, where possible, not at the expense of the environment. We achieve this goal with Intelligent Performance, as epitomized by the Boxster.

Exhaust Emissions Control
Vehicles manufactured by Porsche demonstrate that even high-performance sports cars can achieve moderate fuel consumption and exhaust emissions values in their respective category.

This is achieved, on the one hand, through the use of fuel-efficient technologies such as Auto Start Stop, thermal management, electrical system recuperation, Direct Fuel Injection (DFI), VarioCam Plus, and, in conjunction with optional PDK, coasting mode.

On the other hand, newly developed catalytic converters provide efficient emissions control, while the stereo lambda sensors control and monitor each cylinder bank separately. For each exhaust tract, oxygen sensors, together with the engine electronics and injectors, regulate the composition of the exhaust gas, while lambda sensors on each cylinder bank monitor pollutant conversion in the respective catalytic converter.

...e ecological side, all materials ...are meticulously selected. We use ...nnovative and environmentally ...lly components. All synthetic ...onents are easily recyclable, and ...material is labeled to facilitate ...paration for recycling. The ...tion in the number of plastic ...nts helps to ensure more efficient

recycling. Recycled plastics are used where they meet our exacting technical requirements. In short, the new Boxster is approximately 95 percent recyclable.

In addition, Porsche uses a high proportion of environmentally friendly water-based paints. For us, environmental protection does not begin at the end

of a vehicle's life. It starts at the planning and development stage.

Fuel
Both Boxster models are designed to operate on fuels with an ethanol content of up to 10 percent. Ethanol has a positive impact on the CO_2 balance since the plants grown for the production of this biofuel also absorb

CO_2 from the atmosphere. The release of hydrocarbons from the fuel system has been minimized, thanks to the active carbon filter and the multilayered material from which the fuel tank is made. All fuel lines are made from multilayered plastic, steel, or aluminum.

Servicing
Long service intervals offer clear advantages. For you, they reduce costs and save time. For the environment, they assist in the sparing use of consumables and replacement parts. For full details of service intervals, please contact your Authorized Porsche dealer.

The ideal two-place cockpit.

Interior and comfort.

The interiors of the new Boxster models are purposefully designed to provide its two occupants complete comfort, convenience, and security.

The geometric form of the cockpit follows a clear direction: forward. The elevated center console orients the driver optimally into the vehicle by positioning the shift lever close to the steering wheel for fast and sporty gear changes.

The generously proportioned interior is light and offers plenty of space for driver and passenger comfort. The individual controls are designed to minimize driver distraction and offer simplicity and intuitive ergonomics.

The standard CDR audio system combines with the optional Sound Package Plus to deliver impressive acoustic performance and has a touchscreen for easy operation. Available as an option, the Bose® Surround Sound System creates an authentic sound experience with eight amplifier channels, 10 loudspeakers, and a total output of 445 watts.

The interior materials are high-quality, and the refined tone is enhanced by a wealth of silver-colored details. These are found on the dashboard trim strip, the center console, the door pulls, the glove compartment release lever, the side and center air vent, and the model designation plaque on the center console.

The steering wheel rim and gear lever/selector are sporty and stylish at the same time. The door-pull inlays are typically Porsche. Finished in leather, they represent a balanced blend of design and functionality. In the Boxster S, the door armrests and the center console storage compartment lid are also finished in leather.

For even sportier elegance, you can request the optional leather package for a stylish leather finish on purposefully selected interior features. As always, a comprehensive leather interior package is also available as an option.

Comfort | Interior and comfort

Leather Package

You may have thought the interior of your new Boxster couldn't be any more stylish, but the optional leather package enhances its overall appeal by adding a leather finish to the instrument cowl, center console storage compartment lid, seat centers, side bolsters and headrests, door armrests, and door pulls. With the leather package, all of these feature a silver-colored trim strip, which accentuates the dynamic and sweeping design of the interior.

You have a choice between a minimalist single-tone interior—with one of the standard colors Black, Platinum Grey, Luxor Beige, or Yachting Blue—and a two-tone combination of Agate Grey and Pebble Grey[1] or, exclusively available for the leather package, Agate Grey and Lime Gold. The features in leather (on the seats, only the seat centers) are finished in the contrasting color.

Instruments

The powerful performance of the new Boxster models may be indescribable, but it can be measured. The three circular instruments give you all the information you need. The rev counter with digital speedometer is positioned in the center. In the Boxster S, the dial face is aluminum-colored; in the Boxster, it is finished in minimalist black. The instrument on the left contains the analog speedometer with digital trip meter and total distance display.

A new feature of the right-hand circular instrument is the high-resolution 4.6-inch TFT color screen. It provides you with a continuous stream of data

[1] Additionally available from 07/2012 at the earliest: two-tone combination of Agate Grey and Amber Orange.

The tools of independence.

Additional comfort and convenience features.

Air-Conditioning System
An air-conditioning system with integrated active carbon filter is fitted as standard. The filter traps particles, pollen, and odors. The ventilation pattern is wide and the air conditioning is quiet and effective.

Two-Zone Automatic Climate Control
Two-zone automatic climate control is available as an option. It provides an enhanced ventilation effect and has separate temperature controls for the driver and front passenger. The available air-conditioning modes are gentle, normal, and strong.

The automatic air-recirculation function permanently monitors air quality, reduces humidity, and switches from fresh to recirculated air when required. Another

function makes it possible to use the residual heat of the engine to heat the passenger compartment for up to 20 minutes with the ignition switched off.

Storage Compartments
Ingenious storage solutions create plenty of space: the lockable glove compartment, the compartment with a power socket under the armrest in the rear center console, and the uncovered compartment to the front of it. In conjunction with the smoking package, the uncovered compartment makes way for an ashtray with a lid. Other storage features include two compartments in each door, a net in the passenger footwell, clothes hooks on the seat backrests, and two practical cupholders above the glove compartment.

Light Design Package
The optional light design package comprises dimmable LEDs in the door panels, overhead console, and footwells. LED lighting in the luggage compartments is additionally included.

"Welcome Home" Lighting
The standard "Welcome Home" lighting function automatically switches on the LED daytime running lights for a user-defined period whenever the vehicle is opened or closed using the key remote.

Water-Repellent Side Windows
The surfaces of the side windows are treated with a water-repellent coating so that not only water but also dirt runs away more easily, thereby providing clearer visibility, even in poor weather.

1 Door storage compartments
2 Cupholder
3 Air-conditioning system
4 Two-zone automatic climate control
5 Uncovered center console storage compartment

...m the onboard computer, reminds ...u of your selected communication ...d audio settings, enables you to ...stomize vehicle settings, delivers ...rious warnings including alerts ...m the optional Tire Pressure ...nitoring System (TPMS), and, in ...njunction with the optional PCM, ...plays the navigation system map.

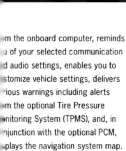

1 Leather package in Agate Grey and Lime Gold
2 Boxster instruments
3 Boxster S instruments

Exterior Mirrors and Rearview Mirror
The new Boxster models come equipped with electrically adjustable and heated exterior mirrors, standard.

Available as an option, electrically folding exterior mirrors with door courtesy lighting on both sides of the vehicle make it easier to find your way in the dark.

An auto-dimming function for the exterior mirrors and rearview mirror with an integrated rain sensor for the windshield wipers is available as an option.

ParkAssist
Optional ParkAssist is activated the moment you select Reverse gear. An audible signal gives a warning if you reverse too close to a large obstacle.

An enhanced version of ParkAssist also provides monitoring of the area to the front of the vehicle. Ultrasonic sensors are neatly integrated into the front and rear aprons. The audible alert is supplemented by a visual warning in the central display of the CDR audio system or optional PCM, which shows a graphical representation of the vehicle from overhead.

HomeLink®
(Programable Garage Door Opener)
The standard programable garage door opener is integrated into the overhead console and remotely controls up to three different garage doors, gates, home lighting, and/or alarm systems.

Anti-Theft Protection
Both new Boxster models are equipped as standard with an immobilizer with in-key transponder. In addition, the Boxster S has an alarm system with contact-sensitive exterior protection. A radar-based interior surveillance system, which enhances protection with the top closed, is available on request.

A combined alarm and radar-based interior surveillance system is available as an option for the Boxster.

Two Luggage Compartments
The two luggage compartments are further proof that the Boxster harmoniously combines the spirit of sport with everyday practicality like never before. The front and rear compartments have a capacity of 5.29 and 4.59 cubic feet respectively, regardless of whether the top is up or down. The interior

surfaces are carpet-lined and the lids are made from aluminum. The two service openings in the rear luggage compartment provide convenient access to the coolant and engine oil filler caps. The separate Porsche Design Driver's Selection catalog contains a selection of matching luggage accessories.

1–3 Loading options with luggage items from the Porsche Design Driver's Selection (items of luggage from the PTS AluFrame and PTS Soft Top series)

Fully Electric Top
Transformation, at the push of a button. The new Boxster models come with a fully electric top, standard. With the engine running, the processes of opening or closing the top are completed in approximately nine seconds. The top is operable at up to a speed of 31 mph (50 km/h).

The newly styled top design blends in elegantly with the contouring of the Boxster models. As a key design feature, it accentuates the new, stretched side view of the vehicle. The top flows backward and sweeps into the body. The especially powerful silhouette promises excellent dynamic performance and delivers impressive aerodynamics. The top stows away compactly above the engine compartment without reducing the luggage compartment volume. The top motor runs exceptionally quietly, and the modern soundproofing fabric is

**We've shown you what rock 'n' roll looks like.
Now you want to know how it sounds.**

Audio and communication.

CDR Audio System

The CDR audio system is an ideal complement to the resonant engine sound of the new Boxster models. It features a seven-inch color touchscreen, giving you quick and easy access to the most important functions and menus.

The integrated CD radio features an FM dual tuner, 30 memory presets, Dynamic Autostore, and speed-sensitive volume control. The system also includes a sound system with four loudspeakers and a total output of 2 x 25 watts.

For an even more intense listening experience, the CDR audio system can be combined with the Sound Package Plus or the Bose® Surround Sound System on request.

HD Radio® Receiver

For the first time, an HD Radio® receiver is now available as an option on the Boxster. HD Radio technology provides access to all of your favorite FM stations plus a broad range of new digital programming. HD Radio also includes advanced audio and data features that enhance your listening experience.

SiriusXM Satellite Radio® Receiver*

Only SiriusXM® brings you more of what you love. The SiriusXM Satellite Radio® receiver, available as an option for Boxster models, includes a three-month free trial period. This service provides over 130 channels coast to coast, including commercial-free music, plus the best sports, news,

talk, comedy, and entertainment. Welcome to the world of satellite radio. Sports and stocks, also provided by SiriusXM®, give you customized updates on your favorite teams and stocks, so you can arrive at your destination well-informed.

The optional NavTraffic® service, available with SiriusXM®, enables PCM to display continuously updated traffic information in over 130 markets. Avoid congestion before you reach it with information on traffic speed, accidents, construction, and road closings.

The optional NavWeather® service, available with SiriusXM®, allows you to stay informed with driver-friendly weather information on the PCM screen.

See storms and severe weather, keep track of weather warnings, and see the current conditions and 3-day forecasts.

CD or CD/DVD Changer

An integrated six-disc CD changer is available for the CDR audio system on request, while an integrated six-disc CD/DVD changer is available for the optional PCM. Both support the playback of tracks in MP3 format.

Sound Package Plus for PCM and CDR

For sophisticated ears: the optionally available Sound Package Plus.

With a total output of 185 watts, seven loudspeakers combine to create the perfect interior sound experience. Audio settings can be customized using the CDR audio system or optional Porsche Communication Management (PCM).

1 CD/DVD changer
2–3 SiriusXM® NavTraffic® and NavWeather®

robust and improves interior acoustics. The large rear window is made from glass and is electrically heated and scratch-resistant, so you can continue to enjoy your freedom whatever the weather.

Wind Deflector

A wind deflector is available as an option. It reduces air turbulence in the cabin and fits easily to the rollover bar.

1 Wind deflector
2–4 Hood

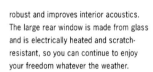

Porsche Communication Management (PCM) Including Navigation Module

The optional PCM is your central information and communication system. It is powerful and multifunctional, yet easy to operate.

The focal point is the intuitive seven-inch high-resolution touchscreen. Almost all functions can be controlled with just your fingertips, although conventional rotary pushbutton controls are still provided. Radio functions include up to 42 memory presets, Dynamic Autostore, and the FM dual tuner, which continuously scans in the background for the best signal.

The CD/DVD drive plays CDs and audio DVDs and is MP3-compatible. Audio playback of video DVDs is also supported. A six-disc CD/DVD changer integrated into PCM is available as an option.

A navigation module with high-speed hard drive is included with PCM. For route guidance, it is possible to select between a 2-D display and a 3-D perspective. In some regions, even land and buildings can be displayed in 3-D. Split-screen mode enables you to view two functions at once, such as the current navigation map and a list of symbols that represent the next navigation instruction.

Electronic Logbook

An electronic logbook is available for PCM as an option. It enables automatic logging on every journey of mileage, route distance, date, time,

starting location, and destination. Data can be downloaded to a USB device and evaluated on your home PC using the software supplied. This information is particularly useful for those who keep logbooks for work- and tax-related purposes.

Voice-Control System

Audio options, route guidance, phone calls, and many other PCM functions can all be controlled using the optional voice-control system. In most cases, you simply say the name of the menu item as seen on the screen. Even lists can be browsed by voice command. For added convenience, there is no need to "train" the system.

Bluetooth® Hands-Free

A standard Bluetooth® interface lets you connect your Bluetooth®-enabled mobile phone to the PCM with Hands-Free Profile (HFP), allowing you to receive and place calls. Basic functions can be controlled via PCM or the optional multifunction steering wheel.

1 Porsche Communication Management (PCM)
1 Electronic logbook
2 Voice-control system
3 Bluetooth® Hands-Free

Universal Audio Interface

In conjunction with PCM, you can access content from your iPod® or any other compatible USB device. The USB port, safely located inside the glove compartment, can also recharge your audio device. You can control your iPod® or USB device conveniently and safely using PCM, the optional multifunction steering wheel, or the optional voice-control system. The USB port is also useful for downloading information from the onboard computer, such as performance data from the Sport Chrono Package or the optional electronic logbook.

Bose® Surround Sound System

The optional Bose® Surround Sound System really strikes a chord.

Developed specifically for Porsche and optimally tuned for the interior of the new Boxster models, it can be combined with the optional Porsche Communication Management (PCM) or the CDR audio system.

This high-end audio system comprises eight amplifier channels with a total output of 445 watts. Its 10 loudspeakers, including an active subwoofer concealed behind the dashboard, deliver a balanced acoustic pattern.

In combination with the optional Porsche Communication Management (PCM), the Bose® Surround Sound System enables audio playback of DVDs and is thus able to make full use of the impressive sound spectrum of 5.1 digital recordings. Of course, you can still play other audio sources, such as CDs and MP3s, in stereo or, at the push of a button, in one of the virtual surround modes generated by Bose® Centerpoint® 2.

The Bose®-patented AudioPilot® Noise Compensation Technology uses a microphone to continuously measure the ambient noise inside the vehicle and adapts music playback instantly and automatically so that a consistent sound is maintained— whatever the driving conditions.

The result is a balanced, faithfully reproduced sound and a captivating 360° acoustic experience.

1 Universal audio interface (AUX, USB, e.g., for iPod®)
  in conjunction with PCM
2 Bose® Surround Sound System

1

2

Chapter 3

The new Cayman arrives

With the new Boxster safely delivered to the showrooms of the world, it was time to push the button to commence the next stage of 981 series evolution – the launch of the Cayman sister car.

Although the first generation Boxster had remained an individual model in the Porsche line-up, engineers had planned a closed coupé in parallel with the development of the second generation, duly bringing about the birth of the Cayman. Sharing many of the same components as the open car, it was released soon after the former's debut in 987 guise, quickly garnering a strong following of its own.

This staggered launch policy was carried over for the 981 variant, too, meaning that the Cayman followed the Boxster's lead several months down the line, eventually making its public debut at the 2012 Los Angeles Show. This was actually where the 987.2s had first taken a bow four years earlier, so it held a great deal of significance for fans of the mid-engined Porsches; the 2012 event took place from 30 November, with the press being allowed in a couple of days earlier. Indeed, it was at just after midday on the 28 November that Matthias Müller stood before a large group of journalists to talk about the grey and yellow coupés placed either side of him. The waiting was over …

The 981 Cayman

There were few surprises in LA, as the Boxster-morphing formula was well-known, and there had even been photographs of the new coupé leaked in the middle of November. This did nothing to dampen spirits, though, with the US launch of the 911 Carrera 4 taking place at the same time to guarantee a few more column inches for the Stuttgart company.

So, what were the differences between the old and the new, and,

apart from the obvious roof panel and the hatchback arrangement aft of it (a more important distinction than ever, given that the 981 convertible was no longer available with a detachable hardtop), what made the Cayman different to its Boxster brethren?

Starting with the styling, naturally, many of the panels were the same as those of the Boxster, as the cost savings this brought about was a salient point in the Cayman's raison d'etre – the chassis code being 981C as opposed to 981 (the Boxster designation not having a suffix) ultimately tells us just how close they were in their make-up. There were plenty of minor differences, though, in addition to the roof, serving as useful distinguishing features that visually separated the mid-engined pair.

As before, the Cayman was given a unique front bumper moulding, with different side vents featuring a signature round driving light in each (quite a contrast to the open car's version, although, like the Boxster, the slats below were black on the S and painted on the smaller-engined models), a dummy central vent section that was wider at the bottom than the top (the opposite being true on the Boxster), and a slightly more aggressive chin spoiler beneath it.

Interestingly, and this was a Cayman only thing, the lower section of the front spoiler (the part that sat below the central 'vent' area and spread horizontally to end underneath the grilles at each side) was black on the base cars, and painted in body colour on the S (unless it was a black car, and then it used the same insert as the 2.7-litre models). Otherwise, looking at the cars head-on, apart

Some of the pictures released to announce the new 981 series Caymans. The white car is a 2.7-litre model, while the yellow one is an S. Both are fitted with optional alloys, by the way, rather than the standard rims.

The Cayman making its debut at the 2012 Los Angeles Auto Show. As it happens, the greater LA area accounts for almost one in five US Porsche sales. *(Courtesy Steve Lyon/Wikimedia Commons)*

from the view above the header rail, the Boxster and Cayman were identical.

Moving around the side, the different roofline and standard wheel designs came into focus. It also highlighted the fact that the 981s shared the same side air intake profile aft of the door, whereas the Boxster and Cayman had unique intakes and surrounding panelwork in the previous generation. The clever use of a cutline in the wing above the intake allowed more panels to be shared, which not only cuts production costs, it keeps insurance companies happy, too.

As such, one had to move further around again to catch the more obvious changes in the car's upper silhouette. In profile, one could see

how well the roof section had been worked into the existing Boxster design, with, quite literally, only the sharper window graphics and the roof above looking any different. The roof sloped elegantly into the tail to finish at the rear spoiler, just as the rear compartment lid did on the Boxster, and even the vents in the front air dam looked similar enough from a side-on angle.

Wheel and tyre sizes were the same as those specified for the equivalent Boxsters, incidentally, although the design was changed, as was the norm. For the base Cayman, there was the 396 rim, which was a cross between the 'Boxster S III' wheel and the 'Carrera S III' one, while the 406 alloys that were standard on the

A series of reference shots of a Cayman S on 'Carrera Classic' rims taken at the same angle as those of the Boxster in the previous chapter. Careful inspection revealed that the roofline was allowed to stretch further back on the 981 Cayman. Although it was only really noticeable when an earlier model was placed alongside it with both viewed fully side-on, as *Autocar* noted: "The new-found elegance and dynamism in the car's silhouette can be traced to that one change."

The standard alloy wheels on the 2.7-litre Cayman (code 396).

The latest 'Cayman S' rims (code 406).

Cayman S were much like the contemporary 'Boxster' rim, but with heavier spokes.

At the back, the Cayman's rear bumper moulding was a touch more shapely in the haunches than that of the Boxster's, although the two now shared the parts surrounding the exhaust. This had previously been another area where the mid-engined cars differed (the detailing in the lower part of the rear apron had been quite different in the 987 series), although people were already used to seeing matching exhaust tips according to engine size rather than model line.

Above the rear bumper, the lights were the same, as was the basic design of the rear spoiler assembly, which been completely different in 987 days. Notwithstanding, the movable section of the Cayman spoiler deployed a touch higher than that of the Boxster, and sat at a steeper angle.

The roofline silhoutte was actually very similar, albeit achieved in a rather different manner. The C-posts looked fabulous from the rear, framing the aluminium hatchback door, which carried the rear window and chrome badging, aping that found on the open car. One big change was the design of the high-mount rear brakelight, which was moved up to

the top edge of the rear screen on the latest Cayman, whereas it had been located on the bottom edge for the previous generation, and sunken into the rear lid on the Boxsters from day one.

Inside, other than the roof area and that behind the seats, the pair were largely the same in terms of layout and design. The only real

Detail image of the rear spoiler mechanism.

Interior of the Porsche Museum car used for the reference photography – an S with a PDK transmission.

difference was in the console aft of the gearshift, with a flat panel where the hood switches are on the open car, and, of course, a 'Cayman' plaque just ahead of it rather than a 'Boxster' one. Turning on the ignition highlighted another change, with the model designation popping up in the TFT screen in the gauge pack, which took away the need for a different instrument shroud for the 981C in the eyes of the designers.

The appearance behind the seats was familiar enough to Cayman fans, with a flat area above the engine, metallic-looking trim between the rear suspension towers (with stylish covers for the oil and water fillers mounted at either end of it), and a deep luggage compartment aft

The rear luggage compartment of the 981 Cayman, with the oil and water fillers neatly hidden beneath the black covers at either end of the central metallic bar.

Body construction

Not surprisingly, most of the body construction was similar to that of the Boxster, especially in the front-end structure, as well as the front lid and doors. Interestingly, though, there were a number of differences, even in areas that appeared to be shared due to their shape. For instance, the upper part of the scuttle was in deep-drawn steel rather than aluminium alloy, while the outer sills were made from the same material as the door pillars and the structure aft of the B-post – the stronger steels were placed in the roof area instead, which makes sense, given the lack of roll-over hoops and the need to hang the aluminium hatchback door off it, and the fact that there was less stress placed on the coupé's rocker panels.

Ultimately, it was all about creating a balance between cost and overall rigidity, with as many pressings as possible given double duty – tooling up for the new mouldings created for the bumper assemblies was a small investment compared to the tooling required for body panels.

Officially, the new Cayman was endowed with a Cd figure of 0.30, which is the same as that quoted for the Boxster, one assumes

with the hood up. As for weight, according to contemporary German data tables, the lightest car was 1310kg (2882lb), with the S grade being 10kg (22lb) more, and PDK adding a further 30kg (66lb) to these DIN numbers. These are the same weights listed for the Boxster, as it happens, translating into a loss of 20kg (44lb) compared to the 987.2 Caymans, although it should be noted that several countries, such as Britain, quoted a kerb weight some 20kg (44lb) higher. Whichever way one looks at it, savings were made that allowed the Cayman to remain a lithe fighting machine.

The new Cayman body, with white depicting deep-drawn steel parts, blue shaded areas the various aluminium-based structures, green showing high-tensile steel panelwork, yellow multiphase steel areas, and red parts that employed 22MnB5 steel.

**Cutaway drawing of the new Cayman:
this illustration showing an S model.**

of that. Officially, this gave 275 litres (9.7 cubic feet) of luggage space at the back, which was a fair bit more than the 130/4.6 quoted for the Boxster.

As before, the Cayman was given a touch more power than the equivalent Boxster model, although the vast majority of the leading specifications were the same as the equivalent 2.7 and 3.4 flat-six engines used in the open car. As such, these more powerful units employed the same MA1/22 and MA1/23 codes, but were usually identified via a C suffix for clarification purposes.

In the strict Cayman, the MA1/22C delivered a healthy 275bhp at 7400rpm (just over the magic 100bhp/litre), and 214lbft of torque at 4500rpm, while the MA1/23C lump in the S pumped out 325bhp at 7400rpm, and 273lbft spread across a curve that was flat from 4500 to 5800rpm.

Several scribes have pointed to the difference coming via an ECU tweak, which is what the author would have assumed, too, although the part number is the same for both fhc and dhc cars, as it is for the main induction components, and even the exhaust backboxes. A full

replacement engine, however, does have a different part number (the I148 'power kit' note being against it), with a second one allocated to a lower c/r version for countries with poor quality fuel.

Ultimately, we may never really get to the bottom of this difference until more years have passed and the tongues of engineers become that bit freer, but the clue seems to be in the higher revs posted against the horsepower increases. It should be noted, though, that the Porsche engines coming off the dyno were probably delivering a lot more than catalogue numbers in any case, as the company always quoted an absolute minimum output for each unit.

Anyway, one thing is for sure – transmission numbers were carried over, as were the internal ratios for each of the four gearbox types, and indeed, the 3.89:1 (MT) and 3.25:1 (PDK) final-drive ratios, too. Chassis components were also basically the same, although the front damper rates were adjusted slightly, and both the spring and shock absorber settings were revised at the back. Otherwise, apart from the alloy wheels that we described earlier, everything else came from the same parts bin as the Boxster.

Press reaction

Car & Driver noted in its report from LA: "We can only guess how Porsche purists dealt with the recent launch of the Cayenne diesel, but we imagine that the addition of the updated Cayman to the brand's line-up will more than make up for it."

Indeed. The author's son runs a sporty diesel from Stuttgart's other famous car brand, and getting past the image of an oil burner in something special is often hard for us traditionalists to take in. A decent test quickly dispels fears of it being like a London taxi from our youth, and ultimately makers need to sell volume models to make the kind of stuff we stick-in-the-muds tend to prefer. But a diesel Porsche?

One could even query the idea of a Porsche SUV, for that matter, but it was the way of the world – building on the success of luxury models like the Range Rover and Benz G-Wagen, it seems as if every maker of note has at least one sport utility vehicle in its line-up. Anyway, that's not what this book is about, and it's the contemporary views of the motoring press corps that really counts, just as they always have.

The 981 Cayman press launch duly took place in Portugal, and when Dickie Meaden tried a manual Cayman S for *Evo* magazine, he was one of several journalists to note that the Cayman should no longer be perceived as a poor man's 911. He went on to say: "For a mid-engined car, the Cayman has always been a magical thing in terms of balance, and the feedback and the feel it gives you. This car has taken it to another level again."

The folks at *Wheels* wrote: "A Cayman S has lapped the 21km Nürburgring in 7:55; that's 11 seconds faster than the previous model and just 15 seconds off the time set by the 991 Carrera S. But like most Porsches, the Cayman is not about numbers. Instead it's about a communicative driving experience and the new car (especially the S) is brilliant. It stays flat during hard cornering, it has an amazingly

One of the strict Caymans at the press launch held at the demanding Autódromo Internacional do Algave circuit and the surrounding area.

Another 2.7-litre car, this one running on 'Cayman S' alloys, and the interior of the same vehicle.

supple ride (even on the optional 20in alloys) and it goes very hard. Oh, and it sounds stunning."

The final words in this section go to Steve Sutcliffe: "Before I started driving this car about an hour ago, I wasn't actually sure whether Porsche was capable of producing a better driver's car than the old Cayman. But I was completely wrong, because this car – the new Cayman S – is absolutely, mind-bogglingly brilliant ... I'd have this instead of a 911 any day of any week."

I think it's safe to say that the Cayman instilled something of a lasting impression, even on the most experienced of testers. Now all that was necessary was translating their obvious enthusiasm for the new mid-engined coupé into sales. The hard work was about to begin ...

A red S being pushed hard on the track ...

The tail and interior of another Cayman S used at the press launch: this one fitted with a PDK transmission and shod with 20in 'Carrera S' alloy wheels.

A final image from the press event, with the red calipers pointing to this being an S model.

Cayman Colour & Trim Guide

These colour variations were listed from the start of 981 Cayman production until June 2013.

Solid coachwork colours
Black (041 Schwarz), White (C9A Weiss), Guards Red (80K Indischrot), and Racing Yellow (1S1 Racinggelb).

Metallic coachwork colours
Basalt Black (C9Z Basaltschwarz) Metallic, Agate Grey (M7S Achatgrau) Metallic, Platinum Silver (M7T Platinsilber) Metallic, Dark Blue (M5X Dunkelblau) Metallic, Aqua Blue (M5R Aquablau) Metallic, Amaranth Red (8L1 Amaranthrot) Metallic, Mahogany (M8Y Mahogani) Metallic, and Anthracite Brown (M8S Anthrazitbraun) Metallic.

Special coachwork colours
GT Silver (M7Z GT-silber) Metallic, Lime Gold (5P1 Limegold) Metallic, and Cognac (M8Z Cognac) Metallic. A 'colour to sample' option was also available.

Leatherette/vinyl trim
Black, Platinum Grey, Yachting Blue, and Luxor Beige. Carpeting, floor mats and the roof lining came in matching hues, except for the blue option, which had a black headliner.

Leather trim
Black, Platinum Grey, Yachting Blue, and Luxor Beige. Carpeting, floor mats and the roof lining came in matching hues, except for the blue option, which had a black headliner.

Regular two-tone leather trim
Agate Grey with Lime Gold, Agate Grey with Pebble Grey, and Agate Grey with Amber Orange. Carpeting, floor mats and the roof lining came in Agate Grey.

Special leather colours and natural leather trim
Agate Grey, Carrera Red, and Espresso monotone: These came with carpeting, floor mats and the roof lining in matching hues, except for the red option, which had a black headliner. Agate Grey with Lime Gold, Agate Grey with Pebble Grey, and Agate Grey with Amber Orange two-tone: Carpeting and floor mats came in the lighter shade, with the roof liner in Agate Grey. A 'colour to sample' option was also available.

The domestic market

In Germany, 981 Cayman sales started on 1 January 2013, although the official European launch was listed as 2 March 2013, after which most EU countries started getting their first deliveries of the new coupé. Including VAT, €51,385 was being asked for the strict Cayman in its native land, and €64,118 for S.

Seemingly five minutes later, a new price list was issued, due to take effect on the first day of June. Although the Cayman RRP remained unchanged on both grades, a small increase was applied to the Boxster line, taking the 2.7-litre model up to €49,243, and the 3.4-litre car to €60,191. Many questioned why the closed coupé was more expensive, given that dropheads usually command a premium, but when one thinks of the cost of a 911 – with prices starting at a hefty €90,417 by this time – buyers saw the Cayman as good value nonetheless.

A rear wiper (option code 425) was a unique item for the Cayman, priced at €345.10. Apart from this and the odd Boxster-specific item, though (and the ability to specify the alloy wheels from the Boxster, of course), all other optional extras were shared across the entire 981 series range.

For the record, as with the Boxster earlier on, most of the Cayman's Exclusive options were not available immediately, despite appearing in the initial January 2013 price list and already being fitted to the open car. Ultimately coming online in the spring of 2013, this included things like the paintwork and leather upgrades, the various wood, aluminium and carbon interior packages and related components, coloured seatbelts and dial faces, door decals, and also the exhaust system parts.

The DBR paint option became available from March 2013, bringing with it colour-keyed side air intake housings, a rear apron in body colour, and fully rather than partially painted door mirrors. In reality, it was a combination of the Exclusive CNL, CAC and CNG options listed earlier on.

New, though, from the following month, and for both the Boxster and Cayman, was the chance to have the PDLS light system washer nozzles painted in a contrast colour (option code CGU), or ask for model designation decals for the doors (CAS for black versions, or CAT for silver). For the record, these stickers were actually listed from October 2012 in the Tequipment catalogue, and were significantly cheaper bought that way, too.

Anyway, for sporting enthusiasts, there was also a new stiffer suspension package (X73), priced at €1011.50 and lowering the car by 20mm/0.8in. This was also available via the Tequipment route a touch earlier, although it was a lot more expensive as a retro-fit. In addition, there was an attractive alloy fuel cap (XYB), and Boxster buyers were now able to specify the alloy wheels fitted as standard to the Cayman pairing.

(Continues on page 96)

Interior of a domestic
2.7-litre Cayman with the
striking grey and orange
two-tone leather trim.

A contemporary Boxster S
with painted alloys.

The optional rear wiper for the Cayman (code 425).

The high-end Burmester audio upgrade seen applied to the Cayman model.

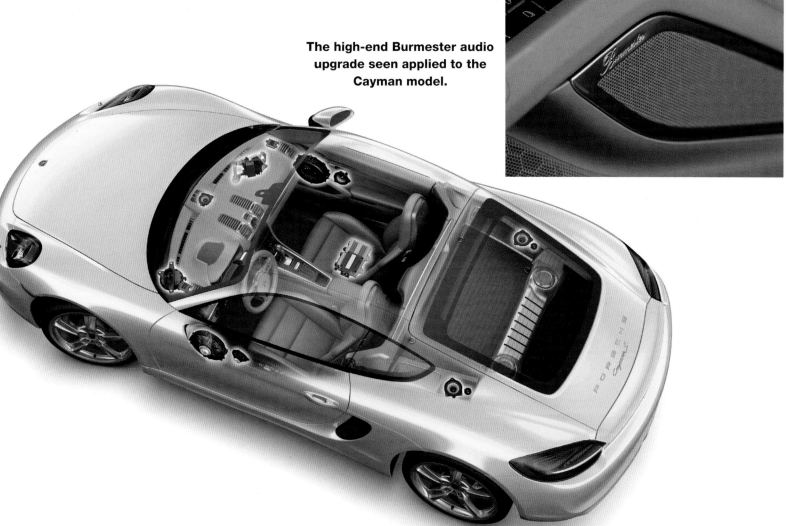

A Boxster S with the optional door decals. Although the brake calipers would seem to confirm this, as they are definitely red if you zoom in on the picture, the wheels are the 18in rims off the 2.7-litre model. Presumably, they were bought as an accessory to go with all-weather tyres, as this was not a combination that was possible when ordering a new car.

On the audio front, the P25 option became available at this time, building on the standard CD/radio unit specifications with seven speakers instead of four and numerous other upgrades for tech-savvy users. The telephone module could be linked to this stereo, by the way, while 691 was a digital radio package for the PCM unit.

Optional extras

With the Cayman's arrival on the marketplace, it makes sense to look at the various options listed for the 981 series as a whole, with domestic prices being provided to form a definitive picture as of 1 June 2013 (quoted with local taxes included), by which time specifications had settled down for both vehicles. To avoid repetition and provide ease of reference, the list has been split into common options, dedicated Boxster ones, and Cayman only options; they have also been listed in numerical/alphabetical order to provide another form of contemporary reference.

Common options

Code	Item	Price (€)
220	Porsche Torque Vectoring (PTV) system	1309.00
250	PDK transmission	2826.25
342	Seat heating	416.50
345	Steering wheel heater	267.75
423	20in 'Carrera S' wheel (for base model)	2856.00
	Ditto (for S model)	1428.00
427	20in 'Carrera Classic' wheel (for base model)	3927.00
	Ditto (for S model)	2499.00
446	Coloured Porsche crest for wheel centres	160.65
450	PCCB ceramic composite braking system	7318.50
454	Cruise control	392.70
456	Adaptive cruise control with PAS system	2011.10
475	PASM active suspension	1428.00
482	Tyre pressure monitor	618.80
490	Sound Package Plus	583.10
498	Model badge deletion	NCO
509	Fire extinguisher	148.75
534	Alarm with interior monitor (for base model)	487.90
	Ditto (for S model)	202.30
541	Seat ventilation	928.20
567	Grey-tinted band on windscreen	113.05
573	Two-zone automatic air-conditioning system	761.60
583	Smoking package	NCO
603	Bi-Xenon lights with PDLS and washers (for base model)	1558.90
	Ditto (for S model)	702.10
608	HomeLink garage door opener	285.60
619	Mobile phone preparation	654.50
630	Light design package	297.50
635	Park Assist (rear only)	511.70
636	Park Assist (front and rear)	880.60
639	Sport Chrono Package (manual, without PCM)	1594.60
	Ditto (with PDK transmission, without PCM)	2023.00
640	Sport Chrono Package (manual, with PCM)	1594.60
	Ditto (with PDK transmission, with PCM)	2023.00
641	Electronic logbook	523.60
658	Power Steering Plus	261.80
666	Telephone module	773.50
669	Cordless handset for telephone module	571.20
671	Voice control for PCM system	452.20
674	Vehicle tracking system	297.50
676	TV tuner	1535.10
680	Bose surround sound system	1178.10
682	Burmester surround sound system	3915.10
691	Digital radio upgrade	476.00
692	Six-CD changer (for cars without PCM)	464.10
693	Six-CD/DVD changer (for cars with PCM)	583.10
748	Folding mirrors (electric) with courtesy lighting	297.50
810	Floor mats	107.10
840	SportDesign steering wheel (manual)	214.20
	Ditto (with PDK transmission)	416.50
844	Multi-function steering wheel	523.60
899	Child seat preparation	178.50
946	Partial leather trim	1094.80
970	Two-tone leather trim	3445.05
980	Leather package (monotone)	1487.50
	Ditto (two-tone)	1666.00
998	Natural leather trim	4266.15
CAC	Side air intake housings painted in body colour	464.10
CAS	Model designation decals on doors (black)	208.25
CAT	Model designation decals on doors (silver)	208.25
CDN	Dashboard air vent slats painted in body colour	821.10
CDT	Seatbelt buckle receivers in leather	440.30
CFX	Personalised floor mats	315.35
CGE	Sport Chrono dial face in yellow	345.10
CGG	Sport Chrono dial face in red	345.10
CGJ	Sport Chrono dial face in white	345.10
CGU	Headlight washer nozzles in contrast colour	202.30
CLB	Manual transmission gearknob in Alcantara	595.00
CLH	PDK selector head in Alcantara	595.00
CLU	Steering wheel rim in a contrasting leather	708.05
CMT	Painted finish for seatbelt slots on P03 seats	452.20
CNG	Rear apron painted in body colour	440.30
CNL	Fully painted door mirrors in body colour	446.25
CPE	Leather key pouch	113.05
CPK	Car key painted in body colour	232.05
CUF	PCM package painted in body colour	1338.75
CUJ	Fuse box lids trimmed in leather	261.80
CUR	PCM package trimmed with leather	1338.75
CVW	Rearview mirror trimmed with leather	464.10
CXC	Personalised stainless steel treadplates with lighting	773.50
CXE	Personalised carbonfibre treadplates with lighting	1071.00
CXM	Door trim package, leather	476.00
CZT	Sport Chrono dial face in beige	345.10
CZV	Dashboard air vent surrounds in leather	821.10
CZW	Dashboard trim package, leather	1059.10
DBR	Exclusive exterior paint package in body colour	1249.50
EEA	Interior package, leather	493.85
EEB	Interior package, mahogany (manual cars)	1481.55
EEC	As per EEB, minus door capping dressing piece	1255.45
EED	Interior package, mahogany (PDK cars)	1481.55
EEF	As per EED, minus door capping dressing piece	1255.45
EEG	Interior package, carbon (manual cars)	1481.55
EEH	As per EEG, minus door capping dressing piece	1255.45
EEJ	Interior package, carbon (PDK cars)	1481.55
EEK	As per EEJ, minus door capping dressing piece	1255.45
EEL	Interior package, brushed aluminium (manual cars)	702.10
EEM	As per EEL, minus door capping dressing piece	595.00
EEN	Interior package, brushed aluminium (PDK cars)	702.10
EEP	As per EEN, minus door capping dressing piece	595.00
EER	Interior package, painted in body colour	470.05
EES	As per EEA, minus door capping dressing piece	374.85
EET	As per EER, minus door capping dressing piece	357.00
EFA	Aluminium alloy pedal set	440.30

Code	Item	Price (€)
P03	Sports bucket seats	3272.50
P04	Two-way power Sports Seats Plus	1898.05
	Ditto (combined with leather interior)	458.15
P06	14-way power sports seats with memory function	2261.00
P07	18-way adaptive sports seats with memory function	3617.60
	Ditto (combined with leather interior)	3272.50
P13	Automatic dimming mirrors with integrated rain sensor	487.90
P23	Porsche Communication Management (PCM) system	3147.55
P25	CDR Plus with Sound Package Plus and universal port	1547.00
UN1	Online services package	178.50
X69	Carbonfibre treadplates	535.50
X70	Stainless steel treadplates	238.00
X73	Sports suspension	1011.50
XDH	Platinum paint finish on wheels	702.10
XFG	Instrument faces in red	487.90
XFJ	Instrument faces in white	487.90
XFL	Instrument faces in beige	487.90
XFR	Instrument faces in yellow	487.90
XHB	Tail of centre console (aft of audio unit) in leather	238.00
XHF	Heated multi-function steering wheel, mahogany	1094.80
XHG	Tail of centre console (aft of audio unit) in mahogany	499.80
XHL	Heated multi-function steering wheel, carbon	1094.80
XHM	Tail of centre console (aft of audio unit) in carbon	499.80
XHN	Seatbelts in yellow	243.95
XHP	Seatbelts in beige	243.95
XHR	Seatbelts in blue	243.95
XLF	Sports exhaust system	2165.80
XLK	SportDesign steering wheel in Alcantara (manual)	380.80
	Ditto (with PDK transmission)	583.10
XLS	Sports tailpipe	535.50
XNG	Leather instrument surround	297.50
XNS	Steering column surround in leather	327.25
XPT	Porsche crest on centre storage box lid	226.10
XRT	20in 'SportTechno' wheel (for base model)	4087.65
	Ditto (for S model)	2659.65
XSC	Porsche crest on seat headrests	202.30
XSH	Seatbelts in silver-grey	243.95
XSX	Seatbelts in red	243.95
XUB	Headlight washer nozzles in body colour	202.30
XUV	Model designation on centre storage box lid	226.10
XWK	P07 seat seatbacks and base in leather	1338.75
XXB	Stainless steel treadplates with lighting	654.50
XXD	Carbonfibre treadplates with lighting	952.00
XYA	PDK gear selector in aluminium	529.55
XYB	Aluminium-look fuel filler cap	130.90
XYE	Tail of centre console (aft of audio unit) in aluminium	238.00
XYG	Tail of centre console (aft of audio unit) in body colour	226.10
---	Metallic paint	821.10
---	Special paint	2344.30
---	Paint to sample	4165.00
---	Leather trim in standard colour	3076.15
---	Leather trim in special colour	3445.00
---	Leather trim to sample	4569.60

Boxster-specific options

Code	Item	Price (€)
396	18in 'Cayman' wheel (for base model)	357.00
400	19in 'Boxster S' wheel (for base model)	1428.00
406	19in 'Cayman S' wheel (for base model)	1428.00
	Ditto (for S model)	357.00
546	Roll-over hoops in exterior colour	505.75
547	Roll-over hoops with aluminium-look finish	505.75
551	Windblocker	267.75

Cayman-specific options

Code	Item	Price (€)
395	18in 'Boxster' wheel (for base model)	357.00
400	19in 'Boxster S' wheel (for base model)	1428.00
	Ditto (for S model)	357.00
406	19in 'Cayman S' wheel (for base model)	1428.00
425	Rear wiper	345.10

NB: Not all items were available in all markets, of course, although any major differences – very few, in reality – have been pointed out in the text.

For the record, almost all of the prices quoted in the sidebar above were correct at the time of the Boxster's launch, with only three items being cheaper back then: painted door mirrors (CNL) were about €30 cheaper, leather trim to the tail of the centre console (XHB) was some €10 less, and the equivalent part in brushed aluminium (XYE) was €5 cheaper.

It was actually very easy to get carried away with options, for as *Auto Motor und Sport* pointed out in an article from the middle of 2013, their €64,118 Cayman S (with costly paint and leather, as well as PDK transmission, but standard brakes) was actually €98,741 as tested! Ticking a few more boxes would have taken the invoice over the 100K mark with ease.

The US market
The 2013 season started on a bright note in the States. The Boxster was selling well, helping keep the momentum going towards a record year for the 191 dealers in that part of the world. Awards kept on coming for the open car, too, with *Autoweek* naming it 'Best of the Best' ahead of the 911, Cadillac ATS, Subaru BRZ and Dodge Dart. The 'World Performance Car' title from the WCA group had also fallen to the 981 series. The 911 would get its revenge in *Motor Trend*'s 'Best Driver's Car' extravaganza, restoring honour for the flagship sports car, but the gauntlet had been thrown.

There was also a groundbreaking ceremony to kick off PCNA's bold plan to create a new US headquarters that included a test track for owners (and potential owners) to experience the Porsche range in a safe, controlled environment. Still in Atlanta, and finally opening in mid-2015, the 'Experience Centre' idea was duly expanded to other areas and countries. Indeed, one recently opened in Chiba, only a few miles south of the author's humble abode in Japan.

The Porsche 918 Spyder

The mid-engined Carrera GT supercar had been shown as a concept at the 2000 Paris Salon, and eventually went into limited production (1500 units were planned) as a showroom model following its international debut at the 2003 Geneva Show. Powered by a 612bhp V10, it had mad levels of performance and a price tag to match, so it was not surprising when Porsche announced the end of the Carrera GT run in the spring of 2006, despite not reaching the sales target originally mooted. That does not mean the car was a failure, though, for it served as a technical tour de force and its styling showed the way forward for the next generation of Porsche design language – indeed, a lot of it can be seen in the 981.

The 918 Spyder duly took on the mantle of the Carrera GT, first appearing as a concept at the 2010 Geneva Show. Production status was granted soon after, but perfecting the advanced plug-in hybrid technology took time, and it would ultimately be the end of 2013 before sales started. Nonetheless, the limited run model ((918 showroom vehicles were planned) would once again give various clues as to the future direction of the Stuttgart maker, with its race-inspired drivetrain being a case in point. A 4.6-litre V8 was augmented by two electric motors to give a

The exotic 918 Spyder.

total power output of 887bhp and the kind of torque one more readily associates with a train than an automobile. Production ended in the middle of 2015, but its blistering performance (0-60 in less than three seconds) combined with an ability to sport 'green' credentials has left an indelible mark on the industry.

Meanwhile, having launched in March, US Cayman deliveries began at the end of April 2013, with the strict Cayman priced at $52,600, and the S grade commanding a further $11,200 on top of that; both cars attracted the usual $950 destination charge. Boxster prices were carried over, by the way, meaning that the closed car was around $3000 more than its convertible stablemate.

Motor Trend tried a Cayman S soon after sales started in the States, and noted: "The last Porsche Cayman won our 'Best Driver's Car' event in 2009. As far as high praise goes for sports cars, that's about as high as it gets. At our test track, the Cayman exceeded expectations ... no production car with under 325bhp has been any quicker in our testing. Braking performance is likewise consistent, [while] its 1.04g lateral acceleration matches that of the last-gen and 200lb lighter Boxster Spyder. It isn't the speed or the grip, though, but the balance of the entire experience. The Cayman certainly punches above its class ..."

Oddly, though, given this level of praise, the 'Best Driver's Car' award went to the Porsche 911 Carrera 4S for 2013, which must have had a few wiping their brow, given the price difference between these Stuttgart thoroughbreds. The Cayman S was still in there with the big

hitters, of course, making many of them look superficial (after all, as Randy Probst said, "the Cayman reminds me of a good race car" with beautiful balance – and he should know), but a few noted a "clinical" lack of emotion in the new version.

Rory Jurnecka perhaps summed things up: "If I had to choose a car to run an unfamiliar road with at speed, it would be the Cayman S. I'd also pick it for a 24-hour endurance race, because it's so easy to drive quickly ... It's a tremendously capable car, perfect in so many ways, but it just doesn't grab me the way the old one did."

Car & Driver felt much the same after testing a manual 2.7-litre model. Although it stated that it was "every bit as magical" as the S grade, the magazine noted: "It's good enough to be too good. The Pirelli P Zero tyres, tasked with wrangling just 275 humble horsepower and the most agile chassis we know, place the limits at improbable heights. You'll assault roads with speed and fluidity, but for some, the Cayman will struggle to instill the deep satisfaction that comes from being challenged. It's a car so exceptional that it renders many corners unexceptional."

The bottom line, however, is that most loved the newcomer, and the modern owner – as we established earlier – is not the traditional

(Continues on page 112)

PORSCHE

The new Cayman

For those who believe life is lived at the apex of a curve.

Cayman concept.

There is a place where driving pleasure reaches its pinnacle. Where the laws of physics are set in asphalt, and where gravity insists on finding its center. It's a point so precisely located, a single degree can be the difference between a perfect moment and profound disappointment. Welcome to the apex of the curve, where the new Porsche Cayman lives.

Cayman is a sports car concept that pursues performance unconventionally.

With its mid-engine design, the Cayman centers weight low in the chassis, so the car's center of gravity is directly beneath the driver seat. The connection between car and driver is pure and undiluted.

And now, the Cayman concept enters its second generation. New chassis developments, new engine developments, and a front-to-tail redesign of its coupe shape create an entirely new Cayman, with enhanced levels of power, efficiency, and handling

agility. Enter a corner and roll on the throttle: Whether you choose the Cayman model with its new 2.7-liter, 275-hp six-cylinder engine or the Cayman S with its 3.4-liter, 325-hp six, pressing the accelerator creates forward propulsion combined with formidable lateral grip.

The new Cayman and Cayman S. There's an apex just waiting for you to arrive.

**Six cylinders. Four heart chambers.
Just 12 inches apart.**

Engineering.

The new Cayman adheres to Porsche's long-held principle of intelligent lightweight construction. The doors, luggage compartment lid, and rear hatch are made entirely of aluminum, with the lightweight material accounting for approximately 44 percent of the entire structure. The chassis has been completely revised and its wheelbase lengthened, helping the new Cayman achieve two of automotive engineering's most coveted aims: an ideal front/rear weight balance, and an optimal power-to-weight ratio.

For enhanced dynamic performance and increased driving stability when the car is pushed to the limit, both

Cayman models are equipped with Porsche Stability Management (PSM). Enhanced Porsche Active Suspension Management (PASM) is available as an option and includes a ride-height reduction of 10 mm. Porsche Torque Vectoring (PTV) with rear differential lock for increased agility and traction in corners is also available on request.

The optional Sport Chrono Package makes the highly responsive handling characteristics of the new Cayman even sportier. For the first time, the package now also includes dynamic gearbox mounts, which make a perceptible contribution to handling

stability in fast corners while ensuring a high degree of ride comfort.

The Cayman model's new 2.7-liter engine and the Cayman S model's 3.4-liter engine are "boxer" designs. Unlike a conventional "V" configuration, in our boxer engines the pistons are horizontally opposed, forming a "flat six." It's a compact yet potent engine that keeps the core weight mass positioned low within the engine—and engine low within the car. It's the ideal design for a mid-engine sports car.

Both engines feature Direct Fuel Injection (DFI) and VarioCam Plus. Power is transmitted to the wheels by a smooth six-

speed manual transmission or the optional 7-speed Porsche Doppelkupplung (PDK).

Fuel efficiency is achieved by a suite of engineering innovations. The Auto Start Stop function, electromechanical power steering, electrical system recuperation, and intelligent thermal management all help reduce the demand for fuel and the level of emissions.

The new Cayman design is unmistakably that of a pure-bred Porsche sports car, with every line and every edge energized in one direction: forward.

The purposeful, now made even more beautiful.

Design.

Exterior

Study the sculpted lines and edges, narrow wheel arches, short overhangs, taut proportions, and sleek silhouette of the new Cayman. What you will observe is a design aesthetic that is unique to Porsche. The family values encoded into the

Cayman genes since the very beginning are evident. No matter where your eye falls, it sees the Porsche character, the Porsche profile, and the unwavering Porsche belief in form following function.

The new front is dominated by the prominent fenders. With its large and dynamic air intakes, the front end signals the powerful persona of the Cayman. Restyled headlights—inspired by the Porsche racing heritage of the 1960s and 1970s—are the windows

to the soul of the Cayman. The ci[r] front light units integrated in the a[ir] intakes are a signature of Cayman styling and incorporate LED dayti[me] running lights and position lights.

Retracted, the separation edge of the rear spoiler makes a seamless transition to the LED taillights. The integrated turn signals are narrow and in line with the fender. The rear fascia with centrally framed stainless steel

tailpipe (dual-tube on the Cayman S) adds the powerful finishing touch.

Compared with that of the previous model, the wheelbase of the new Cayman has been extended by 2.4

inches, the wheels are larger, and the silhouette is sleeker. The effect on the eye is more dynamic. The effect on the road? It's more dynamic too. The side windows are narrow and, if you wish, you can highlight their contours with

optional trim strips in a high-gloss finish. The taut energy of the exterior design is accentuated by a forward-shifted windshield, aggressive air-intake channels, large wheel arches, and a roofline that extends far into the rear.

It's as if the Cayman is moving swiftly, even when it's standing perfectly still.

To help improve aerodynamics and reduce wind buffeting, the exterior mirrors are mounted directly on the

doors. Their dynamic contouring [not] only gives emphasis to the Caym[an] profile—it improves airflow to th[e] side air intakes. The rush of cool[ing] air supplies oxygen to this athlet[ic] beating heart: the boxer engine.

Precise edges stretch backward along the roof to the rear. In conjunction with the wide track, the effect is a sculpted and honed physique. Imposing fenders lend prominence to the wheels. The wide brake light is an integral feature of the large rear window.

The rear spoiler is more than a stunning eye-catcher. It deploys automatically at 75 mph to effectively enlarge the aerodynamic surface area and increase downforce. The firm contact with the road heightens driving pleasure at the limits of performance.

Where the new Cayman wants to go is clear. Every line and every technical detail is focused in one direction: forward.

Our mid-engine coupe now puts the driver even closer to the center.

Design.

Interior

Creating an uncompromising sports car takes conviction. Giving it an unmistakable design takes creativity. Combine both conviction and creativity and apply it to the interior design. What results? An environment where the driver is central in the driving experience.

In the new Cayman, this has been made possible by a new interior architecture that gives a feeling of open space and offers plenty of freedom of movement around the low-positioned standard sport seats.

The central feature of the interior is the redesigned ascending center console. We believe that the gear lever should be positioned close to the steering wheel to enable fast, efficient, and ergonomic gearshifts. It's just one of many principles that we've transferred from the racetrack to the road. As you would expect, the ignition lock is on the left.

The three-spoke sport steering wheel fits the hand perfectly.

Behind it are the three central circular instruments, which give you all the important information you need. The new and generously proportioned luggage compartment is located underneath the wide rear window. The large rear hatch above the exquisitely styled luggage compartment has a wide opening angle. The luggage protection bar is finished in Brushed Aluminum just like the inlay between the upper and rear luggage spaces. Storage compartments on both sides offer additional storage room.

To further enhance the interior, we offer a comprehensive range of personalization options and a wide selection of colors and materials. All to create your unique vision.

A sports car that does more with less. How very Porsche.

The new Cayman.

At Porsche, it's never our aim to pursue efficiency purely for its own sake. Our rationale is always to use any savings in size or weight to help make a better sports car. A more agile sports car. A quicker sports car, whether accelerating or braking. A safer sports car, able to use its razor-sharp reflexes to avoid accidents in the first place. It's an approach to engineering we call Intelligent Performance. And in the new Cayman model, it results in a sports car that simply does more with less.

The Cayman model's new 2.7-liter boxer engine is actually smaller in terms of displacement than the engine it replaces. The six-cylinder boxer engine is as compact as possible. After all, the less weight an engine carries, the more the car it propels is able then to translate that weight savings into brisk acceleration and responsive handling.

We're not the first company to put the letter "S" on our high-performance models.

Just the most qualified.

The new Cayman S.

When you start at an already-high level, where do you go next? At Porsche, we go to the 19th letter of the alphabet. With the new Cayman S, this is exactly what we did—in every respect. Its 3.4-liter flat-six engine with DFI and VarioCam Plus generates 325 horsepower. It accelerates from 0–60 mph in 4.7 seconds and achieves a top track speed of 175 mph. With PDK and the Sport Chrono Package, both of which are optional, it reaches 60 mph in just 4.4 seconds.

Improved performance demands capable components. The chassis of the new Cayman S is matched specifically to

e secret to the engine's less-is-more
os is a suite of engineering innovations
t optimize power. This six-cylinder
gine uses Direct Fuel Injection (DFI)
 VarioCam Plus to help it produce
5 horsepower, with a top track speed
165 mph. With its precisely geared
speed manual transmission, the

Cayman accelerates from 0–60 mph in
5.4 seconds. Add the optional 7-speed
Porsche Doppelkupplung (PDK) combined
with the Sport Chrono Package, and the
Cayman model's 0–60-mph acceleration
time is cut to a mere 5.1 seconds.

The 18-inch Cayman wheels, a new front
end, brake calipers finished in black,

and, of course, the central tailpipe in
brushed stainless steel are unmistakable
ways to identify the Cayman model.
Come to think of it, so is the sound
coming from that singular exhaust.

the high power output of the engine.
Even greater levels of agility, traction,
and control in corners can be achieved
with Porsche Active Suspension
Management (PASM), Porsche Torque
Vectoring (PTV) with rear differential
lock, and the dynamic gearbox mounts

of the Sport Chrono Package, all of
which are available from our list of
options. For added safety, the front
axle is equipped with larger brake discs
to cope with the increased engine
power. The brake calipers are finished
in red. Imposing 19-inch Cayman S

light-alloy wheels with a classic five-
spoke design are fitted as standard.
On the new Cayman S, Bi-Xenon™
headlights are also standard. The
precisely styled LED front light units
accentuate the front air intakes finished
in black. At the rear, the twin tailpipe
in brushed stainless steel is located

in the center and produces the
typically resonant Porsche sound.

The new Cayman S. Because
Porsche engineers gave it their all,
we're able to give it the letter S.

We're behind the driver 100 percent. Or in this case, about 12 inches.

Boxer engines.

The new Cayman models are powered by compact, mid-mounted boxer engines positioned no further than 12 inches behind the driver. This unorthodox approach yields unique attributes. A substantial amount of the weight of the Cayman is concentrated close to the middle of the vehicle. The center of gravity is low and central, and weight is distributed uniformly between the front and rear axles. The tangible effect—a truly stunning level of agility, with well-balanced handling, particularly in corners.

The new engine concept is defined by high power plus reduced fuel consumption and emissions figures compared with the previous model. We call it Intelligent Performance, a philosophy that applies the engineering principles of the racetrack to the road.

Both engines are equipped as standard with VarioCam Plus and Direct Fuel Injection (DFI) as well as efficiency-enhancing technologies such as Auto Start Stop, electrical system recuperation, and advanced thermal management.

What can you expect from the Cayman driving experience? Direct responses to every burst of acceleration. Dynamic handling in every corner. Oh yes, and one more thing: the inevitable pain of separation at the end of every drive.

Wheels
Performance needs sustained stability. Standard on the new Cayman model are 18-inch alloy wheels that maintain the bond between the vehicle and the road. A minimalist dual-arm spoke design

accentuates the sporty character of the wheels. Tire sizes are 235/45 ZR 18 at the front and 265/45 ZR 18 at the rear.

The Cayman S comes standard with 19-inch wheels with a classic

five-spoke design. The tire size at the front is 235/40 ZR 19 and 265/40 ZR 19 at the rear.

Wheels up to 20 inches are available from our list of options.

The large rolling circumference helps to improve comfort. At the same time, the rolling resistance of the new generation of tires has been reduced, which, in turn, helps to reduce fuel consumption.

Tire Pressure Monitoring System (TPMS)
The Tire Pressure Monitoring System (TPMS) sends warnings to the onboard computer's display screen in the event of low tire pressure. The TFT screen

in the instrument cluster enables the driver to check the pressure in all fo tires. The system updates quickly ar accurately after an engine start, tire pressure correction, or wheel chang for increased comfort and your safe

Airbags

To protect the driver and passenger, the new Cayman models come standard with full-size airbags, which are inflated in two stages depending on the severity and type of accident (e.g., frontal or offset frontal). In less serious accidents, the airbags are only partially inflated, thereby minimizing discomfort to the occupants.

In addition to the central airbag control unit on the transmission tunnel, a pair of impact sensors is located near the headlights. This allows a crash to be detected and evaluated far sooner and with considerably greater accuracy.

Porsche Side Impact Protection (POSIP) System

Both new Cayman models are equipped as standard with the Porsche Side Impact Protection (POSIP) system. It comprises two side airbags on each side and knee airbags. An integral thorax airbag is located in the outer side bolster of each seat, while the door panels each contain an upward-inflating head airbag. Each thorax airbag has a volume of 2.6 gallons and each head airbag 4.0 gallons, ensuring excellent protection in the event of a side impact. POSIP additionally includes steel side impact protection elements in the doors.

1 18-inch Cayman wheel
2 19-inch Cayman S wheel

Airbags and Porsche Side Impact Protection (POSIP) system

Fuel Economy and Recycling

Intelligent lightweight construction is, and always has been, a fundamental aspect of the Porsche philosophy—for both technical and ecological reasons. This combination forms the basis for achieving low fuel consumption values in conjunction with high performance. On the technical side, various components are made with a high proportion of aluminum, magnesium, plastics, and super high-strength sheet steel. The materials used have been selected for their ability to withstand load, yet they are considerably lighter than conventional steel. As a result, the bodyshell of the new Cayman models has a light alloy content of approximately 44 percent.

On the ecological side, all materials used are meticulously selected. We use only state-of-the-art components, with priority given to products manufactured in a sustainable manner when possible. All synthetic components are easily recyclable and each material is labeled to facilitate its separation for recycling. The reduction in the number of plastic variants helps to ensure more efficient recycling. Recycled plastics are used when they meet our exacting technical requirements.

In short, the new Cayman is approximately 95 percent recoverable.

In addition, Porsche uses a high proportion of environmentally friendly water-based paints. For us, environmental protection does not begin with the vehicle manufacturing process. It starts at the planning and development stage.

Fuel

The new Cayman models are designed to operate on fuels with an ethanol content of up to 10 percent. Ethanol has a positive impact on the CO_2 balance since the plants grown for the production of this biofuel also absorb CO_2 from the atmosphere. The release of hydrocarbons from the fuel system has been minimized thanks to the active carbon filter and the multilayered material from which the fuel tank is made.

Servicing

Long service intervals offer clear advantages. For you, they reduce costs and save time. For the environment, they assist in the sparing use of consumables and replacement parts. For full details of service intervals, please contact your local Authorized Porsche dealer.

Feeling relaxed is all about feeling in control.

Interior and comfort.

Leather Package

The new optional Leather package enhances the interior of your new Cayman, with additional items finished in Leather.

You have a choice between a minimalist single-tone interior, with one of the standard colors Black, Platinum Grey, Luxor Beige, or Yachting Blue, and a two-tone combination of Agate Grey and Pebble Grey, Agate Grey and Lime Gold, or Agate Grey and Amber Orange. With these combinations, the features in Leather (on the seats, only the seat center) are finished in the contrasting color.

The package adds a Leather finish to the instrument surround, center console storage compartment lid, seat centers, side bolsters and headrests, door armrests, and door pulls. With the Leather package, the door pulls feature a silver-colored trim strip, which accentuates the dynamic and sweeping design of the interior.

Instruments

Forward thrust is measured by your heart rate. Or it can be displayed in numbers. The three circular instruments give you all the information you need. The rev counter with digital speedometer is positioned in the center. In the Cayman S, the dial face is Aluminum-colored; in the Cayman, it is finished in minimalist black. The instrument on the left contains the analog speedometer with digital trip meter and total distance display.

A new feature of the right-hand circular instrument is the high-resolution, 4.6-inch TFT color screen. It provides you with a continuous stream of data from the onboard computer, reminds you of your selected communication and audio settings, enables you to customize vehicle settings, delivers various warnings including alerts from the Tire Pressure Monitoring System (TPMS), and, in conjunction with the optional PCM, displays information from the navigation system.

1 Leather package in Agate Grey and Amber Orange
2 Cayman instruments
3 Cayman S instruments

Practicality makes perfect.

Storage Compartments

The new Cayman models afford you the everyday practicality that makes Porsche exceptional among sports cars. In addition to the luggage compartment at the front, the luggage space under the wide-opening rear hatch is impressively roomy.

The lockable glove compartment and the compartment with a power socket under the armrest in the center console provide plenty of space. As does the open compartment to the front of it. In conjunction with the smoking package, the open compartment makes way for an ashtray with a lid. Other storage features include two compartments

Our engineers made certain Cayman was pure Porsche. Now you make certain it's all yours.

Personalization.

A comprehensive range of customization options is available for the new Cayman. So you can configure it to your personal preference even before you have placed your order.

The following pages feature all of the available options. For your ease of reference, each one has been arranged in the appropriate category—exterior or interior.

The extensive color palette, for example, enables you to make your Cayman even more individual. It gives you the choice of four solid colors, eight metallic colors, four special colors, and 10 interior colors, as well as the selection of two-tone combinations for the Leather packages and Leather interiors.

Of course, you can choose to have your Cayman finished in virtually any other color of your choice. For further information, please refer to the Porsche Exclusive Cayman catalog. It offers an even more comprehensive selection of personalization options for your Cayman and a way to turn something special into something unique.

With our Porsche Tequipment range of accessories, you can always customize your Porsche at a later time. Please consult your Authorized Porsche dealer for more details.

Using the Porsche Car Configurator at **porscheusa.com**, you can transform your ideas into reality. Here, you can design your very own Cayman model from the ground up. The choice of color or additional equipment, as always, is up to you.

in each door, a net in the passenger footwell, clothes hooks on the seat backrests, and two practical cupholders above the glove compartment.

Front Luggage Compartment
With its mid-engine design, Cayman has room where you wouldn't ordinarily expect to find it: up front. The front luggage compartment has a capacity of 5.3 cubic feet and is lined with black carpet.

Rear Luggage Space
Comprising the shelf above the engine cover and the luggage compartment behind, the rear luggage space of the Cayman is both convenient and functional. With a total capacity of approximately 9.7 cubic feet, it comfortably holds even long items of luggage such as sports equipment. As part of the interior, it is lined with carpet in the interior color. The luggage protection bar and inlay are made of Brushed Aluminum. Concealed by the inlay are the service openings for the coolant and engine oil tanks. Storage compartments in the upper luggage compartment provide additional space for your belongings.

To see the selection of matching luggage accessories available from Porsche, consult the separate "Driver's Selection by Porsche Design" catalog available at your Authorized Porsche dealer.

Porsche Exclusive

A Distinctive Identity Is Another Form of Exclusivity
Everything starts with the right advice to complement your exclusive wishes and requirements. We offer personal support and individual expert advice to each and every customer. So, why wait? Make an appointment with your Authorized Porsche dealer to discuss your requirements.

For the truly personal touch, contact our Porsche Customer Consultation Specialists at **customerconsultations@porsche.us**.

You can see what we really mean by "customization" by making an appointment to visit our Customer Consultation Center in Beverly Hills, California. Here, you can select the materials, such as Leather, Wood, Carbon, or Aluminum, and the paint finish you desire. With the advanced Porsche Car Configurator, you will be able to see a nearly life-size wall display of your creation. The Porsche New-Vehicle Limited Warranty applies for all Porsche Exclusive options and special designs. Please understand that some Porsche Exclusive options may require a longer delivery lead time.

Porsche buyer from the eighties and nineties, and far removed from those of the sixties and seventies. Times change. *Road & Track* even went as far as to say: "It might be the ultimate weapon for an all-back-roads coast-to-coast road trip." Also named as 'Best Car to Buy' by *Motor Authority*, there was plenty to be happy about back in Weissach, and just enough constructive criticism to help hone the pocket rocket in the future.

Regular folks tend to vote with their wallets, of course, and there was no shortage of people lining up to part with their money to be seen behind the wheel of the new Cayman and its sister car. By the end of 2013, sales of the middies had reached 7953 units – a 137 per cent increase over the previous year's figure, which helped Porsche Cars North America Inc break through the 40K sales barrier for the first time ever. Without doubt, this was the ultimate commendation …

As far as the Boxsters were concerned, the summer of 2013 saw Platinum Silver replaced by Rhodium Silver, and Aqua Blue by Sapphire Blue. In addition, Emerald Green was dropped from the colour palette, while Black with Luxor Beige two-tone leather was added as another trim alternative.

Even though the Cayman price list was slow to pick up on the change, the same was actually true for the coupé range, with June 2013 heralding a new era, as per the open car (dealers were told 31 May for the last Platinum Silver orders, thus confirming the situation). As such, there were the silver and blue paintwork revisions, along with the Black/Luxor Beige leather trim addition to take note of at this point; Emerald Green was not offered on the 981 Caymans, incidentally.

The rhd markets

UK prices were carried over on the 981 Boxster, so the cost of entry into Porsche motoring remained pegged at £37,589. This is because the new Cayman, listed from March 2013, hit the forecourt at £39,694

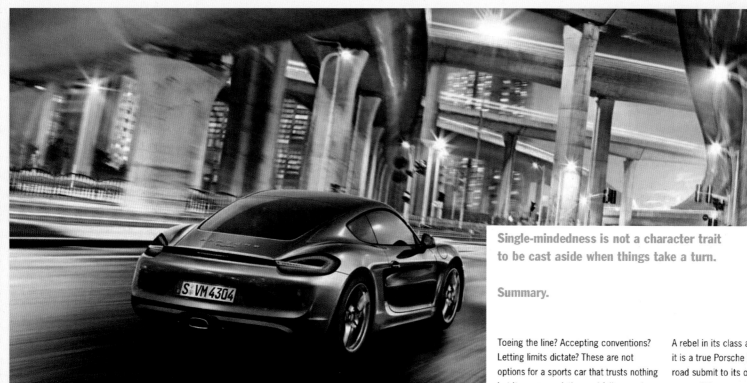

Single-mindedness is not a character trait to be cast aside when things take a turn.

Summary.

Toeing the line? Accepting conventions? Letting limits dictate? These are not options for a sports car that trusts nothing but its own conviction and follows only one thing: the code of the curve.

A rebel in its class and in its family, it is a true Porsche that makes the road submit to its own will. In every corner, it is preoccupied by one thing above all: reaching the next.

The new Cayman challenges the limits of physics. It exploits the potential of every corner and interprets the mid-engine concept more purposefully, more independently, and in a more contemporary way than ever before—in its design, in its performance, and in its handling.

The new Cayman.

in 2.7-litre guise, and £48,783 with the larger S engine. This made both coupés a fraction more expensive than their 987 predecessors, but only by a relatively small amount – in the hundreds rather than the thousands.

Autocar tested a 6MT base Cayman soon after the UK launch, clocking a 0-60 time of 5.9 seconds with it, and recording a creditable average fuel consumption of 29.2mpg along the way. Interesting options included a 19in wheel and tyre transplant (£971) and trick PDLS headights (£1060), although every effort was made to keep the sticker price down. The navi system made the biggest splash on this particular car, but adding things like 18-way P07 seats at £4318 and PCCB brakes at £4977 would have soon bumped up the invoice; even a tyre pressure monitor was listed at £421.

Anyway, giving the new Cayman a five-star rating, the magazine praised the "sensational handling" and "cabin quality and layout," and was only really upset by the level of standard equipment. It added: "The smaller flat-six is no pale shadow; it's a stirring boxer engine in Porsche's grand tradition, and what it lacks in tractability, it makes up for in high-rev sparkle and road-biased usability."

Andrew Frankel was less impressed with the base car. Although "quite giddy" after running around in the Cayman S, the *MotorSport* man had obviously been spoilt by it, and found the smaller six (albeit smooth, and perfectly fine in normal driving) lacking the torque-induced punch of its bigger brother when pushing hard: "It seems mean to sound critical of a car that I still liked very much and perhaps I'd have not put it this way had I driven it before the Cayman S. Still, I must report as I find."

There were no changes on the Boxster front Down Under, with prices starting at $101,500, but the arrival of the Cayman in late April 2013 was significant. The base car was listed at $107,100, while the Cayman S came in at $139,900; the seven-speed PDK gearbox added about $5000 to the invoice. Edged out from the *Wheels* 'Car of

(Continues on page 116)

Boxster Colour & Trim Guide

These colour variations were available from June 2013 until March 2014.

Solid coachwork colours
Black (041 Schwarz), White (C9A Weiss), Guards Red (80K Indischrot), and Racing Yellow (1S1 Racinggelb).

Metallic coachwork colours
Basalt Black (C9Z Basaltschwarz) Metallic, Agate Grey (M7S Achatgrau) Metallic, Rhodium Silver (M7U Rhodiumsilber) Metallic, Dark Blue (M5X Dunkelblau) Metallic, Sapphire Blue (M5J Saphirblau) Metallic, Amaranth Red (8L1 Amaranthrot) Metallic, Mahogany (M8Y Mahogani) Metallic, and Anthracite Brown (M8S Anthrazitbraun) Metallic.

Special coachwork colours
GT Silver (M7Z GT-silber) Metallic, Lime Gold (5P1 Limegold) Metallic, and Cognac (M8Z Cognac) Metallic. A 'colour to sample' option was also available.

Hood (convertible top) colours
Black, Blue, Red, and Brown.

Leatherette/Vinyl trim
Black, Platinum Grey, Yachting Blue, and Luxor Beige. Carpeting and floor mats came in matching hues, with the headlining in black.

Leather trim
Black, Platinum Grey, Yachting Blue, and Luxor Beige. Carpeting and floor mats came in matching hues, with the roof liner in black on all but the Luxor Beige option (this came with a beige headlining).

Regular two-tone leather trim
Agate Grey with Lime Gold, Agate Grey with Pebble Grey, and Agate Grey with Amber Orange. Carpeting and floor mats came in Agate Grey, with the roof liner in black.

Special leather colours and natural leather trim
Agate Grey, Carrera Red, Espresso, Agate Grey with Lime Gold, Agate Grey with Pebble Grey, Agate Grey with Amber Orange, and Black with Luxor Beige. Carpeting and floor mats came in matching hues (being the lighter shades on the two-tone options), with the roof liner in black, or dark grey on the Agate Grey-based two-tone trim. A 'colour to sample' option was also available.

Cayman Colour & Trim Guide

These colour variations were available from June 2013 until March 2014.

Solid coachwork colours
Black (041 Schwarz), White (C9A Weiss), Guards Red (80K Indischrot), and Racing Yellow (1S1 Racinggelb).

Metallic coachwork colours
Basalt Black (C9Z Basaltschwarz) Metallic, Agate Grey (M7S Achatgrau) Metallic, Rhodium Silver (M7U Rhodiumsilber) Metallic, Dark Blue (M5X Dunkelblau) Metallic, Sapphire Blue (M5J Saphirblau) Metallic, Amaranth Red (8L1 Amaranthrot) Metallic, Mahogany (M8Y Mahogani) Metallic, and Anthracite Brown (M8S Anthrazitbraun) Metallic.

Special coachwork colours
GT Silver (M7Z GT-silber) Metallic, Lime Gold (5P1 Limegold) Metallic, and Cognac (M8Z Cognac) Metallic. A 'colour to sample' option was also available.

Leatherette/vinyl trim
Black, Platinum Grey, Yachting Blue, and Luxor Beige. Carpeting, floor mats and the roof lining came in matching hues, except for the blue option, which had a black headliner.

Leather trim
Black, Platinum Grey, Yachting Blue, and Luxor Beige. Carpeting, floor mats and the roof lining came in matching hues, except for the blue option, which had a black headliner.

Regular two-tone leather trim
Agate Grey with Lime Gold, Agate Grey with Pebble Grey, and Agate Grey with Amber Orange. Carpeting, floor mats and the roof lining came in Agate Grey.

Special leather colours and natural leather trim
Agate Grey, Carrera Red, and Espresso monotone: These came with carpeting, floor mats and the roof lining in matching hues, except for the red option, which had a black headliner. Agate Grey with Lime Gold, Agate Grey with Pebble Grey, Agate Grey with Amber Orange, and Black with Luxor Beige two-tone: Carpeting and floor mats came in the lighter shade, with the roof liner in Agate Grey on all but the Black/Luxor Beige combination (this had a black headlining). A 'colour to sample' option was also available.

A strict Cayman for the UK market, fitted with optional 20in 'Carrera Classic' alloy wheels. Note the exhaust pipe shape, which followed the Boxster's lead according to engine size.

the Year' title, the coupé nonetheless enthralled testers. There were the odd gripes about the EPS steering, and even the heavy clutch, but most were quite literally reaching for a thesaurus in a bid to find alternative ways to wax lyrical, not just about the new car, but also Porsche's philosophy in general.

In Japan, the cost of Boxster motoring increased by 120,000 yen on base cars and 130,000 yen on the S grade during the spring of 2013, although they were still a fair bit cheaper than their Cayman equivalents even then. Introduced in December 2012, the 2.7-litre Cayman commanded 6,120,000 yen in manual guise, while the Cayman S was listed at 7,730,000 yen; a PDK transmission added 470,000 yen to the price on all 981 series cars.

With no major changes to the specification sheet, prices were carried over in Germany for the 2014 Model Year proper, as they were in most EU markets, and Australia and Japan, as it happens. In Britain, the cost of Cayman motoring remained unchanged, although the Boxsters had a small increase applied to them (less than two per cent), closing the price gap between the open and closed versions a touch. It was the same story in America, with the convertibles only getting hit with an increase, in this case an average of just over $1000.

Whilst listed a few months earlier, option XXR became available from November 2013 – just as the Macan was making its world debut at the Los Angeles Show (it was also displayed at the Tokyo Motor Show, as it happens, but with less fanfare). Costing €440.30, specifying this Exclusive item brought a dark tint to the rear combination light units. At the same time, specifying the CTX option brought a gearknob in a contrasting leather colour, while CTL was the same thing for the PDK transmission shifter; both were listed at €714.00.

It should also be said here that the XD9 and XDA wheel painting options (with a body colour finish and a black finish, respectively, on the main part of the wheel, minus the outer bead rim) were listed in the first Boxster price list, but then failed to appear in the original Cayman one. Sure enough, a footnote stating that they were available

The Caymans were ideally suited to the VLN endurance races held at the Nürburgring. This car is pictured at the German track in October 2013, although appearances of the 981 series models became more prolific from the 2014 season onwards.

from November 2013 appeared in later lists, so this is the date that should be kept in mind when considering these €1178.10 options in the future; the same is true of the short-lived CRX option that brought a contrast colour to the wheels.

Another oddity was the Porsche Entry & Drive option (625), which was listed in the first Cayman catalogue, but failed to appear in any 981 series price lists beyond the spring of 2013. Priced at €880.60, it would eventually resurface in January 2014, bringing keyless entry and engine starting to Boxster and Cayman owners via a different transponder key, revised door handles with sensors (plus an equivalent at each end of the car for the luggage compartment lids) and a dummy key not much smaller than the original that could be left in the ignition barrel. It seems a lot to pay to build on the existing remote entry system, which came as standard, but for those who can't be bothered to put their hand in their pocket once in a while, it must have been a real godsend …

Cover from a contemporary Japanese model range catalogue, showing how the Porsche range had grown. From left to right we have the Boxster, the Cayman, the 911, the new Macan, the Panamera, and the Cayenne.

Chapter 4
Expanding the range

Earlier, we mentioned the growing importance of the Chinese market. The international launch of the 981-based GTS variants at the 2014 Beijing Show (which opened on 21 April) confirms the situation beyond any doubt ...

The GTS models at the time of their announcement, with a Boxster GTS on the left, and a Cayman GTS on the right.

The GTS line was announced on 19 March, just a few days after the 2014 Geneva Show closed its doors. The fact this timing was chosen quite deliberately, rather than unleashing the Boxster GTS and Cayman GTS in more familiar Swiss surroundings, which would have been easy enough to do given that we're talking about days and not months, proves beyond doubt that China had – almost overnight – become a real heavyweight in import car circles.

The red pairing making their debut in Beijing (or Peking as the German press preferred to call it) certainly attracted a lot of attention in amongst an array of domestically-produced and foreign automobiles, despite no fewer than 118 world premiers taking place at the event; 31 of them from makers based outside China.

Interestingly, while Jan Roth remained Project Manager (and would into the 718 run), a remarkably young Dr Stefan Weckbach became the new head of the Boxster and Cayman model lines in 2013 before moving across to electric vehicles. As such, the GTS came out on his watch, and his marketing skills would be much appreciated in what was still a challenging era in the global marketplace. But what exactly was the GTS?

Stefan Weckbach (seen here seated in a Cayman GTS) would become an important figure in the fate of the mid-engined cars.

The GTS in detail

Available on both the Boxster and Cayman bodies – and for the first time as it happens, the GTS grade (by now common in other Porsche lines, with the historically significant moniker standing for Gran Turismo Sport, although the I011 code was used internally) was basically a sportier package that built on the S specification in a number of ways.

As the press release on these more powerful variants noted: "With uprated engines and excellent PASM chassis, the Boxster GTS and Cayman GTS set new benchmarks for sportiness in their segment. The [new front-end] and a modified rear-end, blackened Bi-Xenon headlights – with the Porsche Dynamic Light System (PDLS) as standard – and exterior lettering in silky black gloss are subtle yet unmistakable features of the new top models.

"The combination of PASM and the Sport Chrono package as standard enables the driver to switch between progressive sportiness on the one hand and long-distance comfort on the other at the press of a button. The tyres, measuring 235/35 at the front and 265/35 at the rear, on 20in 'Carrera S' wheels, provide the perfect setup for both. Both two-seaters come with sports seats and leather interiors as standard. Like other GTS models from Porsche, they are refined with Alcantara elements."

Starting with the powerplant, the GTS six was based on the 3.4-litre S unit, and "thanks to optimised fine-tuning," delivered an additional 15bhp – this meant 330bhp for the Boxster GTS, and 340bhp for the Cayman GTS, which was considered enough of a jump to justify the fitting of a third radiator up front. Torque output was also increased

by around 7lbft on both models, the maxima arriving at 4500rpm in the open car and 4750rpm in the tin-top – the latter being the only difference noted in the engine revs for peak values.

Sure enough, the I011 spec brings forth a different part number for a replacement engine, but it's frankly difficult to see the make-up through individual components, and reliable information is decidedly thin on the ground. As with the Cayman 'Power Kit', we just have to trust our friends in Stuttgart, and perhaps all will become clear in the future.

With the same manual or PDK gearboxes as the S and the Sport Chrono package as standard, as well as the XLF sports exhaust system, the extra horses translated into a top speed of over 175mph (280km/h), and a fractional gain in 0-60 times. The regular S brakes were more than capable of handling this, so they were retained (complete with red calipers), hidden behind 'inch-up' 423 'Carrera S' alloys with a natural finish (many chose to order a black rim, but this was not the catalogue specification). As noted in the press release, the GTS line also came with the PASM active suspension, which lowered the car by 10mm (0.39in).

As for the styling changes, the trim around the inner workings of the PDLS headlights was darkened to give a smoked impression, while the light units below them were completely revised, being shaped like those of the Boxster for both 981 series models and given dark lenses at the same time. Although the side repeater lens remained clear, the theme chosen for the GTS was continued at the back of the car, with tinted rear combination lights (available via option code XXR as a rule).

The first Porsche to carry the GTS moniker was the 904 – spiritual grandparent of the Cayman.

The frontal changes for the GTS, seen here on a Porsche Museum car, as the press pictures were attractive but not very useful from a reference standpoint, being too dark to pick out details. This is a Cayman, obviously, but the fresh lights and air dam arrangement were the same for the Boxster GTS.

The revised front air dam, which added 30mm (1.2in) to the car's overall length, was much like the strict Cayman one in shape, but with a black frame around the upper part of the central vent (open in the recessed centre section), and edgier-looking black inserts in the air vents off to the sides. It was the same for both the Boxster GTS and the Cayman GTS, the merging of designs explaining the driving light change.

Black 'GTS' decals adorned the doors, and while 'Carrera S' wheels were the norm, as already mentioned, the other 20in rims were available as a heavily subsidised option; indeed the 427 'Carrera Classic' wheel was listed as a no-cost option on the Cayman GTS (but not the Boxster GTS for some reason). Caymans had gloss black side window trim, by the way, while the roll-over hoops on the Boxsters remained in their regular dark grey.

Meanwhile, around the back, the 'Porsche' script was now in black, matched up with a 'Cayman GTS' or 'Boxster GTS' one with the same finish, fitting in nicely with the darker taillight units. The dual exhaust tips were black, poking out from a new diffuser-style rear apron, which was also in black.

Moving inside, the GTS came with the sportier P04 seats, with Alcantara inlays and a 'GTS' logo in the headrest; cheaper upgrades were available for those that wanted them. Black leather trim was used as the foundation stone, with Alcantara elements everywhere, from the centre armrest lid, through to the lower section of the dash, on the doors, and even the Cayman's headlining. 'Galvanosilber' trim was applied to the fascia, door cappings and centre console, and, if owners wanted, the interior could be toned down, with less Alcantara-trimmed areas upon request, or with all leather upholstery free of charge.

A SportDesign steering wheel was used, with Alcantara trim on the rim to continue the sporting theme (usually option XLK) and shift paddles on PDK cars, although a multi-function or regular SportDesign wheel could be specified at no extra cost; the two gearshift types were also trimmed in Alcantara as standard. A black tachometer with a 'GTS' logo on it was the norm, with model-specific treadplates finishing things off. For the record, the standard GTS-spec Alcantara gearshifts were duly made available on the other 981 series models (option code XLM for manual cars, and XLN for those fitted with PDK), priced at €309.40 apiece.

Officially, the weight was listed at 1345kg (2965lb) for both cars, although some markets put the Cayman version 10kg (22lb) higher. This seems like a very small gain considering the amount of additional items included, such as the third radiator, but the list also highlights what good value the GTS grade offered for those wanting a road burner.

There were several GTS-specific options created at this time,

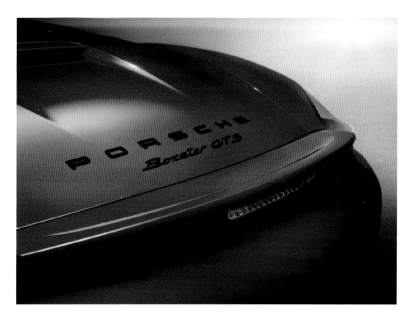

The tail badging on a Boxster GTS.

as well as the odd one related to the GTS – standard on the more powerful car, but made available on the base and S grades for the first time.

Writing 712 on the order form deleted the 'GTS' decals on the doors (free of charge), while CLP was an extended leather and Alcantara door trim package, priced at €476.00. Code 089 brought a GTS-only exterior package (front spoiler, front and side intakes, door

Interior of the Porsche Museum's Cayman GTS, which had the GTS interior package (code 088) with red contrast stitching. Note the model-specific logo in the TFT screen to the right of the tachometer.

A publicity photograph of the Boxster GTS that somehow managed to avoid the catalogue. For us, if nothing else, the lighting is much more useful for reference than the arty press shots.

Boxster Colour & Trim Guide

These colour variations were available on regular base, S and GTS models from March 2014 until the end of production. However, not all options were listed in the final months, and a note on discontinued paint and trim can be found in the next chapter. One should also note that the GTS was offered with regular upholstery, but only GTS buyers were allowed to specify the special GTS trim package.

Solid coachwork colours
Black (041 Schwarz), White (C9A Weiss), Guards Red (80K Indischrot), and Racing Yellow (1S1 Racinggelb).

Metallic coachwork colours
Jet Black (C9X Tiefschwarz) Metallic, Carrara White (B9A Carraraweiss) Metallic, Agate Grey (M7S Achatgrau) Metallic, Rhodium Silver (M7U Rhodiumsilber) Metallic, Dark Blue (M5X Dunkelblau) Metallic, Sapphire Blue (M5J Saphirblau) Metallic, Mahogany (M8Y Mahogani) Metallic, and Anthracite Brown (M8S Anthrazitbraun) Metallic.

Special coachwork colours
GT Silver (M7Z GT-silber) Metallic, Lime Gold (5P1 Limegold) Metallic, and Carmine Red (M3C Karminrot) Metallic. A 'colour to sample' option was also available.

Hood (convertible top) colours
Black, Blue, Red, and Brown.

Leatherette/Vinyl trim
Black, Platinum Grey, Yachting Blue, and Luxor Beige. Carpeting and floor mats came in matching hues, with the headlining in black.

Leather trim
Black, Platinum Grey, Yachting Blue, and Luxor Beige. Carpeting and floor mats came in matching hues, with the roof liner in black on all but the Luxor Beige option (this came with a beige headlining).

Regular two-tone leather trim
Agate Grey with Lime Gold, Agate Grey with Pebble Grey, and Agate Grey with Amber Orange. Carpeting and floor mats came in Agate Grey, with the roof liner in black.

Special leather colours and natural leather trim
Agate Grey, Garnet Red, Espresso, Agate Grey with Lime Gold, Agate Grey with Pebble Grey, Agate Grey with Amber Orange, and Black with Luxor Beige. Carpeting and floor mats came in matching hues (being the lighter shades on the two-tone options), with the roof liner in black. A 'colour to sample' option was also available.

GTS model-specific trim
Black leather with matching Alcantara inserts and red or silver contrast stitching. Carpeting and floor mats came in black (with red or silver accents), while the rooflining came in black cloth.

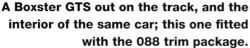

A Boxster GTS out on the track, and the interior of the same car; this one fitted with the 088 trim package.

mirror undersides and rear apron painted in gloss black) for €999.60, while 088 was a GTS interior package (carbonfibre trim pieces on the dashboard, doors and centre console, plus red or silver contrast stitching, with a matching tachometer dial, headrest logo, seatbelt edges and floormat trim); the latter was €2963.10 on the open car, but a no-cost option on the fixed-head coupé.

From June, GTS buyers could obtain the P2A and 809 aluminium trim parts. These were given a black finish, with the former bringing dashboard and door capping sections for €821.10, and the latter adding the console surrounding the gearshift for a further €238.00. Finally, the GTS version of the XXB-type stainless steel treadplates eventually came online in November 2014.

Meanwhile, the opportunity was taken to review the colour and trim listing with the introduction of the GTS grade. The Basalt Black paint option was replaced by Jet Black Metallic (also known as Deep Black), while Amaranth Red gave way to Carrara White Metallic. These two changes didn't take place until June, although Cognac was replaced by Carmine Red with immediate effect. In addition, the Carrera Red trim option was superseded by Garnet Red natural leather, and the headliner became black on all Boxsters except for those with a Luxor Beige leather interior.

Fun in the sun

The international GTS press launch took place in Majorca. Put any journalist in a nice motor on magnificent roads, and you're almost guaranteed to get some enthusiastic words on paper.

Scott Burgess wrote for *Motor Trend*: "The all-new GTS versions

corners and get the rear moving round so that you can pick up the throttle smartly as you hit the apex."

There was absolutely no doubt that the GTS was indeed a super tool, with endless prose saying how good the new pairing was. But regarding everyday use back in the real world, with speed cameras everywhere and an endless variety of dawdlers in the gaps, *Auto Express'* Mat Watson came up with some sensible comments, noting that it was difficult to discern extra power on normal roads, and things like launch control were goodies that you use once, put the video up on *YouTube*, and then forgot about.

Henry Catchpole in his *Evo* piece also suggested some shorter gearing as an option, which would make a lot of sense, bringing the gears closer at the cost of losing a bit of top speed that hardly anyone on the planet will be able to experience outside a racetrack, and there's not many circuits with suitable straights in any case.

The author used to be of the opinion that more is automatically better; that faster is obviously better, and so on, but things have got to the point nowadays where most high-performance vehicles are simply too

of the Boxster and Cayman are more than howling mid-engine two-seaters. They are the sum total of what a small Porsche can be, and could make the decision between a fully-loaded Cayman GTS and a base 911 much more difficult ... As much as I like the 911, these two GTS models offer a lot to consider.

"They are lighter, more nimble, and have great power-to-weight ratios." Having moved off the mountain roads to the local circuit, he added: "While I have never considered myself much of a track driver, the Cayman GTS will make most people feel like a good one."

The guys at *Evo* were certainly impressed by the Cayman's fine yet forgiving handling: "One road that we find is exceptionally bumpy and tight, but the GTS seems happy to tackle it at speed and never loses its composure. Then through a particular set of smoother corners, the Cayman deals with quick left-right direction changes sublimely, never leaving you guessing as you load the suspension one way then the other. It will even allow you to brake deep into the

powerful and too fast to be exploited in regular use, with owners lulled into a false sense of security by an array of gadgets controlling cornering and braking. For me, at least, the fun comes with unfiltered feedback and pure control, even if it bites. Of course, the GTS would go on to sell very well, and not just as a status symbol – further proof, if ever it were needed, that the marketplace had moved on, while I obviously haven't ...

Home market update

With the first domestic deliveries expected in May 2014, the Boxster GTS was listed at €69,949 in its native country, while the Cayman GTS commanded €73,757 including taxes. As it happens, the RRP on the existing four models (or eight if you want to class the PDK versions as separate) increased by around two per cent at the same time, so the price gap on the S was ultimately a bit less than the jump from a 2.7-litre car to a 3.4-litre one.

A selection of pictures from a VLN endurance event at the Nürburgring in the summer of 2014 – the ADAC Reinoldus-Langstreckenrennen. Soon, 981 Caymans would be seen all over Europe, competing in all manner of GT4 events, including the Britcar GT series, and various American races, too. But it was the Nürburgring 24-hour Race (sometimes held as part of the VLN championship, sometimes a stand-alone competition) that attracted the mid-engined two-seater in droves.

The new 20in '911 Turbo' alloy wheel option (code 429), actually on a 911 in this picture.

The cost of options was, in the main, carried over. Interestingly, the PDK transmission was significantly more expensive on the GTS model for some reason (€3456.95 against €2826.25), while the price of the sports exhaust (code XLF) rose to €2249.10, and €30 was added to the cost of XXR-type rear lights at the same time. The latter two items were both standard on the GTS models, of course, so it was very much a case of robbing Peter to pay Paul.

Apart from the cost of leather trim going up by an average of four per cent and platinum painted wheels being landed with a hefty €125 price hike, the other changes were all fairly small, being applied to coloured seatbelts, the painted rear apron option (CNG), painted dash vent slats (CDN), a couple of leather dash trim options (CZV and CZW), and a colour-keyed master keyfob. We should also be aware that the CLB/CLH Alcantara-trimmed gearshifts were superseded by the newer – and significantly cheaper – XLM and XLN versions we mentioned earlier in order to fit in with the standard GTS specification, while the CRX painted wheel option fell by the wayside.

All 981 series cars (base, S and GTS) were given black front air

Cayman Colour & Trim Guide

These colour variations were available on regular base, S and GTS models from March 2014 until the end of production. However, not all options were listed in the final months, and a note on discontinued paint and trim can be found in the next chapter. One should also note that the GTS was offered with regular upholstery, but only GTS buyers were allowed to specify the special GTS trim package.

Solid coachwork colours
Black (041 Schwarz), White (C9A Weiss), Guards Red (80K Indischrot), and Racing Yellow (1S1 Racinggelb).

Metallic coachwork colours
Jet Black (C9X Tiefschwarz) Metallic, Carrara White (B9A Carraraweiss) Metallic, Agate Grey (M7S Achatgrau) Metallic, Rhodium Silver (M7U Rhodiumsilber) Metallic, Dark Blue (M5X Dunkelblau) Metallic, Sapphire Blue (M5J Saphirblau) Metallic, Mahogany (M8Y Mahogani) Metallic, and Anthracite Brown (M8S Anthrazitbraun) Metallic.

Special coachwork colours
GT Silver (M7Z GT-silber) Metallic, Lime Gold (5P1 Limegold) Metallic, and Carmine Red (M3C Karminrot) Metallic. A 'colour to sample' option was also available.

Leatherette/vinyl trim
Black, Platinum Grey, Yachting Blue, and Luxor Beige. Carpeting,

floor mats and the roof lining came in matching hues, except for the blue option, which had a black headliner.

Leather trim
Black, Platinum Grey, Yachting Blue, and Luxor Beige. Carpeting, floor mats and the roof lining came in matching hues, except for the blue option, which had a black headliner.

Regular two-tone leather trim
Agate Grey with Lime Gold, Agate Grey with Pebble Grey, and Agate Grey with Amber Orange. Carpeting, floor mats and the roof lining came in Agate Grey.

Special leather colours and natural leather trim
Agate Grey, Garnet Red, and Espresso monotone: These came with carpeting, floor mats and the roof lining in matching hues, except for the red option, which had a black headliner. Agate Grey with Lime Gold, Agate Grey with Pebble Grey, Agate Grey with Amber Orange, and Black with Luxor Beige two-tone: Carpeting and floor mats came in the lighter shade, with the roof liner in Agate Grey on all but the Black/Luxor Beige combination (this had a black headlining). A 'colour to sample' option was also available.

GTS model-specific trim
Black leather with matching Alcantara inserts and red or silver contrast stitching. Carpeting and floor mats came in black (with red or silver accents), while the rooflining came in Black Alcantara.

vent grilles from this time, and a tyre pressure monitor (using the RDK moniker in Germany) was added to the domestic market specification. In addition, the net windblocker device moved from the option column to the standard equipment list on the Boxster S and Boxster GTS, although it remained an extra on the 2.7-litre convertible.

New options for the Boxsters and Caymans included the Porsche Dynamic Light System Plus lighting package (code 632, and priced at between €452.20 and €2011.10 depending on the grade). The PDLS+ system took oncoming traffic and the distance from the car in front into consideration to adjust the beam more thoughtfully, while specifying the 631 option code brought with a speed limit indicator. Costing a hefty €416.50, it's doubtful many went for that one!

The rather ornate '911 Turbo' wheel design (429) was another newcomer, priced at between €1309.00 and €4165.00 according to the vehicle they were to be fitted to. A carbonfibre-trimmed gearshift was also listed now, with EHH being the manual car version and EHJ the one for PDK machines; both versions were listed at €499.80.

A new parking assistance package (638) became available in June, combining the former 635 and 636 options and adding a rear camera into the equation for €1535.00. In the same month, one could ask for wheels to be fully painted (rim bead included) in silk black (code 344) for €737.80, or gloss black (XDG) for €1178.10, and the inner door sill guards could be trimmed in leather (XTG) after handing over €458.15. Another €226.10 allowed owners to specify either Porsche script (XLG) or a Porsche crest (XLJ) on an Alcantara centre armrest/storage box lid.

The export markets

Hot on the heels of the news that the Boxster and Cayman had made *Automobile* magazine's 'All-Star' list yet again, the arrival of the GTS grades in American showrooms was another cause for celebration.

Motor Trend's Scott Mortara tried both GTS models at the Laguna Seca track, and declared: "Getting more power out of the Boxster or Cayman engine would be easy for Porsche, but it will never pass the 911, and it doesn't need to. As enjoyable as the Boxster GTS is in every way, for me, it just can't match its fixed-roof sibling. The Cayman GTS has the perfect balance of power and capability, much like the Ferrari 458 Italia. It's not the most powerful or fastest, but, out of the line-up, it is arguably the most enjoyable car to drive."

Praise indeed, and with the Boxster GTS listed at $73,500 and the Cayman GTS at $75,200, they were sensibly priced, too. The strict 2014 MY Boxster had been listed at $50,400 at the start of the season, while the S commanded $62,100 (all plus a $995 destination fee, of course). However, the difference was easy to justify, and for many who would have ordered the options anyway, the choice was something of a no-brainer, meaning the GTS became extremely popular.

Interestingly, Cayman and Cayman S prices had been left alone, allowing the pricing gap to close, and the same thing happened again for the 2015 season, with only the strict Boxster and Boxster S prices increasing (by $1000 and $1200, respectively, this time around).

Incidentally, a windblocker was added to the Boxster's spec sheet in the States for 2015, adjusting the various PCNA packages accordingly, and there were plenty of those. In the main, though,

(Continues on page 135)

Selected pages from the international version of the Boxster GTS catalogue (pages 127-133).

PORSCHE

The new Boxster GTS
Purist

If it's not open air, it's not real rock 'n' roll.

The Boxster GTS concept.

Real life is played out in the open air. It's where legendary rock concerts have been staged. It's where legendary races have been won. Legendary driving sensations are the emotions that the Boxster evokes. It lets us feel the wind against our skin – and enjoy pleasure in every corner.

Can sensations like these be further heightened? Could driving possibly get any more intense? The answer from our engineers has three letters: GTS. Three letters that we adopted for the first time in 1963 with the 904 GTS, a sports car equipped with a mid-mounted engine. Three letters that have since become an emblem for racetrack performance and

incredible sportiness on everyday drives. So it's only logical that they would eventually adorn another mid-engined sports car, this time the Boxster. Their promise is delivered without compromise: increased horsepower, a much more exquisite specification and even greater driving pleasure. Making the experience of driving a roadster even more emphatic and direct.

The result is the new Boxster GTS. A design classic with an acute desire for freedom. A mid-engined sports car that truly strikes a chord. A roadster for the ultimate driving experience.

Those who can boast of a prestigious track record are entitled to quote from their own experience.

Exterior.

The 550 Spyder and 718 RS 60 Spyder are both inspiring examples of freedom behind the wheel. The Boxster is also a symbol of independence. We've made some refinements and given freedom an even sharper appearance.

The new Boxster GTS displays an insatiable desire for acceleration and it's evident at the very first glance. The distinctively designed front end, with largely dimensioned air intakes characterised by their imposing geometry, exudes pure sportiness. The effect is strengthened by the

GTS specific smoked daytime running lights and position lights built on LED technology. Bi-Xenon headlights, including the Porsche Dynamic Light System (PDLS), are fitted as standard. The black inner trims lend further prominence to the vertical arrangement of the headlights – an unmistakable reference to the motorsport era of the 60s and 70s. The Carmine Red special colour is a particularly expressive touch. Available for the first time with the GTS model of the Boxster, it nicely accentuates the exterior parts finished in black.

The stretched silhouette is sleek and wedge-shaped. The side air intakes give clues to the mid-engine concept within. 20-inch Carrera S wheels are fitted as standard with their impressive, dynamic 10-spoke design. A black painted finish is available on request. Equally as eye-catching are the optional 20-inch 911 Turbo wheels with rim well painted in titanium colour and centre spokes in polished aluminium.

The fully electric hood opens and closes in just nine seconds, and remains operable up to a speed of 50 km/h. Pure independence – at the touch of a button.

The smoked LED taillights lend expressive accents. The black 'Boxster GTS' logo puts a name to this intensified sporty design. The restyled rear apron makes the new Boxster GTS appear even wider and sportier. The unadulterated Porsche sound blasts out of the black tailpipes of the sports exhaust system, which is fitted as standard.

1) Available from 06/2014 at the earliest.

20-inch Carrera S wheels painted in high-gloss black (partially)

20-inch Carrera S wheels painted in satin black (complete)1)

20-inch 911 Turbo wheel

Where do truly powerful emotions come from? The inside, of course.

Interior.

The interior delivers exactly what the exterior promises: the insatiable urge for acceleration.

The 'Boxster GTS' logo on the door sill guards makes the first statement. The interior integrates the driver perfectly into the vehicle. The ascending centre console positions the gear lever/selector close to the SportDesign steering wheel, which is fitted as standard. This is the pure sports car. Also faithful to the concept is the use of Alcantara, a particularly high-grip material derived from motorsport. It complements the standard black leather interior on the lower section of the dashboard, the doors, the lid of the centre console storage compartment, the steering wheel and the gear lever/selector. Alcantara is also found on the seat centres of the Sports seats Plus. Fitted as standard, their prominent seat side bolsters and sporty firm padding provide even better lateral support. The headrests are embroidered with 'GTS' logos.

Boxster GTS

GTS interior package.

Wouldn't it be nice if the authentic sports car feel could be further intensified? It can be – with the optional GTS interior package.

The sporty contrast of the exterior theme is continued in the interior. The standard black interior of the Boxster GTS is supplemented by sporty accents in Carmine Red or Rhodium Silver. These include 'GTS' logos embroidered on the headrests in the contrasting colour. Also in the contrasting colour are the dial face of the rev counter, selected decorative seams, the 'PORSCHE' logo on the floor mats and the edges of the seat belts. The sporty, progressive impression is purposefully reinforced by the material carbon, which is used for the decorative trims of the dashboard and doors as well as for the centre console, resulting in sharply refined sportiness for enhanced driving pleasure.

There are no speed limits for a racing heart.

Drive.

Engine.

The uprated 3.4-litre flat-six engine with direct fuel injection (DFI) and VarioCam Plus delivers 243 kW (330 hp). That's 11 kW (15 hp) more than that of the Boxster S. Purposeful lightweight construction has achieved a weight-to-power ratio of just 5.5 kg/kW (4.1 kg/hp). With the 6-speed manual gearbox and the Sport Chrono Package integrated as standard, the new Boxster GTS accelerates from 0 to 100 km/h in a mere 5.0 seconds and achieves a top speed of 281 km/h. This sporty performance is beaten only with the optional Porsche Doppelkupplung (PDK), which makes it possible to complete the 0 to 100 km/h sprint in 4.7 seconds.

Sports exhaust system.

The sound of the new Boxster GTS is particularly resonant, thanks to the selectable sports exhaust system featuring a distinctive two-tract sports tailpipe in black. It produces an even more intense sports car sound at the push of a button. A chrome-plated sports tailpipe is available as an option.

6-speed manual gearbox.

Fitted as standard, the smooth and precise 6-speed manual gearbox is optimally adapted to the high power output of the engine. Shift throws are short and the gear lever is easy to operate. The upshift indicator located in the central round instrument helps you to maximise fuel efficiency.

Porsche Doppelkupplung (PDK).

The 7-speed Porsche Doppelkupplung (PDK), which features a manual and an automatic mode, is available as an option. Gearshifts take place in milliseconds with no interruption in the flow of power. Not only does it help to deliver even faster acceleration than the manual gearbox, it improves comfort and even reduces fuel consumption.

With both feet firmly on the ground, you can feel the wind on your face with peace of mind.

Chassis.

The lightweight adaptive chassis of the new Boxster GTS operates with precision to deliver impressive driving dynamics with practically zero pitch and roll. In short, it offers increased levels of comfort and safety.

Porsche Active Suspension Management (PASM).
PASM is an electronic damping control system and is fitted as standard. It regulates the damping force based on current road conditions and driving style.

Two modes are available: 'Normal', which is a blend of performance and comfort, and 'Sport', where the setup is much firmer. In addition, the body is 10 mm lower than that of the Boxster S.

Sport Chrono Package including dynamic gearbox mounts.
Integrated as standard, the Sport Chrono Package not only features a digital and an analogue stopwatch for recording lap times, it offers a firmer setup for the engine, chassis and gearbox. The SPORT

PLUS button gives the option of a harder damper setting and a more direct steering response. In short, it delivers a particularly pure driving feel.

The Sport Chrono Package also includes dynamic gearbox mounts. Selectable by the SPORT or SPORT PLUS button, they reduce the perceptible oscillations and vibrations of the drivetrain and the engine. The result is sporty cornering – and even greater comfort.

Porsche Torque Vectoring (PTV).
Optional PTV with rear differential lock is designed to provide a further improvement in dynamic performance. To be more specific, when the car is driven assertively into a corner, moderate brake pressure is applied to the inside rear wheel. For greater angular momentum in the direction of steering. When accelerating out of the corner, the rear differential lock provides increased traction.

You're not the only one thinking about the next bend …

Safety.

When we work, we look ahead. That's how we came to develop an ingenious safety concept that is just as performance-oriented as the power aspect of the new Boxster GTS.

Occupant protection is provided by the bodywork design, which has been optimised for stiffness, and by dual roll-over protection, two full-size airbags fitted as standard and the Porsche Side Impact Protection System (POSIP) featuring two side airbags and steel side impact protection elements, respectively. To match the considerable engine power of the Boxster GTS, the front and rear axles are

equipped with four-piston aluminium monobloc fixed brake calipers. Other control systems, including Porsche Stability Management (PSM) and Porsche Active Suspension Management (PASM), offer additional reinforcement to the customary Porsche safety concept.

Bi-Xenon headlights including Porsche Dynamic Light System (PDLS).
Integrated as standard, PDLS comprises Bi-Xenon main headlights with halogen auxiliary main-beam headlights, headlight cleaning system and automatic dynamic range control. Dynamic cornering lights provide even better visibility.

Porsche Dynamic Light System Plus (PDLS+).

The optional Porsche Dynamic Light System Plus offers an additional function: the dynamic main-beam feature detects vehicles driving in front as well as oncoming traffic and adapts the range of the light cone automatically to the prevailing situation. This provides a stepless transition between dipped and main beam.

Speed limit display.

The optional speed limit display informs the driver about speed restrictions and the start and end of no overtaking zones. The information is recorded by a camera located near the rear-view mirror and is shown on the screen in the instrument cluster or on the screen of the optional Porsche Communication Management (PCM). If a traffic sign is missed – for example due to heavy rain or darkness – the speed limit stored in the navigation module is automatically displayed. The benefit of this function is that it allows you to concentrate fully on the road ahead.

Open air concerts are best enjoyed from the front row.

CDR audio system.

Fitted as standard, the CDR audio system with 7-inch touchscreen is intuitive to control. It features a CD radio with FM twin tuner with RDS, 30 memory presets, dynamic autostore and speed-sensitive volume control. The AUX interface in the glove compartment enables you to connect external sources such as a compatible MP3 player.

Porsche Communication Management (PCM).

Optional PCM is your control centre for audio, communication and navigation functions. Thanks to a high-resolution 7-inch touchscreen, it is intuitive to use and includes a navigation module with fast hard drive. The CD/DVD drive is MP3-compatible. An AUX interface and a USB port for connecting suitable external devices are provided in the glove compartment.

Sound systems.

Available as an option, the BOSE® Surround Sound System produces an impressive listening experience. The only way you can make it even more intense is with the optional Burmester® High-End Surround Sound System.

Reversing camera.

Comfort, even in reverse. The image from the optional reversing camera is superimposed with dynamic guidelines to facilitate precise parking and manoeuvring.

You should trace every neural pathway to its end.

Summary.

A sports car doesn't necessarily have to be driven with a roof on. It's more about driving with a character and direction of your own. These are principles that the new Boxster GTS has embedded in its genes. Just like the ancestors from which it draws inspiration.

They are all united by the insatiable desire for freedom. It's what drives us, too.

That's why we developed the concept further, bringing it into sharper focus and exposing it more and more to the driving wind. Right until the moment we achieved our goal: more Boxster than ever.

The new Boxster GTS.
Purism without sacrifice.

PORSCHE

The new Cayman GTS
Purist

Design

Greater sharpness. Greater precision.
Pure inspiration. That, in essence, is what
the new Cayman GTS is all about. And it
displays these attributes in every twist
and turn – without compromise.

GTS

Performance

Performance is another area where we
kept compressing and driving forth the
GTS concept until it eventually ignited:
purism as the sum of its parts, with one
result – the pure driving experience.

GTS

Comfort

The goal is the pure sports car feel. On
every straight, in every curve, in every
moment. What does it require? A clear
concept and tone-setting technologies.

GTS

Both covers and the title pages from the US Cayman GTS catalogue, which was almost the same as the Boxster GTS version, but featuring a closed rather than an open car in the photography.

apart from the US-specific bundles outlined earlier, most of them were interior trim sets.

On the other side of the Atlantic, *Auto Express* tried a manual Boxster GTS on home territory, with Jonathan Burn noting: "It takes guts to tamper with an already-perfect recipe, but Porsche has done just that with the Boxster – and improved it.

"If we're honest, the incremental power hike isn't immediately obvious, but power delivery is flawlessly linear, with maximum grunt at 6700rpm. There's a throaty snarl from the standard-fit sports exhaust – usually a £1530 option – and the harder you push it through the rev-range the deeper the bellow, with crackling pops and bangs when you lift off the throttle."

Having remarked on the car's balance and "infectious" six-speed transmission, Burn added: "For a car which is so focused and direct, the ride is still fairly forgiving, even with the standard 20in alloys."

UK 981 series prices had been the same as those at the start of the 2014 Model Year just prior to the GTS launch, but crept up with the arrival of the new pairing. By the time the 2015 season kicked off, the strict Boxster was listed at £39,350, with the S at £47,725, and the GTS £53,569; the equivalent Caymans were £40,234, £49,473 and £56,087, respectively, although another price hike in the spring closed the gap between the open and closed cars once more, with almost two per cent added to the RRP of the Boxsters, but only a fiver premium applied to the Cayman range.

In Australia, things had been quiet until the GTS arrived in June. As soon as it landed, the price of the 981 series convertibles went up a little, taking the strict Boxster up to $102,800 and the S to $128,900, while the Cayman's price dropped by $500; the PDK option was just under 5K on all four of these vehicles. As for the newcomers, the Boxster GTS was listed at $145,500, while the Cayman GTS was quoted at $160,900 – a full $21,500 more than the S, and $54,300 more than the 2.7-litre Cayman. As with other markets, the PDK transmission cost more on the GTS grades, being a $6290 option Down Under.

Few complained. Writing for *Drive*, Mike Costello noted that while the Boxster GTS with PDK was just as happy to potter around town as it was hovering around the red-line, "It's not about raw speed or the thump in the back of a supercar, rather it's about driver involvement and the kind of clinical yet somehow also visceral interaction of man and machine. The sound of the engine and the delivery of its power is emblematic of this."

There was heaps of praise for the handling and EPS rudder, with Costello summing things up thus: "Performance cars rarely offer such involvement alongside such raw ability as the Porsche Boxster GTS. It's not a price-leader like the regular car, but in its own way it remains just about perfect."

Introduction pages from a contemporary Japanese range brochure, with the new GTS models stealing the limelight.

Further south, in Japan, the April 2014 price list saw the strict Boxster move up to 6,220,000 yen in manual guise, with the S 1,540,000 yen more, and the GTS coming in at 8,850,000 yen. Likewise, the Cayman was also more expensive, with the equivalent models costing 6,290,000 yen, 7,950,000 yen and 9,150,000 yen; a PDK gearbox added 490,000 yen on the existing cars, but 640,000 yen on the GTS models. Considering you could buy a complete JDM Suzuki Every van for less than 1,000,000 yen at that time, this kind of puts the latter into perspective!

Following a test of the Cayman GTS, *Car Graphic* noted: "You can feel the mechanical precision in every part. Of course the engine and chassis are perfect, as we'd expect from Porsche, but it's the small details – even the idling-stop system – that come together to make this a special vehicle that is so easy to drive well."

Some new extras

While the new cars were finding their feet in the various corners of the globe, things were carried over in Germany for the 2015 season. However, the options just kept on coming, with another extended leather trim package (the €4272.10 DHB version) and leather sunvisors (XMP) arriving in the second half of 2014, priced at €410.55; an Alcantara-trimmed sunvisor set (XLU) was listed at the same money, as it happens, but this alternative was delayed until June 2015.

Polished aluminium side window trim (559) was made available for the strict Cayman and Cayman S for €404.60, but not the Boxsters or Cayman GTS. Meanwhile, the SportDesign bodykit that was standard on the GTS (code XAT,

Cars awaiting delivery pictured in October 2014.

A Boxster S after being given the Exclusive treatment.

including a new front air dam and diffuser-style rear apron) at last became available in November on the base cars (€2499.00) and S grades (€2100.00), while an Alcantara headlining (594, and already fitted to the Cayman GTS) was listed for the base Cayman and Cayman S models at €1005.55.

A little further down the line, the price of the 089 exterior package for the GTS went up by around €120, while the cost of the silk black wheel option (344) had increased to €827.05 by the spring of 2015.

In the meantime, Porsche announced it had sold 189,849 cars in the 2014 CY, up 17 per cent on the figures recorded in the previous year, and surely set to climb again with the Macan augmenting the ever-expanding line-up. America remained the biggest market, but now China was less than 100 units behind in terms of sales, and looked set to become Porsche's best customer. However, vastly more important announcements were about to be made for diehard fans of the 981 series models …

A Boxster S from 2015 that was part of the 'Leichtbau' project. This 6MT car had carbonfibre lids, a manual soft top and the PCCB braking system to reduce weight, although the Alcantara-trimmed interior remained fairly standard. However, a more dramatic diet plan was already on the cards …

Chapter 5

End of the line

The 'saving the best 'til last' pattern had been established in other Porsche lines, and in the case of the 987s the policy had brought forth the Boxster Spyder and Cayman R at the end of the 987.2 run. The 981 was still a relatively new model, though, and, as such, one had every right to expect a 981.2 face-lift at this stage in the proceedings rather than a swan song. With the benefit of hindsight, however, the sudden deluge of flagship grades all begins to make sense …

The Cayman GT4 making its debut at the 2015 Geneva Show.
(Courtesy Norbert Aepli, Switzerland/Wikimedia Commons)

First, visitors to the 2015 Geneva Show in early March 2015 were presented with a bright yellow Cayman GT4 on the Porsche stand, their appetites whetted by a barrage of publicity that had started rolling out at the beginning of February. Unlike the earlier Cayman R model, this 3.8-litre manual-only beastie was basically a racing car for the road, much like the mighty 991-series 911 GT3 RS launched alongside it, and was expected to hit European showrooms in the summer.

Then, only four weeks later, the 981 Boxster Spyder made its world debut at the New York Show, which opened its doors on 3 April that year. While Alfa Romeo again stole some of the glory with its recently-launched 4C model, backed up by an array of exotica from the past, the white Stuttgart contender, using the same powertrain as the Cayman GT4, drew plenty of admirers from the press and public alike.

The UK's respected *Car* magazine noted: "The new Boxster Spyder is great news for car enthusiasts. It bears significance beyond its likely driver-hero status, for it indicates that Volkswagen understands how Porsche must amplify its sporting DNA if it is to carry off the enduring shift into SUVs and saloons ... We'll excuse such financial pragmatism if that means we continue to see cars such as the Spyder, Cayman GT4 and 991 GT3 RS. All three have been launched inside a month. Happy days!"

Indeed, these were exciting times in the Porsche camp, with domestic GT4 deliveries starting at the end of March, and orders being taken for the Spyder immediately after its US debut.

The Cayman GT4

The clue is in the name – following on from the success of the GT3 series, the GT4 motorsport Class was becoming more and more popular amongst enthusiastic amateurs in Europe, able to enter vehicles in racing at reasonable cost (at least compared to the higher echelons of the sport) and against drivers of a similar level. This type of racing would soon become a global hit, and the Cayman provided an ideal base car on which to create a GT4 warrior ...

Much of the technology was borrowed from Porsche's extensive GT3 experience, with its lap time around the Nürburgring proving far better than the 4.4 second 0-60 time that the GT4 was an awful lot more than a marketing gimmick. While the engine, chassis components and bodywork had all been breathed on, it was also worth noting that the GT4 remained practical enough for everyday use.

The key part in the transformation was the 3.8-litre engine – a modified 911 Carrera S flat-six that delivered 385bhp. Hooked up to a 6MT gearbox with dynamic mounts (there was no PDK option on this car), the MA1/24 lump had nowhere near the output of the rarefied GT3

GT4 racing may not have the glamour of the higher categories, but at least it allows folks to go racing on a reasonable budget in an age of escalating costs. These pictures were taken at the VLN event at the Nürburgring in July 2015.

engine (or the Carrera S unit, for that matter), but it was ample for a car tipping the scales at just 1340kg (2948lb).

Looking at the all-alloy 24v engine in a little more detail,

Some of the first pictures released of the Cayman GT4, with an interior shot included. Note the GT4 logo spread across the cockpit on the tachometer face, the two screens and the plaque aft of the gearbox, as well as on the seat headrests and treadplates.

it had a 102mm bore and a 77.5mm stroke, thus giving a 3799cc displacement. With a 12.5:1 compression ratio and the direct fuel-injection system managed by the familiar SDI 9 black box, it delivered 385bhp at 7000rpm, and 309lbft of torque from 4750rpm onwards. Incidentally, due to the GT4's track-orientated focus, a third radiator was deemed necessary.

The gearbox was the G81/20 unit employed in the Cayman S, which says a lot for the original unit's strength. While the part numbers for a replacement 'box and clutch are different (probably due to the lighter flywheel employed), the serial numbers are the same as those for the regular run. The internal ratios were carried over, though, as was the 3.89:1 final-drive; not surprisingly, a limited-slip differential (coming courtesy of the PTV system) and a reworked Sport Chrono package more suited to track events were included on the GT4 spec sheet.

Larger brakes, the PSM and PASM systems, fat tyres mounted on new alloys, and a revised aerodynamic package on the lower body helped keep the power in check. Up front, aluminium alloy six-pot calipers worked on huge 380mm (15.0in) composite discs, while at the back, the discs were the same diameter, but slightly thinner, and teamed up with four-pot calipers; the ceramic disc PCCB option was always there for those wanting the ultimate in anchors.

The PASM active suspension package was used as a starting point, but because of the GT4's track bias (and the fact that the majority of Porsche GT-series buyers venture onto circuits), the toe, camber and anti-roll bar settings were made readily adjustable. Various other motorsport-inspired tweaks, including such things as the adoption of uprated wheel carriers and reinforcing the crossmember joining the rear suspension towers and other areas, ultimately brought about a 9mm (0.35in) longer wheelbase and a car that was lower by roughly 30mm (1.2in); there was also a wider track measurement up front due to the bigger wheel and tyre combination.

The 20in 'Cayman GT4' rims (code 473) were an 8.5J width at the front, and 11J at the rear, shod with 245/35 and 295/30 VR-rated rubber; only colouring options were listed in the catalogue, with a platinum shade classed as standard. The steering ratio was also changed on the EPS rack, incidentally, as was the steering wheel diameter, which was 10mm (0.39in) less than normal on the GT4 to increase feedback.

The new front bumper moulding was actually similar to that employed on the GTS models, featuring three large apertures of the same basic shape, and dark driving lights in the outer ones. The vents were filled with titanium-coloured net-type grilles, though, and there was another cut-out just ahead of the 'bonnet' lid on the GT4 to extract air from the central radiator. The monotone colouring and full-width flexible lip spoiler also helped lend a different impression.

The 'Cayman GT4' alloy wheels (code 473) on a car fitted with the lightweight PCCB brake system.

Around the side, it became clear that the lip spoiler extended into the lower part of the wheelarch, while the wheels themselves were unique to the GT4 – a variation on the 'Carrera S' alloys in reality, albeit with shapelier spokes. There were heavy covers over the air intakes on the flanks to enhance airflow through to the engine bay, and careful inspection revealed different SportDesign door mirrors with two narrow posts – it was much easier to spot the new tail spoiler arrangement, though.

At the back, the regular combination lamps had a deeper and fixed ducktail spoiler placed between them, and the black badging was moved off the rear hatch to a new position below the reversing lamp enclosure. The reinforced hatchback door now played host to a pair of body-coloured supports for the carbonfibre rear wing (adjustable for angle of attack) that sat high off the body; the aluminium posts could be painted black, incidentally, for those wanting to highlight their functional status. Rounding things off was a new, more purposeful black diffuser section in the rear apron, with net inserts and twin black exhausts poking out from the centre.

At Cd 0.32, the GT4 was not quite as slippery through the air as the stock coupé, but it was the first Cayman to display downforce on

The Porsche Museum's Cayman GT4 provides us with some ideal reference shots of the front and rear bodywork changes, as well as a close look at the new rear spoiler arrangement. Although the angle of adjustment on the rear spoiler was small, settings were not to be taken lightly. Indeed, with the wing mounted in the one position, a couple of trim pieces had to be removed up front to balance the aerodynamics.

Interior of the Porsche Museum car, with a yellow highlight package allowing a little relief from the predominantly black surfaces.

both axles. As for other leading specifications not already mentioned, thanks to the front lip spoiler and extended diffuser at the back, it was a fraction longer than the Cayman GTS (measuring 4438mm/174.7in), and came as standard with a slightly smaller 54-litre (11.9 imperial gallon) fuel tank.

Far from being a stripped-out racer, the GT4 remained quite luxurious. The standard P04-type seats came with black leather on the bolsters and headrests, with Alcantara inserts. Alcantara was also employed on the steering wheel rim and gearlever, door handles, door armrests and centre storage compartment lid, as well as the headliner, with contrast stitching in silver-grey. Seatbelts and the fabric door pull loops were black, while the dash and centre console

Cayman GT4 Colour & Trim Guide

Compared to the regular Cayman models, the series-production GT4 had a subtly different colour and trim guide. These are the options available for this particular car.

Solid coachwork colours
Black (041 Schwarz), White (C9A Weiss), Guards Red (80K Indischrot), and Racing Yellow (1S1 Racinggelb).

Metallic coachwork colours
Jet Black (C9X Tiefschwarz) Metallic, Carrara White (B9A Carraraweiss) Metallic, Agate Grey (M7S Achatgrau) Metallic, Rhodium Silver (M7U Rhodiumsilber) Metallic, Dark Blue (M5X Dunkelblau), and Sapphire Blue (M5J Saphirblau) Metallic.

Special coachwork colours
GT Silver (M7Z GT-silber) Metallic, and Carmine Red (M3C Karminrot) Metallic.

Basic upholstery
Black leather with matching Alcantara inserts, although an all-leather package was available, also in black.

trim came in brushed aluminium, with 'Galvanosilber' parts used elsewhere.

The leather option listed for the GT4 brought forth smooth black hide trim to most areas except the lower part of the fascia (Alcantara was used instead), and an aluminium strip was added to the door cappings. Grey stitching on black was the norm, but options were available to go for red or yellow highlight packages, which incorporated contrast stitching, and the 'GT4' logo on the headrests and door pull loops in these alternative hues. Oddly, while the yellow option was possible for both interior styles, the red one was listed against black leather upholstery only.

Interesting details worth noting are the 'GT4' logo on the titanium-coloured tachometer, the same model logo on the centre console badge, and the lack of a rear spoiler control button aft of it – something no longer necessary given the new aerodynamic arrangements on the tail.

The Cayman GT4 ("old school, but not old-fashioned" according to the man who created it, Andreas Preuninger) was available to order almost as soon as it was announced in February, with home market deliveries starting at the end of March 2015. Including taxes, it was priced at €85,779 in Germany.

Compared to the regular Caymans, options were relatively few, with 'relatively' being the operative word. With its sporting intent clearer than ever, quite a lot of the extras were for enthusiasts who might venture onto the track, or simply for those who wanted it to look like they did. Either way, there was some serious kit made available to satisfy both camps.

As far as the run-of-the mill options were concerned, the PCCB braking system was an obvious one, while cruise control was most certainly not. Nonetheless, it was in there, along with metallic or special paintwork, a grey-tinted windscreen, automatic dimming lights, colour-keyed headlight washer nozzles, an alloy fuel filler cap, dual-zone air-conditioning, an aluminium pedal set, black leather trim (a €1975.40 alternative to the stock upholstery), the CLP extended leather and Alcantara trim package from the GTS grade, the P07 seats (with a 'GT4' logo in the headrests), seat heating, coloured seatbelts (in silver-grey, red or yellow), Alcantara or leather sunvisors, a Porsche crest or Porsche script on the Alcantara centre armrest, a carbonfibre centre console and treadplates, stainless treadplates with lighting, a fire extinguisher, the 630 light design package, audio upgrades (including the PCM package and telephone-related items), an interior monitor for the alarm, a vehicle tracking system, garage door opener, floor mats, a smoking package, a painted car key and a leather pouch for it, and model badge deletion.

GT4 model-specific items included a special version of the Sport Chrono setup with a lap trigger and so on (643), silver- or silk black-painted wheels with the GT4 logo on the centres (option code 346 and XDK, respectively), GTS-style darkened headlights (620), black-painted rear spoiler supports (802), a different fuel tank (085), full bucket seats trimmed in black leather and Alcantara with a carbonfibre shell (P11), a black leather steering wheel with a centre mark and matching gearshift (878), two carbonfibre trim packages (EGA for the dash and doors, and EGB for the fascia trim only), the same thing in black aluminium (P1A and P1B, although both packages came with a centre console in this case), the return of the passenger footwell net map pocket (581), deletion of the stereo (609, although the standard four-speaker CDR audio unit was itself classed as a no-cost option), and deletion of the air-conditioning (574).

There was also the Clubsport (CS) package. Ordered via the 003 code and in conjunction with the P11 bucket seats, this included a rear rollcage, fire extinguisher, and a six-point harness (available separately via the 579 option code); a front rollcage could be ordered from the factory for those who took their motorsport seriously.

As *Road & Track* pointed out following the Portuguese press event: "This new car is pure old-school hot-rod: Stuff a big engine in a little car with a stick." The article went on to note that "production capacity constraints will limit the GT4 to about 2500 units worldwide,

(Continues on page 151)

The new Cayman GT4
Rebels, race on

First it takes your breath away.
Then the fun begins.

Cayman GT4 concept.

The new Cayman GT4 sports cars is the long-awaited step beyond the boundary. The step over to the other side of the frontier – onto the racetrack. It's our tribute to all the motorsport enthusiasts and performance motivators. To all those who really do mean business. To all the victories of tomorrow, to all the personal bests still to be achieved.

For this reason, we've given it everything it needs – not just to survive on the racetrack, but to blow it away. More downforce. More traction. More capacity. More thrust. More power. More than any Cayman has ever had before. That's what makes it the Cayman GT4: the super GT with the distinctive mid-engine layout; the hero of weekends; the rebel of the racetrack.

The new Cayman GT4. Rebels, race on.

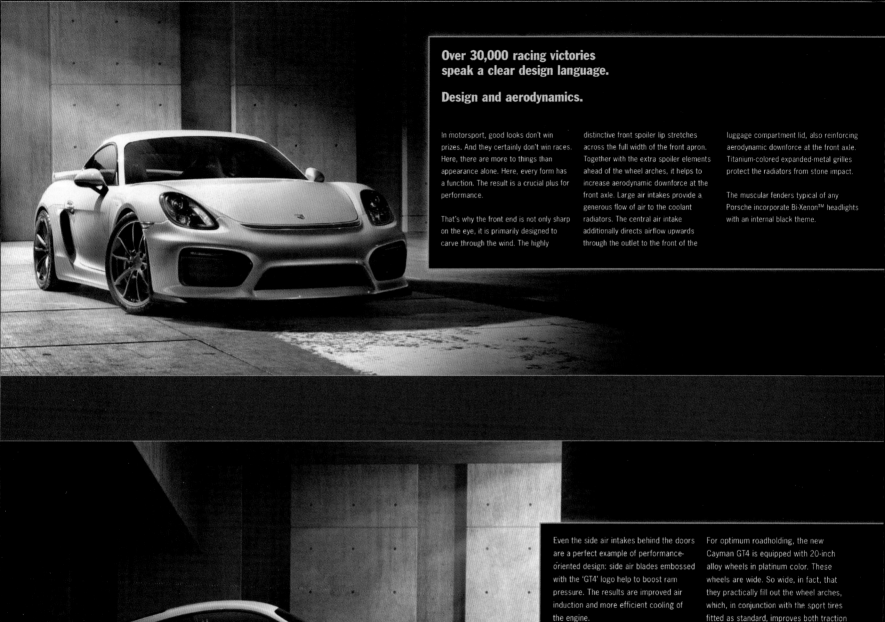

Over 30,000 racing victories speak a clear design language.

Design and aerodynamics.

In motorsport, good looks don't win prizes. And they certainly don't win races. Here, there are more to things than appearance alone. Here, every form has a function. The result is a crucial plus for performance.

That's why the front end is not only sharp on the eye, it is primarily designed to carve through the wind. The highly distinctive front spoiler lip stretches across the full width of the front apron. Together with the extra spoiler elements ahead of the wheel arches, it helps to increase aerodynamic downforce at the front axle. Large air intakes provide a generous flow of air to the coolant radiators. The central air intake additionally directs airflow upwards through the outlet to the front of the luggage compartment lid, also reinforcing aerodynamic downforce at the front axle. Titanium-colored expanded-metal grilles protect the radiators from stone impact.

The muscular fenders typical of any Porsche incorporate Bi-Xenon™ headlights with an internal black theme.

Even the side air intakes behind the doors are a perfect example of performance-oriented design: side air blades embossed with the 'GT4' logo help to boost ram pressure. The results are improved air induction and more efficient cooling of the engine.

The new Cayman GT4 gets closer to the tarmac: its body sits 30 mm lower than that of the Cayman. The advantage being a lower center of gravity for especially sporty handling.

For optimum roadholding, the new Cayman GT4 is equipped with 20-inch alloy wheels in platinum color. These wheels are wide. So wide, in fact, that they practically fill out the wheel arches, which, in conjunction with the sport tires fitted as standard, improves both traction and cornering performance. The v-shaped design of the wheel spokes is reflected in the styling of the SportDesign exterior mirrors, also fitted as standard.

The origins of the new Cayman GT4 are most clearly discernible at the rear end. The fixed fender, with uprights in aluminum, is the very epitome of motorsport. In conjunction with the spoiler underneath featuring an integral separation edge – the Gurney flap – it produces a noticeable amount of downforce at the rear axle. The sideplates of the fender are tuned for optimum aerodynamics. Further proof that all details have been deliberately designed to co-exist in harmony.

The powerful finale is presented by the black rear apron in diffuser look with two centrally positioned tailpipes, also in black. The sound is nothing short of explosive – thanks to the sport exhaust system fitted as standard.

Every element of the exterior combines to produce one and the same result: rampant performance. Summed up and cut straight to the point by the black rear logo: 'GT4'.

Hard on the outside.
Hard in the middle.

Engine and transmission.

Drive concept.
In the new Cayman GT4, typical Porsche GT performance is united with the great agility and cornering dynamics of a proven mid-engine concept.

The flat-six engine is equipped with direct fuel injection (DFI), VarioCam Plus and integrated dry-sump lubrication. These are supplemented by a variable intake manifold with switchable resonance valve

for a healthy supply of air. From its capacity of 3.8 liters, it delivers an imperious 385 hp at 7,400 rpm. Maximum torque of 309 lb.-ft. is available in the range from 4,750 to 6,000 rpm.

When combined with a low weight-to-power ratio of 7.6 lbs/hp, this leads to a veritable explosion of power. And a sprint to 0–60 mph that takes just 4.2 seconds. Top track speed is 183 mph.

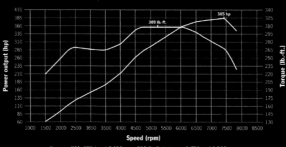

Cayman GT4: 385 hp at 7,400 rpm, 309 lb.-ft. between 4,750 and 6,000 rpm

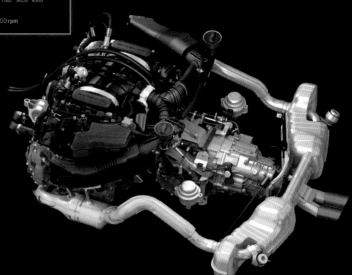

Sports exhaust system.

The sound of the new Cayman GT4 makes a statement of its own thanks to the selectable sport exhaust system with two-tract sports tailpipe in black. It produces an even more powerful sports car sound at the push of a button.

Six-speed manual transmission.

The high power output of the engine is transmitted to the road by the exact and particularly lightweight six-speed manual transmission with its specially tuned gear ratios. It also happens to sustain an exceptionally engaging driving experience. Every corner and every burst of throttle becomes a trial by fire – where every success is your own – for a performance measured not merely in figures, but also in an abundance of driving pleasure.

SPORT button.

The SPORT button activates automatic throttle-blipping for downshifts and provides sporty gear changes.

The ideal line is not up for negotiation.

Chassis.

The entire chassis has been engineered for the harsh demands of racetrack use. This makes the new Cayman GT4 sports car a tougher proposition, gets it through the corner faster and helps it onto the ideal line sooner.

To deliver high levels of agility, stability and directional accuracy, the front axle is equipped with a reinforced McPherson strut suspension featuring racetrack-proven kinematics and independent wheel suspension with longitudinal and transverse links. With additional reinforcements and specialized wheel hubs, the rear axle has also been adapted to handle the super-sporty performance of the new Cayman GT4. Individual ball joints on both axles establish a particularly firm connection between the chassis and the body, making it possible to locate the wheels with even greater precision.

Height, camber, toe angle and the anti-roll bars of the chassis can be individually adapted for use on the racetrack. That's vital because, on the circuit, every millimeter makes a difference. A difference that could mean hundredths of a second shaved off each lap, and more adrenaline in the bloodstream.

Dynamic transmission mounts.

This electronically controlled system not only minimizes the oscillations and vibrations of the entire drivetrain, particularly the engine, it also adapts its damping force and stiffness to driving style and road surface conditions. In this way, it is possible to exploit the benefits of both a hard and a soft engine mounting arrangement.

Handling is perceptibly more stable and precise under load change conditions and in fast corners. At the same time, the vertical oscillations of the engine that occur under full-load acceleration are reduced. The results are greater and more uniform drive force at the rear axle, increased traction and better acceleration. Whenever a less assertive driving style is adopted, the dynamic transmission mounts automatically soften to enhance comfort.

Wheels and tires.

The 20-inch alloy wheels of the new Cayman GT4 come painted in platinum color. A silver-colored or satin black finish is available as an option. The tires have been sized for performance: 245/35 ZR 20 tires on 8.5 J x 20 wheels at the front and 295/30 ZR 20 tires on 11 J x 20 wheels at the rear. That's a large contact patch and a lot of grip for road-legal sports tires. Please bear in mind, however, that the reduced tread depth does mean an increased risk of aquaplaning on wet surfaces.

Porsche Active Suspension Management (PASM).

This variable damping control system actively and continuously regulates the damping force for each wheel according to the road conditions and driving style.

Integrated in the new Cayman GT4 as standard, Tire Pressure Monitoring System (TPMS) issues warnings in the event of pressure loss. It also features a racetrack mode, which takes into consideration the pressure and temperature characteristics of the tires out on the circuit and precisely monitors the pressure set in each individual tire.

At the push of a button, you can select one of two sporty modes: 'Normal' mode for sporty driving on public roads, and 'Sport' mode for maximum lateral acceleration and the best possible traction on the racetrack. In addition, the body is droppped by 30 mm to maintain a low center of gravity. The resulting suppression of pitch and roll means enhanced dynamic performance and extraordinary longitudinal and lateral acceleration.

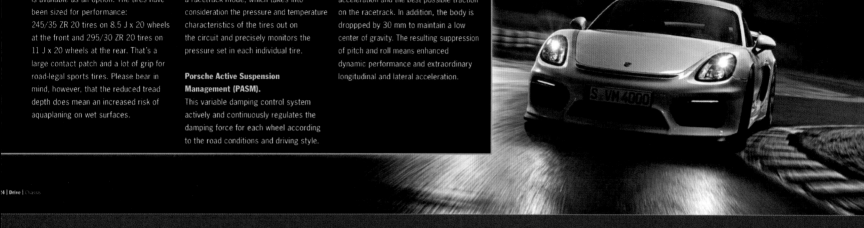

Porsche Stability Management (PSM).

PSM helps to maintain stability even at the limits of dynamic driving performance. In addition to the anti-lock braking system (ABS), this system also includes electronic stability control (ESC) and traction control (TC). Sensors continuously monitor the direction, speed, yaw velocity and lateral acceleration of the car. Using this information, PSM is able to calculate the actual direction of travel at any given moment. If the car begins to oversteer or understeer, PSM applies selective braking on individual wheels. What's special about PSM in the new Cayman GT4? The sporty setup works in tandem with extremely sensitive and precise control

interventions. In addition, the systems can be completely deactivated in two stages.

Porsche Torque Vectoring (PTV) including rear differential lock.

Fitted as standard, PTV further enhances dynamic performance. The rear differential lock helps to provide greater traction and a significant increase in both lateral dynamics and driving stability under load changes in corners and during lane-change manoeuvres. When the car is driven assertively into a corner, selective braking of the inside rear wheel quickly induces an additional rotational pulse in the direction of the turn.

Unleashed, not unchecked.

Active safety.

Brakes.

Acceleration values are not the only markers of GT heritage. With the new Cayman GT4, braking performance is also a key to success on the racetrack.

That's why six-piston aluminum brake calipers with a red finish are fitted to the front axle and four-piston equivalents are fitted at the rear. Their monobloc design makes them extremely resistant to deformation and enables a more rapid response and release of the brake, even under heavy loads.

With a diameter of 380 mm front and rear, the brake discs are generously dimensioned. They are cross-drilled and internally vented to offer a high level of braking power, even in adverse weather conditions. To ensure excellent stability under load, the brake system also benefits from an efficient brake ventilation and cooling concept in the form of independent cooling channels as well as brake air spoilers and air deflector blades.

Porsche Ceramic Composite Brake (PCCB).

The optional Porsche Ceramic Composite Brake (PCCB) is a proven motorsport solution. Boasting particularly large brake disc diameters of 410 mm at the front and 390 mm at the rear, it offers an even more formidable braking performance.

The use of six-piston aluminum monobloc fixed brake calipers on the front axle and four-piston units at the rear ensures extremely high brake forces, which, crucially, are exceptionally consistent. PCCB enables shorter braking distances in even the toughest road and race conditions.

Another key advantage of the ceramic braking system is its extremely low weight. The brake discs are approximately 50% lighter than standard discs of similar design and size. As well as enhancing performance and fuel economy, this also represents a major reduction in unsprung and rotating masses. The consequence of this is better roadholding and increased comfort, particularly on uneven roads.

Alongside the regular servicing work performed within the standard service intervals, additional servicing should be performed if used on the racetrack.

Designed for the most important performance factor of all: the driver.

Interior.

Now it's about exploiting performance potential to the max. With an interior that gives the driver the best possible chance of setting superlative standards. With driver-centric solutions such as the ascending center console, which positions the gear lever close to the Sports steering wheel – fitted as standard. Or, for driving information at a glance, three round instruments featuring a 4.6-inch color screen and a centrally located titanium-colored tachometer with 'GT4' logo. Clarity is enhanced by yellow

needles and increment markings. Ideal prerequisites to those critical split-second decisions.

Even the materials in the black-themed interior breathe motorsport. The door openers are belt straps. Alcantara® provides good grip – and a motorsport feel. It is found on the steering wheel rim and gear lever, on the door pulls of the door panels, on the lid of the storage compartment in the center console and on the A-pillars and roof lining. It is also

used for the seat centers of the Sports seats Plus, which are fitted as standard. The bolsters and headrests of the seats are upholstered in black leather. The character of the new Cayman GT4 is further reinforced by Platinum Grey decorative stitching on the gear lever boot, on the door armrests and on the seats, as well as by elements in brushed aluminum on the decorative trims of the dashboard and center console. As an option, the trims in brushed aluminum are also available in Anodized Black.

With the optional leather interior package, a leather trim is additionally applied to the upper section of the dashboard, the instrument shroud, the upper section of the door panels and the sides of the center console. For contrast, the use of Alcantara® is extended to include the dashboard lower section and door center panels, while brushed aluminum is used for the decorative strips on the door trims. In conjunction with the leather interior package, there is also the option to swap the Platinum Grey deviated stitching for contrasting seams in red or yellow.

Sport Chrono Package including Porsche Track Precision app and lap trigger preparation.
The optional Sport Chrono Package marks the start of a new kind of time reckoning – for ever new personal bests. In addition to a stopwatch on the dashboard, it includes the newly developed Porsche Track Precision app for your smartphone. Timings – accurate to one hundredth of a second – are displayed on the Sport Chrono stopwatch and in the instrument cluster. The stopwatch is operated by the control stalk for the on-board computer.

In conjunction with Porsche Communication Management (PCM, page 45), Sport Chrono Package functionality is enhanced by a performance display in PCM and the ability to display, store and evaluate recorded lap times.

With the newly developed GPS-enabled Porsche Track Precision app, you can have your lap timer stop automatically the moment you cross the line. Lap times are recorded and managed on your smartphone and can be shared with other drivers for comparison. On the racetrack,

dynamic performance is also visualized on your smartphone and, in addition to sector and lap times, the app is also able to show how your current lap compares with a reference lap of your choice. The app uses highly precise vehicle data acquired by a control unit on-board. In the process, graphical analyses of driving data plus a video analysis help the driver to improve driving performance.

For even greater precision in your lap time measurements, a lap trigger is available from Porsche Tequipment. This can be placed next to the start/finish line on the circuit where it will clock and share your lap times automatically.

Up to now your life has simply been a warm-up.

Summary.

No sooner do we reach our destination than the next is already in sight. No sooner do we achieve one victory than it's time to compete for the next.

The new Cayman GT4 sports car does not exist to stand still, but to be driven to the max. Engine power has been increased and aerodynamics have been optimized for downforce. The chassis and brake system have been engineered for performance. For a hunger to explore sporty new territory. For your personal best. For a race that never ends.

Rebels, race on.

Summar

about half of which will come to US dealers. And from what we're hearing, they're all accounted for."

But what was it like? The same article observed: "The single best part of the GT4 is its powertrain calibration. The engine is a masterpiece with a haunting, deafening, flat-six wail … [And] if you're co-ordinated enough to drive a stick in the first place, you'll master every shift on your own. It feels like the computer helping you, but it's not – this is Porsche's magic at work once again."

Gavin Conway was equally impressed. Writing for *Driving* (from *The Sunday Times*), he said: "Oh lordy, is it quick! It feels as if every one of my senses is being assaulted (in a good way), from the shrieking wail of the engine as it spins to nearly 8000rpm, to the vicious shove in the back from the acceleration, and then the telepathically good feedback through the steering wheel … It's the phenomenal agility of the GT4 that stays with me the longest, though. The balance is confidence-inspiring, which is largely down to near-perfect weight distribution and the engine

Porsche Exclusive.

Another kind of pole position in terms of individual creativity. With the range of options featured in this catalog, you can personalize your Porsche even further. Introducing

Porsche Exclusive. Have your vehicle individually and exclusively tailored to your wishes, even before it leaves the factory. Aesthetically and technically, inside and outside, using fine materials

and with customary Porsche quality. The principle? To ensure your car is uniquely handcrafted to your taste. You will find a wide range of design options in the separate Porsche Exclusive Cayman catalog.

For the truly personal touch, contact our Porsche Customer Consultation Specialists at customerconsultations@porsche.us for visit us your authorized Porsche dealer.

For those wanting something extra special, naturally, the Exclusive programme was still open to GT4 owners.

Master wheelman Walter Röhrl pictured at the Autódromo Internacional do Algarve in March 2015.

A Cayman GT4R was planned and tested in 2015 with a view to creating a one-make series. Here, we can see this exotic model in the storage facility attached to the Porsche Museum.

being mid-mounted. As you'd expect, the ride is quite firm, albeit not punishingly so."

Having noted that the car would flatter any driver, Conway did say that it was probably more suited to track days than everyday use, which, of course, was its raison d'etre. It didn't stop folks lining up at dealers for it, though! Another measure of its success was that almost overnight the aftermarket tuning brigade was busy making bolt-on goodies to give owners of 'lesser' machines the chance to blag away …

Along came a Spyder

Although the Cayman GT4 and Boxster Spyder made their world debut within weeks of each other, unlike the GT4, which had started arriving in domestic showrooms some months earlier, the Spyder was ultimately classed as a 2016 car due to its late availability. Indeed, it wasn't until July that the first Spyders began filtering through to dealerships – too late to make the most of the convertible season, but then typical Spyder buyers were less concerned about warmer climes than the value of owning such a rare and desirable beast.

The formula was a familiar one, and tied-in with the Cayman GT4 in a number of ways on this latest incarnation, both cosmetically and mechanically. *Car & Driver* summed it up beautifully: Not to be left sucking the Cayman GT4's wake, the Spyder trim returns to the "Boxster line-up bearing a 3.8-litre flat-six good for 375bhp. The minimalist top of the previous Spyder is gone in the current 981 gen; a conventional manual-folding top subs in. It's not as light as the old Spyder's canvas bikini, but it does save pounds over a power top … Like the GT4, [it] comes exclusively with a six-speed manual and 911 brake hardware."

Up front, the front bumper moulding was pure GT4, including the 'titanium' grille inserts, upper slot, the elongated lip spoiler and lighting arrangements. Headlights with black highlighting on the internal parts were the norm, with the two PDLS options available as extras, while SportDesign mirrors were visible beyond them.

The side view brought the unique 20in ten-spoke 'Boxster Spyder' (393) wheels into focus, as well as the new hood and various revisions to the tail area. The hood was actually similar in concept to the first Spyder one, though an altogether neater design. The lightweight black hood (11kg, or 24lb, lighter than the standard rag-top) was now a single piece, for instance, with the header rail lock being electrically operated. The tails of the convertible still needed to be worked by hand (located on small black panels attached to the rear lid with 'Spyder' badges on), and one had to lift said aluminium panel in order to manually drop or raise the hood. There were also a couple of trim pieces behind the seats that needed dealing with, but it was all simple enough, and a far superior arrangement to the 987 Spyder top.

The lid itself was a similar panel to that of the first Spyder, with a pair of fairings continuing the lines of the roll-over hoops behind the seats, and the third high-mount brakelight module set in a bar between them. The automatic rear spoiler aft of the lid was a deeper version of the regular 981 Boxster one, framed by the darker rear combination lamps, and the black badging on the tail followed the pattern established by the GT4; the rear diffuser insert was also GT4-inspired, as was the smaller fuel tank.

Inside, things were kept fairly standard compared to the first Spyder. A black interior was taken as read, with Alcantara detailing on the steering wheel, gearlever, door pull (the release was a black fabric one, by the way), and door and centre armrests. Dashboard and door capping trim, as well as the console surrounding the gearbox, were finished in body colour. The P03-style bucket seats were classed as the norm, trimmed in black hide and Alcantara, and featuring 'Spyder' script on the headrest area; the same logo was repeated on the treadplates, centre console badge and tachometer. Air-conditioning and the CDR audio systems were considered no-cost options, meaning they weren't fitted as standard in order to save weight.

Power came from the normally-aspirated MA1/24 flat-six used in the GT4, but listed with 375bhp instead of 385 for this particular application; torque output was unchanged at 309lbft. The 6MT transmission was also the same, with a limited-slip diff, dynamic gearbox mounts and no PDK option, although the chassis details were quite different.

The wheel and tyre combination was 235/35 rubber on silver 8.5J rims at the front, and 265/35 ZRs mounted on 10.5J alloys at the other end. In addition to tauter sports suspension and lowering the car by 20mm (0.8in), there was a quicker and completely different steering ratio on the variable EPS (15.0:1 on-centre), mated to a three-spoke steering wheel borrowed from the GT4. Brake discs were 340mm (13.4in) diameter up front and 330mm (13.0in) at the back, serviced by six- and four-pot calipers respectively, which were duly painted in red; PSM was standard, looking after a lot of the braking aids.

For the record, the Boxster Spyder was catalogued at 1315kg (2895lb), and this low weight combined with the power and gearing (and the standard Sport Chrono system) to deliver an official 0-60 time of 4.5 seconds, and a top speed of just over 180mph (290km/h). As it happens, the original press release noted 4.3 seconds to sixty, but whichever way one looks at it, the newcomer was quick off the line by any measure!

Before options, this latest 981 series variant was listed at €79,945 in Germany. Not surprisingly, though, there were plenty of ways to make the bottom line on the invoice rapidly swell.

(Continues on page 157)

Exterior of the 981 version of the Boxster Spyder, as illustrated in the first press shots of the new car: those of the tail and the hood arrangement are the really important ones.

The 'Boxster Spyder' alloys (code 393) fitted to a US-spec vehicle judging by the repeater lens on the wheelarch.

The two pictures below show the unique rear lid used on the Boxster Spyder, along with a good view of the car's tail badging.

Boxster Spyder Colour & Trim Guide

Compared to the regular Boxster models, the Spyder had a simplified colour and trim guide. These are the choices available for this particular car, with the optional red Spyder Classic interior package not recommended on blue, red or yellow vehicles.

Solid coachwork colours
Black (041 Schwarz), White (C9A Weiss), Guards Red (80K Indischrot), and Racing Yellow (1S1 Racinggelb).

Metallic coachwork colours
Jet Black (C9X Tiefschwarz) Metallic, Carrara White (B9A Carraraweiss) Metallic, Agate Grey (M7S Achatgrau) Metallic, Rhodium Silver (M7U Rhodiumsilber) Metallic, and Sapphire Blue (M5J Saphirblau) Metallic.

Special coachwork colours
GT Silver (M7Z GT-silber) Metallic. A 'colour to sample' option was also available.

Hood (convertible top) colours
Black.

Basic upholstery
Black leather with matching Alcantara inserts, although a special 'Spyder Classic' package featuring Garnet Red leather with black Alcantara was also listed.

Interior of a blue Spyder for the domestic market, chosen as it shows off the standard colouring better than a white car.

Air-conditioning (to replace the conventional heating and ventilation system employed for the Spyder), P04 or P07 seats, leather steering wheel and gearshift, a windblocker, the CDR stereo setup, passenger-side footwell net, contrast stitching on the door release loops, the smoking package, a standard fuel tank, and model badge deletion were all classed as NCO items. There was also a brushed aluminium dash panel trim set, with or without matching door pieces, which was free of charge, as was the XYE centre console trim to suit, and the 809 version, too, as it happens.

Metallic or special paint, colour-keyed side air intakes, painted headlight washer nozzles for the optional 620 or 632 PDLS lights, XXR rear light units, gloss black detailing on the door mirrors, a platinum or black finish on the wheels, a coloured Porsche crest on the wheel centres, colour-keyed roll-over hoops, an alloy fuel cap, grey-tinted windscreen, automatic dimming mirrors (with rain sensor), the PCCB braking system, sports exhaust, cruise control,

(Continues on page 164)

Selected pages from the Boxster Spyder catalogue, including the one covering the 'Spyder Classic' interior option.

PORSCHE

The new Boxster Spyder
Unfiltered

Boxster Spyder concept

**If the world is a stage,
this is Stage Diving.**

Boxster Spyder concept.

This roadster is not a roadster. At least not like any we have come to expect these days. No more soft breeze, no more cruising, no more clichés. Typical Boxster, you might think. And yet our engineers have managed to sharpen this attitude even more. The new Boxster Spyder is a radical return to the origins of the Roadster: two seats, high performance, no room for any distractions. It's openly direct, unadulterated and unconditional. It's hot, cold, stormy, wild. Whichever way you look at it: unfiltered.

The new Boxster Spyder is the original interpretation of a legend that began life in the fifties with the 550 Spyder and continued into the sixties with the 718 RSK – on the racetrack of course. Described to this day as extremely agile with consistently lightweight construction. Taken to the limit in a mid-engined sports car with 276 kW (375 hp) and 3.8-litre displacement – more power than ever before in a Boxster. And you can feel exactly what that means when the world is blowing, unfiltered, around your ears.

The new Boxster Spyder.

True beauty needs no filter.

Design.

Unfiltered. Which means that you could barely get a sheet of paper between you and the world. That every detail of the exterior brings you closer to the true driving experience. With no unnecessary ballast. Instead just clearly defined forms that follow function above all else.

The result: a design that's focused on the countless challenges of the past. And the tireless endeavours of our engineers.

No wonder then that the front of the new Boxster Spyder literally says competitive athlete. Straight away, the large air intakes show how seriously it means it – as well as being extremely effective at cooling. The middle air intake also directs the air upwards through the vent in front of the luggage compartment lid. To reduce aerodynamic lift on the front axle.

Other striking features are the black Bi-Xenon headlights and the SportDesign exterior mirrors. The 20-inch wheels designed especially for the new Boxster Spyder combine lightweight construction with a unique design.

**Like a bungee jump.
Only horizontal.**

Engine and transmission.

The new Boxster Spyder just can't hold back. Its six-cylinder boxer engine, with 3.8-litre displacement, VarioCam Plus and integrated dry-sump lubrication, produces 276 kW (375 hp) at 6,700 rpm. The maximum torque of 420 Nm is available from 4,750 to 6,000 rpm. And it sprints from 0 to 100 km/h in just 4.5 seconds. With a top speed of 290 km/h. The low centre of gravity in the middle of the car – typical of a mid-engine – provides great cornering performance. The sports exhaust system provides an even more resonant sound at the press of a button. Sound good? Sounds even better: the

power-to-weight ratio is a mere 4.8 kg/kW (3.5 kg/hp).

Power is transmitted to the wheels by the precise six-gear manual transmission which has been optimally designed for the high power. Shift throws are short and snappy, the ratios tuned for dynamic performance. The drive is especially active, intensive and pure. When you press the SPORT PLUS button, throttle-blip downshifts make changing gear as emotional as it is perfect, for unfiltered driving enjoyment.

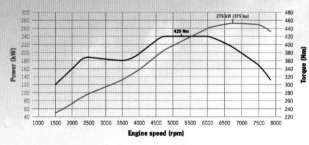

Boxster Spyder: 276 kW (375 hp) at 6,700 rpm, 420 Nm between 4,750 and 6,000 rpm

The new Boxster Spyder also shows its muscles at the rear. Most clearly on the streamliners, two powerful bulges on the rear. They visually continue the form of the black roll-over bars and lend the new Boxster Spyder its originality.

The distinctive rear spoiler underlines the performance-driven design and its lines flow seamlessly into the smoked taillights. It deploys automatically when the speed reaches 120 km/h, to reduce lift and increase stability.

All dynamically rounded off by the black rear apron in diffusor look. Integrated into the centre is the twin tailpipe from which bursts the unfiltered Porsche sound. Which, thanks to the sports exhaust system, has become an unambiguous call for freedom.

Open to all.
Although sometimes you might want to drive with it closed.

Hood.

With such a radically open car you might almost forget about it: the hood. The new Boxster Spyder cuts a dynamic figure even when it's closed. With side contours flowing seamlessly into the streamliners on the rear lid, the hood runs back into two taut fins.

And it's not just visually that the hood has developed. Compared to the previous model, it has become much more practical for everyday use. And it can be driven at top speed, with no constraints. It unlocks electrically and then the lightweight hood can easily be stowed away by hand

beneath the rear lid – without restricting the luggage compartment volume of course. As an option, the roll-over bars can also be painted in the exterior colour. And there's a net-type wind deflector available at no extra cost.

www.porsche.com/boxster-spyder-top

The comparative form of road?
Roadster.

Chassis.

The new Boxster Spyder can definitely be described as extreme. After all, not for a long time has a roadster stuck so radically to its roots: to every centimetre of road. And so to an especially unfiltered driving experience.

This is aided, not insignificantly, by the lightweight sports chassis. The long wheelbase that's characteristic of the

Boxster, the wide track, taut shock absorbers and a suspension that's 20 mm lower than the Boxster, make every drive an exciting ride. Body roll and pitch are practically non-existent. Porsche Torque Vectoring (PTV) with mechanically locking rear differential improves traction and further increases cornering performance.

Once again, the steering has been made much more direct – and is therefore setting a new standard amongst the Boxster models. For the driver this means an even more dynamic and responsive drive. To ensure even greater stability when cornering, the rear wheels are two inches wider than the front wheels. The 20-inch Boxster Spyder wheels therefore have the promising specification of 235/35 ZR 20, 8.5 J x 20 front and 265/35 ZR 20, 10.5 J x 20 rear. As an option, the wheels are also available painted in satin platinum or satin black.

Porsche Stability Management (PSM) provides additional stability – especially at the limits of dynamic driving performance. The new Boxster Spyder not only keeps to its course – it also keeps your adrenalin levels up.

Designed for the open road.

Interior.

No air conditioning. No radio. No distractions. Missing them? Don't. Every kilo that we've taken out of the Boxster, has an effect on performance. The ascending centre console means only a short distance from the small sports steering wheel, a typical feature of racing cars, to the gear lever, while the three round instruments with central rev counter provide you with all the relevant information.

The shell of the Sports bucket seats[1] is made from glass-/carbon-fibre reinforced plastic. For even more of a weight advantage. The 'Spyder' logo is stitched on the headrests. The Alcantara seat centres are reminiscent of motorsport. An impression that is enhanced by the minimalist door pull loops.

Overall, the interior has an impressively clear design style. The colour is black with the only exceptions being the pointers in the round instruments which are white and the trim strips on the dashboard and centre console which are painted in the exterior colour. Alcantara on the door pulls, armrest, steering wheel and gear lever provides a good grip.

[1] Child seats are not compatible with the Sports bucket seats.

Note: image shows black leather interior with additional Alcantara trim.

A leather interior with extended leather and Alcantara trim is available as an option. A visual treat is provided by the dashboard trim strip painted in the exterior colour which continues on the doors.

Combined with the leather interior, the optional decorative stitching package introduces additional contrast. The stitching package is available in silver, red or yellow and includes the 'Spyder' logo on the headrests. The door pull loops and seat belts can also be in a matching colour if required.

The carbon-fibre reinforced plastic full bucket seats are available as an option to further increase the sporty appearance. In addition to the manual fore/aft adjustment, which the Sports bucket seats also have, there is an electric height adjustment to provide the best sitting position. For more comfort, the

Sports seats Plus with electric backrest adjustment are available at no extra cost.

Despite the minimalism, air conditioning, radio and other equipment are available as options.

Modern materials, classic design.

Spyder Classic interior package.

The Spyder Classic interior package pays homage to the legendary Spyder models: back in 1958, in its second year, the 718 RSK Spyder took third and fourth place in the 24 Hours of Le Mans and won the European Hill Climb Championship. In 1959 there followed victory in the Targa Florio. A huge amount of power despite the small cubic capacity and only four cylinders. Another member of this famous series is the 718 RS 60 Spyder which Porsche put on the racetrack in

1960. Together they dominated the Hill Climb Championships for years.

The optional Spyder Classic interior package means that the legends live on in the new Boxster Spyder. The predominant feature in the interior is Garnet Red leather – based on the colour that caused a stir in the historic Spyder models – and then contrasting with that, black Alcantara like in motorsport.

Trim strips painted in GT Silver Metallic counter the impressive combination of colours with simple elegance and are deliberately reminiscent of the race cars of the sixties. If you want to make it especially authentic you'll choose the Spyder Classic interior package in conjunction with the exterior colour GT Silver Metallic.

After all, life doesn't hold back.

Summary.

Lighter. Stronger. More radical. The new Boxster Spyder is a roadster that's bringing new life to this tradition. Its powerful 3.8-litre boxer engine and the unquestioning approach to weight take driving dynamics to the limit. And the feeling of an unimaginable amount of freedom. Every drive becomes a contest with the elements. The sporting big event for all of the senses. The road cannot be experienced in a more authentic, more unfiltered way.

The new Boxster Spyder.

dual-zone air-conditioning, a black leather trim package similar to the GT4 one (with silver, red or yellow contrast stitching available) plus numerous extended leather trim items, the CLP leather/Alcantara trim and P2A options from the GTS (the latter was actually split for the Boxster, augmented by a P2B black aluminium trim listing – putting the two together gave the full GTS version at the same money), various Alcantara, carbonfibre and aluminium goodies listed against the GT4, new gearknobs, alloy pedals, P11 seats, seat heating, grey, red or yellow seatbelts, painted seatbelt guides on the seats, body-colour painted dash vent slats, PCM surround and car key, stainless treadplates, speed limit warning system, interior monitor for the alarm and tracking system, the 630 lighting package, fire extinguisher, various audio upgrades, a garage door opener and floor mats were familiar items; there was also a rear camera without the parking assistance package – something new that duly spread across the other model lines.

One other option that was totally unique to the new open car was the €2124.15 'Spyder Classic' package, which brought with it red leather and black Alcantara two-tone trim. Seat upholstery came in red hide with Alcantara centres; red leather graced the upper trim sections, with Alcantara below and on the centre box lid, while dash pieces, door capping inserts and the centre console were painted in silver.

Press reaction was understandably buoyant. Ben Miller wrote in *Car* magazine: "So, essentially it's the cutest, lightest and most powerful Boxster you can buy. Good then? Really good – think diametrically opposed to rubbish." Enough said …

The regular 981 series line-up

With all the excitement surrounding the newcomers, it was all too easy to forget the existing range continued to run alongside them. Anthracite Brown had been dropped from the Boxster colour palette in the spring of 2015, with Lime Gold also falling by the wayside in July of that year. On the trim front, the Platinum Grey and Yachting Blue leatherette and leather options were not listed beyond July 2015. Likewise, the Garnet Red upholstery and three of the four two-tone trims on offer were also discarded at this point.

As such, from the summer of 2015, the only Boxster trim options available on the regular base and S grades were Black vinyl or leather, Luxor Beige vinyl or leather, Black with Luxor Beige two-tone leather, Agate Grey leather, and Espresso natural leather; the GTS model continued with the same upholstery options as before.

It was much the same story with the Cayman, with the two paintwork changes carried out at the same time, and most of the upholstery ones, too. The only difference was that the Garnet Red leather option was allowed to continue until the end of production on the closed coupé.

Other than prices increasing on 1 June 2015, there was nothing

For those who are never satisfied, the Exclusive team was ready and willing to help out, as always ...

Porsche Exclusive.

With the range of options featured in this catalogue, you can make your Porsche even more special. Introducing Porsche Exclusive. Have your vehicle individually and exclusively tailored to your wishes even before it leaves the factory. Aesthetically and technically, inside and outside, using fine materials and with customary Porsche quality. Our principle? That your car is uniquely handcrafted to your taste. You will find a wide range of design options in the separate Porsche Exclusive Boxster catalogue.

Your Porsche Centre will be happy to answer any questions about Porsche Exclusive that you may have. Or contact the Customer Centre in Zuffenhausen at customercenter-exclusive@porsche.de or telephone +49 711 911-25977.

Part of the Porsche Exclusive and Tequipment display at Zuffenhausen, pictured in April 2015.

else happening worthy of note in domestic showrooms on the 981 series line. From this date forward, the 2.7-litre Boxster cost €50,909 (including VAT), the S €62,452, and the GTS €71,258; the base Cayman commanded €51,385, the S grade €64,118, and the Cayman GTS €73,757 – dangerously close to Boxster Spyder money, but still significantly cheaper than a GT4.

It is worth noting here, however, that another potential 981 model was being investigated – the Boxster-based Bergspyder. Sadly, this one didn't make the showrooms, but it was a fascinating project nonetheless, with a team of engineers in Weissach given the brief of making the lightest car possible. As a result, the single-seater Bergspyder was born, with no top (only fairings on the carbonfibre rear lid), and a low wraparound aeroscreen following the shape of the tonneau cover over the minimalist cockpit. Powered by a 3.8-litre

six, the Bergspyder finally tipped the scales at a remarkable 1130kg (2486lb). Further development ended when it was realised that type approval would be difficult in a number of major outlets, thus limiting sales potential to numbers that were ultimately considered too risky for the beancounters.

The Black Edition

For followers of Porsche lore, the launch of the I013 'Black Edition' would have come as no surprise. First, the 2.7-litre Boxster version was released in May 2015, launched alongside a gaggle of 911 models, with a black exterior and interior, and the choice of a manual or PDK transmission. Then, five months later, the Cayman 'Black Edition' rolled into view.

Solid Black paintwork was standard, with Jet Black Metallic as an

A Cayman GT4 alongside one of the last 918 Spyders in the delivery hall at Zuffenhausen in July 2015.

Exterior and interior views of the stunning Bergspyder
concept vehicle, along with an indoor shot from the '25 years
of the Boxster' exhibition held at the factory.

Dynamisch. Richtungsweisend. Zeitgemäß.

Dynamic. Trendsetting. Modern.

1996

option. In addition, the €59,477 Boxster had a black hood and gloss black roll-over hoops, while the €59,596 Cayman came with polished aluminium side window trim to make it stand out from the regular fhc run, although standard surrounds could be specified for no extra cost. PDLS lights and automatic dimming mirrors were employed, and 20in 'Carrera Classic' wheels rounded off the exterior features.

Inside, there was dual-zone air-conditioning, cruise control, a leather-wrapped SportDesign steering wheel, leather-trimmed heated seats with a Porsche crest embossed into the headrest, a windblocker,

front and rear parking assistance, special treadplates and floor mats, and the PCM setup with the Sound Package Plus and navigation module included. Most of the regular options were still there for those who wanted something more.

In the background, while Angela Merkel provided consistency in Germany as a whole (ultimately serving as Chancellor for four

The Boxster section from the English language brochure for the first 'Black Edition' models.

Boxster Black Edition

evours looks, like bends.

oxster Black Edition.

e Boxster is more than a roadster, ore than a go-getting mid-engined orts car. It is a symbol of freedom hind the wheel. So we have taken the erty of making you an almost indecent oposal: the new Boxster Black Edition.

d it will attract attention: large air ets. Wings with typical Porsche shape. de air inlets behind the doors. A aracteristically long wheelbase. And the ering silhouette. As if that was all.

Optimum visibility is provided by Bi-Xenon headlights including Porsche Dynamic Light System (PDLS), while optimum looks are ensured by the roll-over bars which are also painted black. The urge for freedom of the Boxster Black Edition is further emphasised by the 20-inch Carrera Classic wheels. It does it with style. Without being pushy.

This also applies to the black interior. From the door sill guards with 'Black Edition'

logo, through the SportDesign steering wheel, to the Sports seats with embossed Porsche Crest on the headrests. After all, the whole trim package has been put together exclusively by the designers responsible. Including Porsche Communication Management (PCM) with navigation module.

That's the new Boxster Black Edition. Dynamically elegant, you might say. Dynamically agile everyone will say if they ever drive one.

Black Edition

Boxster Black Edition

Boxster Black Edition

terms), there was a great deal of upheaval at VW as the 'Dieselgate' scandal came to a head. Things first started to unravel in mid-2014, with Martin Winterkorn duly resigning with a number of others in September 2015, only days after the face-lifted 911 (the 991.2) was unveiled at the Frankfurt Show. Matthias Müller was appointed the new CEO of Volkswagen, this move allowing VW-Audi man Oliver Blume to become Porsche's new boss at the same time. Interestingly, as part of the reshuffle, Detlev von Platen, who'd headed Porsche's US operations for several years with a good measure of success, was appointed the Sales & Marketing Director at head office in Germany.

The US market

The 2016 season would be an exciting one. Available from July 2015, as *Road & Track* noted: "The Cayman GT4 is a near-perfect arrangement of the Porsche Lego set." At $84,600, though (an open and closed Ford Mustang GT bought together, with a lot of change), it was aimed at a very specific kind of buyer.

Just lead yourself into temptation.

Boxster Black Edition – the engine.

There are some moments when there is only the six-cylinder mid-mounted engine, sitting not 30 cm behind you. And your foot on the gas pedal. Any movement has an immediate effect. On the speedometer. And on the endorphins in your bloodstream.

- 2.7-litre, six-cylinder aluminium boxer engine
- 195 kW (265 hp) at 6,700 rpm
- Maximum torque: 280 Nm between 4,500 and 6,500 rpm
- Direct fuel injection (DFI)
- Resonance intake manifold
- Integrated dry-sump lubrication
- VarioCam Plus
- Thermal management
- Auto start/stop function

- Top speed: 164 mph
- Acceleration from 0 to 62 mph: 5.8 secs
- Acceleration with Porsche Doppelkupplung (PDK) and Sport Chrono Package (optional): 5.5 secs

Boxster Black Edition: 195 kW (265 hp) at 6,700 rpm, 280 Nm between 4,500 and 6,500 rpm

For fuel consumption and CO₂ emissions, please refer to page 27.

12 | Boxster Black Edition | Engine

The main feature?
Enthusiasm.

Equipment.

- Exterior paint in black; Jet Black Metallic as an option
- Black hood
- Net-type wind deflector
- Roll-over bars painted in the exterior colour
- Bi-Xenon headlights including PDLS
- 20-inch Carrera Classic wheels
- 'Boxster' model designation on the rear
- Door sill guards with 'Black Edition' logo
- Black interior
- 6-speed manual transmission; 7-speed Porsche Doppelkupplung (PDK) as an option
- Partial leather seats
- Porsche Crest on headrests

- Seat heating
- SportDesign steering wheel
- Cruise control
- ParkAssist front and rear
- Automatically dimming mirrors with integrated rain sensor
- Two-zone automatic climate control
- PCM including navigation module
- Sound Package Plus
- Mobile phone preparation
- Floor mats

More information on these and other options can be found with the Porsche Car Configurator at www.porsche.co.uk, in the Boxster Catalogue or in the Boxster Black Edition price list.

1 Partial leather seats with Porsche Crest on headrests
2 PCM including navigation module, two-zone automatic climate control and seat heating
3 Boxster Black Edition interior

10 | Boxster Black Edition | Equipment

The supremely elegant Cayman 'Black Edition' model in profile.

The Boxster 'Black Edition' released in the same month, however, was much easier to access, being listed at $59,100 plus delivery. With prices increasing a fair bit on the other Boxsters, this represented good value, for the base 2.7-litre car was $52,100 for the 2016 season, while the S was now $63,900, and the GTS a further $10,700 on top of that.

Of course, from October 2015, one could opt for the $82,100 Boxster Spyder, assuming you were one of the 823 lucky peeps to get hold of one in the States. *Car & Driver* described it as "a hardcore Boxster with a soul-filled loud pedal." *Motor Trend* added: "Even when driving down to Starbucks for a latte, it's like you're on the way to winning the Targa Florio. And that's exactly how a sports car should make you feel."

On the Cayman front, the 2.7 base model remained at $52,600 for the 2016 season, with the S going up by $300 to $64,100, and the GTS ("one highly desirable ride," according to *Car & Driver*) continuing as before at $75,200.

Klaus Zellmer filled the gap left by Detlev von Platen on the first day of November 2015, becoming PCNA's new CEO after running the Asia-Pacific offices. He must have been counting his blessings given the buoyant mood in the showrooms, and a constant stream of new vehicles to add to the armoury, including the $59,200 Cayman 'Black Edition' that arrived at US dealers in January 2016.

Other export markets
In the UK, by the spring of 2015, the cheapest Boxster was commanding £40,098, while the entry-level Cayman was a fraction more at £40,239. Most attention was being directed towards the top Cayman, though, which was priced at £64,451. Only around 50 GT4s made it to UK shores, and they were all sold almost as soon as folks got whiff of it.

In a September 2015 issue, *Autocar* noted: "Poise and balance are from the top drawer of chassis control. This is one of those cars that just feels 'right' ..." A five-star rating was never really in question. What was remarkable for the author, though, was a car that would cover the standing-quarter in less than 13 seconds yet still return an average of 27.9mpg – exceptional economy figures that not long ago would have been good for a family saloon!

By this time, the £60,459 Spyder had entered the arena, of course. Steve Sutcliffe tried one for *Auto Express*, and declared: "This thing is awesome." The good folks at *Autocar* added: "Extra firepower and pared-down kerb weight conjure even greater brilliance from the Boxster's chassis. That this is the best Boxster you can buy is hardly in question."

The BBC's *Top Gear* also pitched in by saying that the Spyder was "a thing of uncommon beauty" and "a truly brilliant driver's car." I think we all get the picture by now, but, like the GT4, this was hardly a mainstream model and with a new Boxster in the wings, not destined to be around for long – something quite a few people found out to their dismay as they unsuccessfully tried to place an order.

In Australia, May 2015 saw the release of the $189,900 Cayman GT4. As *Wheels* wrote a few months after: "This is the first Cayman to be fettled by Porsche's iconic motorsport division, and trust us, it's been worth the wait. This is no light upgrade – the GT4 looks and

The Cayman GT4 in North American guise, hence the speedo being marked up in miles per hour.

feels every bit as focused as the bigger, and more expensive, 911 GT3.

"Porsche's entry-level GT car is a masterclass of sublime dynamics and track-honed thrills pitched at serious performance car enthusiasts. But you better get in quick – it's almost sold out."

This new arrival provided the Aussie importers with the chance to update the prices on the other 981 series models, with the Boxsters going up by between $1900 and $2700, while the Caymans were actually reduced by $400. Prices now started at $104,700 for the entry-level convertible, and $106,200 for the 2.7-litre coupé.

A studio shot of the US-spec Boxster Spyder, seen here with its hood in place. The white paintwork nicely shows up the Federal-style amber side lenses.

Interestingly, on the 'Black Edition' cars, the Boxster was the more expensive of the pair by a small amount (listed at $110,400), which is perhaps the way things should always have been, and it was actually the same story in Britain – the £46,164 Boxster being £175 less than the Cayman version, and commanding a £6611 premium over the regular 2.7-litre drophead, which had been reduced in price slightly for the 2016 season.

A few $168,600 Spyders made their way Down Under, but one had to wait until the new generation cars for any meaningful changes to the mid-engined range beyond that.

Apart from the 10,640,000 yen Cayman GT4 being available to order in Japan from the spring of 2015 (with deliveries taking place in the summer), there wasn't much happening in the Land of the Rising Sun. Notwithstanding, 981 series prices increased in April 2015, taking the Boxsters from 6,340,000 yen for a manual base car up to 9,660,000 yen for a GTS when equipped with a with a PDK transmission; the cheapest Cayman commanded 6,290,000 yen by this time.

The 'Black Edition' cars were sold in Japan for a premium of around 1,000,000 yen over the vehicles they were based on, with the

Boxster version released in June 2015 and the Cayman one following in early October; lhd and rhd models were available. The Boxster Spyder was also imported in very small numbers at 10,120,000 yen apiece, all sold almost as soon as they were announced. Things continued the same then until the spring of 2016 …

The GT4 Clubsport

The Cayman GT4 Clubsport was announced at the end of 2015, and was basically an FIA-approved off-the-peg racer based on the GT4 road car. Although its world debut was at the LA Show rather than a competition-related event, the contact details in the catalogue were enough to tell the story, with the Motorsport Department in Weissach and Porsche Motorsport North America Inc being listed as the people for interested parties to get in touch with.

Delivered in white, the €132,090 machine came with a modified PDK transmission, limited-slip differential, slick Michelins or rain tyres mounted on special 18in rims, suspension modifications for pure circuit use, a 90-litre (19.8 imperial gallon) fuel tank (although a selection of other sizes were available), a welded-in rollcage, fire extinguisher system, and a racing bucket seat with a six-point safety harness. Taking away most of the interior and noise insulation allowed the 385bhp car's weight to be reduced to 1300kg (2860lb), giving a remarkable power-to-weight ratio and a top speed of 184mph (295km/h).

It was a fitting end to a perfect year for Porsche – SUV sales (particularly those of the Macan) had bumped up worldwide deliveries to just beyond the 225,000 mark, beating the previous record set in 2014 by quite some margin. Remarkably, China became Porsche's

Optional extras

A list of the later options, to be used in conjunction with the sidebar in Chapter Three to avoid repetition. As with the earlier list, it has been laid out to show common options and those dedicated to specific models, all in numerical/alphabetical order to provide another form of contemporary reference. (The domestic prices quoted were current as of 1 June 2015, and include local taxes).

Common options

Code	Item	Price (€)
7X9	Rear parking camera only	654.50
344	Wheels painted in silk black	827.05
429	20in '911 Turbo' wheel (for base model)	4165.00
	Ditto (for S model)	2737.30
	Ditto (for GTS model)	1309.00
625	Porsche Entry & Drive	880.60
631	Speed limit indicator	416.50
632	PDLS+ lighting system (for base model)	2011.10
	Ditto (for S model)	1154.30
	Ditto (for GTS model)	452.20
638	Park Assist front and rear, with rear camera	1535.00
CRX	Wheels painted in a contrast colour	1535.10
CTL	PDK gear selector in contrasting leather	714.00
CTX	Manual transmission gearknob in contrasting leather	714.00
DHB	Extended leather trim package	4272.10
EHH	Manual transmission gearknob in carbonfibre	499.80
EHJ	PDK gear selector in carbonfibre	499.80
XAT	SportDesign bodykit (for base model)	2499.00
	Ditto (for S model)	2100.00
XD9	Wheel spokes and centres in body colour	1178.10
XDA	Wheel spokes and centres in black	1178.10
XDG	Wheels painted in gloss black	1178.10
XLG	Porsche script on centre storage box lid, Alcantara	226.10
XLJ	Porsche crest on centre storage box lid, Alcantara	226.10
XLM	Manual transmission gearknob in Alcantara	309.40
XLN	PDK gear selector in Alcantara	309.40
XLU	Sunvisors in Alcantara	410.55
XMP	Sunvisors in leather	410.55
XTG	Inner door sill guards in leather	458.15
XXR	Tinted rear combination lamps	470.05

Cayman-specific options

Code	Item	Price (€)
559	Polished aluminium side window garnish	404.60
594	Headlining in Alcantara	1005.55

GTS-specific options

Code	Item	Price (€)
088	GTS interior package (for Boxster GTS)	2963.10
	Ditto (for Cayman GTS)	NCO
089	Exclusive exterior paint package in gloss black	1118.60
712	Deletion of door decals	NCO
809	Tail of centre console in black aluminium	238.00
CLP	Extended door trim in leather and Alcantara	476.00
P2A	Dashboard and door trim, black aluminium	821.10

Cayman GT4-specific options

Code	Item	Price (€)
003	Clubsport (CS) package	3927.00
346	Wheels painted in silver with 'GT4' logo	NCO
574	Deletion of air-conditioning	NCO
579	Spare race harness for the CS package	416.50
609	Deletion of audio equipment	NCO
643	Sport Chrono Package (special version)	1594.60
802	Rear spoiler supports in silk black	NCO
P1A	Black aluminium trim package, including doors	238.00
P1B	Black aluminium trim package, minus doors	238.00
XDK	Wheels painted in silk black with 'GT4' logo	577.15
---	Black leather trim package for GT4	1975.40
---	Red accent set for black leather trim package	1178.10
---	Yellow accent set for black leather trim package	1178.10

Boxster Spyder-specific options

Code	Item	Price (€)
505	Contrast stitching on the door release loops	NCO
546	Body-coloured roll-over hoops	505.75
572	Return of air-conditioning	NCO
696	Return of audio system	NCO
CLP	Extended door trim in leather and Alcantara	476.00
EGC	Brushed aluminium trim package, including doors	NCO
EGD	Brushed aluminium trim package, minus doors	NCO
P2A	Black aluminium trim package, including doors	464.10
P2B	Black aluminium trim package, minus doors	357.00
XCS	Gloss black paint on SportDesign mirrors	285.60
XHH	Carbonfibre and leather gearshift	499.80
XYC	Aluminium and leather gearshift	238.00
---	Classic trim package	2124.15

GT4 & Spyder shared options

Code	Item	Price (€)
085	64-litre (14.1 Imp. gallon) fuel tank	NCO
581	Return of passenger-side map net	NCO
620	Black-accent PDLS headlights	702.10
878	Black leather steering wheel and gearknob	NCO
EGA	Carbonfibre interior package, including doors (GT4)	981.75
	Ditto, for Spyder model	517.65
EGB	Carbonfibre interior package, minus doors (GT4)	755.65
	Ditto, for Spyder model	398.65
P11	Full bucket seats	2802.45

NCO = No cost option

Der neue Cayman GT4 Clubsport

Cover and tasteful opening page from the Cayman GT4 Clubsport brochure. The text was of little use as a form of reference, as it was rather flowery ...

largest single market, taking 58,009 vehicles, against 51,756 for the USA, which was second in the league table, despite continued growth and another PCNA record year.

The 718

Porsche decided not to use the internal 982 designation for the face-lifted cars, instead opting to revive the 718 moniker of yore for use in the showroom – a blatant attempt at trying to link the new models with glories of the past. It had been the same case with the GTS, of course, and why not? Makers have a habit of reviving old nameplates on cars that are totally unsuited or undeserving of a hallowed badge just because they own the rights to it and want to add kudos to something mediocre – Porsche's new mid-engined machines were anything but mediocre, and in this case, it was just a proud nod to company heritage rather than dubious marketing.

The 718 was, in fact, much more than a face-lift, for the NA horizontally-opposed six-cylinder engines were dropped in favour of turbocharged flat-fours with a significantly smaller cubic capacity – a sign of things to come under Volkswagen.

While VW's diesel campaign was somewhat chequered (the high-profile scandal probably killing off any remaining plans to introduce a CI lump to rival the oil-burner version of the Mercedes-Benz SLK/SLC), the company's efforts on downsizing petrol engines were undoubtedly successful, with the excellent supercharged and

turbocharged TSI unit being a case in point. The Porsche 919 Hybrid racer was another example of what can be done with a small four, bringing back some Le Mans glory to the Stuttgart company via a win at the Sarthe track in 2015, which would ultimately turn into three consecutive victories.

For the 718 series, 1988cc and 2497cc displacements were chosen (the latter featuring a bored-out version of the two-litre block), rated at 300bhp and 350bhp, respectively – rather different numbers to those posted by the last Porsche flat-fours used in the 912E and 914 series! The equally impressive torque was delivered through a six-speed manual or a seven-speed PDK transmission, with an excellent balance between speed and economy.

It's perhaps ironic to be calling for a ban on internal combustion engines just as they're delivering high levels of performance in a clean manner, but with Volkswagen about to overtake Toyota as the world's number one car manufacturer, the general shift towards EVs in the corridors of power would have a huge bearing on the group's engineering direction.

Styling revisions were subtle, but effective nonetheless, with new front and rear ends lending the 718s a sharper look, deeper intakes at the sides, and revised door handles; the 18in wheels were carried over, but there were fresh designs for the 19in rims employed on the S grades. Inside, the main changes could be seen in the top roll, with new air vent shapes and a relocated Sport Chrono clock, as well as

The 981 Cayman in action during a VLN race meeting held at the Nürburgring in the summer of 2016. With the arrival of the Clubsport, even more people were turning to the Cayman for their weekend of fun.

A Japanese advert announcing the debut of the 718 series.

Arrival of the 718 models may have spelt the end for the road cars, but the 981 was still very active on the world's race tracks. These pictures were taken at the Nürburgring at the end of 2017. For the record, a 981 Cayman GT4 won the GT4 Class in the coveted 24-hour race at this legendary circuit that year, driven by Carlos Gomez, Ronny Lethmate, Mustafa Mehmet Kaya and Gabriele Piana.

the steering wheel, which was a different design to that used on the 981s.

Naturally, the arrival of the 718 signified the imminent end of the 981 run, and indeed all the niche models (the GTS grades, the GT4 and the Spyder) disappeared from price lists with the stablemates that had spawned them the moment the newcomers were announced – although the Geneva Show was chosen for the public debut, the hefty German 718 Boxster price guide was valid from 27 January 2016, and this is the date to bear in mind; the Cayman one was more straightforward, with the 25 April tying in with the 2016 Beijing Motor Show world première.

Domestic 718 Boxster deliveries began in April, with the 1335kg (2937lb) 2-litre car priced at €53,646, and the S at €66,141. This time, with the same power as its drophead brethren, the Cayman became the cheapest of the mid-engined pair, with base model listed at €51,623 and the S at €64,118; the first of the 718 Caymans were scheduled to be in German dealerships by September 2016.

The 718 range evolved quickly, with a basic T grade joining the expected exotica, but that's a story that will have to wait for another book …

A final picture to round off, with a Cayman racing in the ADAC GT4 event held at the Nürburgring in the middle of September 2019. By this time, the 981 Cayman GT4 had also served as a mule to create a new Cayman rally car based on the 718 series. Whichever way one looks at it, the 981 may have had a short run, but it certainly left a lasting impression …

Appendix I

Year-by-year range details

Here are the brief specifications of all the 981-type Porsches, arranged in chronological and engine size order. Column one shows the model, the second column carries engine details (to be used in conjunction with Appendix II), while the third contains useful notes. Only production road cars are listed for each Model Year. Therefore, prototypes, market-specific limited editions and pure racing variants are not shown:

2012

Boxster	MA1/22 (2.7)	Sales started February 2012, and in German dealerships from April. PDK version available. Classed as an early 2013 model in many markets due to a summer 2012 introduction.
Boxster S	MA1/23 (3.4)	Sales started February 2012, and in German dealerships from April. PDK version available. Classed as an early 2013 model in many markets due to a summer 2012 introduction.

2013

Boxster	MA1/22 (2.7)	PDK version available.
Boxster S	MA1/23 (3.4)	PDK version available.
Cayman	MA1/22C (2.7)	Sales started January 2013, and in German dealerships from March. PDK version available. Classed as an early 2014 model in many markets due to a spring 2013 introduction.
Cayman S	MA1/23C (3.4)	Sales started January 2013, and in German dealerships from March. PDK version available. Classed as an early 2014 model in many markets due to a spring 2013 introduction.

2014

Boxster	MA1/22 (2.7)	PDK version available.
Boxster S	MA1/23 (3.4)	PDK version available.
Boxster GTS	MA1/23 (3.4)	Sales started March 2014, and in German dealerships from May. PDK version available. Classed as an early 2015 car in some markets.
Cayman	MA1/22C (2.7)	PDK version available.
Cayman S	MA1/23C (3.4)	PDK version available.
Cayman GTS	MA1/23C (3.4)	Sales started March 2014, and in German dealerships from May. PDK version available. Classed as an early 2015 car in some markets.

2015

Boxster	MA1/22 (2.7)	PDK version available.
Boxster Blk Ed	MA1/22 (2.7)	Sales and domestic availability started May 2015. PDK version available. Classed as a 2016 model in some markets.
Boxster S	MA1/23 (3.4)	PDK version available.
Boxster GTS	MA1/23 (3.4)	PDK version available.
Boxster Spyder	MA1/24 (3.8)	Sales started April 2015, and in German dealerships from July. Manual gearbox only. Classed as a 2016 model in all markets.
Cayman	MA1/22C (2.7)	PDK version available.
Cayman Blk Ed	MA1/22C (2.7)	Sales and domestic availability started October 2015. PDK version available. Classed as a 2016 model in all markets.
Cayman S	MA1/23C (3.4)	PDK version available.
Cayman GTS	MA1/23C (3.4)	PDK version available.
Cayman GT4	MA1/24 (3.8)	Sales started February 2015, and in German dealerships from March. Manual gearbox only. Classed as an early 2016 car in some markets.

2016

Boxster	MA1/22 (2.7)	To February 2016. PDK version available.
Boxster Blk Ed	MA1/22 (2.7)	To February 2016. PDK version available.
Boxster S	MA1/23 (3.4)	To February 2016. PDK version available.
Boxster GTS	MA1/23 (3.4)	To February 2016. PDK version available.
Boxster Spyder	MA1/24 (3.8)	To February 2016. Manual gearbox only.
Cayman	MA1/22C (2.7)	To May 2016. PDK version available.
Cayman Blk Ed	MA1/22C (2.7)	To May 2016. PDK version available.
Cayman S	MA1/23C (3.4)	To May 2016. PDK version available.
Cayman GTS	MA1/23C (3.4)	To May 2016. PDK version available.
Cayman GT4	MA1/24 (3.8)	To May 2016. Manual gearbox only.

Appendix II
Engine specifications

The following is a survey of all the engines employed in the 981 series, complete with the leading specifications, and any other notes of interest. Only power-units employed in series production road cars are covered by this appendix.

Type MA1/22	
Production (MY)	2012-2016
Cylinders	Six, water-cooled
Main bearings	Seven, in alloy block
Valve operation	Dohc per bank, in alloy heads
Bore & stroke	89.0 x 72.5mm
Cubic capacity	2706cc
Compression ratio	12.5:1
Fuel delivery	Direct fuel-injection
Hp @ rpm	265bhp DIN @ 6700
Torque @ rpm	206lbft (280Nm) @ 4500
Serial numbers	6*C 00501-, 6*D 00501-, 6*E 00501-, 6*F 00501- & 6*G 00501-
Notes	*Used in the strict Boxster models (MT & AT).*

Type MA1/23	
Production (MY)	2012-2016
Cylinders	Six, water-cooled
Main bearings	Seven, in alloy block
Valve operation	Dohc per bank, in alloy heads
Bore & stroke	97.0 x 77.5mm
Cubic capacity	3436cc
Compression ratio	12.5:1
Fuel delivery	Direct fuel-injection
Hp @ rpm	315bhp DIN @ 6700
Torque @ rpm	266lbft (360Nm) @ 4500
Serial numbers	6*C 00501-, 6*D 00501-, 6*E 00501-, 6*F 00501- & 6*G 00501-
Notes	*Used in the Boxster S models (MT & AT). Developed 330bhp at 6700rpm and 273lbft (370Nm) of torque at 4500rpm when used in the Boxster GTS model (I011).*

Type MA1/22C

As per MA1/22, except:	
Production (MY)	2013-2016
Hp @ rpm	275bhp DIN @ 7400
Torque @ rpm	214lbft (290Nm) @ 4500
Serial numbers	6*D 00501-, 6*E 00501-, 6*F 00501- & 6*G 00501-
Notes	Fitted with the I145 Power Kit for use in the strict Cayman models (MT & AT).

Type MA1/23C

As per MA1/23, except:	
Production (MY)	2013-2016
Hp @ rpm	325bhp DIN @ 7400
Torque @ rpm	273lbft (370Nm) @ 4500
Serial numbers	6*D 00501-, 6*E 00501-, 6*F 00501- & 6*G 00501-
Notes	Fitted with the I145 Power Kit for use in the Cayman S models (MT & AT). Developed 340bhp at 7400rpm and 280lbft (380Nm) of torque at 4750rpm when used in the Cayman GTS model (I011).

Type MA1/24 (MDB.XA)

Production (MY)	2015-2016
Cylinders	Six, water-cooled
Main bearings	Seven, in alloy block
Valve operation	Dohc per bank, in alloy heads
Bore & stroke	102.0 x 77.5mm
Cubic capacity	3799cc
Compression ratio	12.5:1
Fuel delivery	Direct fuel-injection
Hp @ rpm	385bhp DIN @ 7000
Torque @ rpm	309lbft (420Nm) @ 4750
Serial numbers	DBX 00501-
Notes	Used in the Cayman GT4 models (MT only).

Type MA1/24 (MDB.XB)

As per MA1/24 (MDB.XA), except:	
Production (MY)	2016
Hp @ rpm	375bhp DIN @ 6700
Notes	Used in the Boxster Spyder model (MT only).

Appendix III

Chassis numbers

Please note that the following are start of run sanction numbers, with the first Boxsters classed as early 2013 models, and the first Caymans as early 2014 models. An 'S' as the 11th digit in the chassis code indicates that the car was built in Stuttgart, while a 'K' was used for those built at the old Karmann works in Osnabrück.

D-Serie models

2013 MY	
Boxster	WP0ZZZ 98ZDS1 00061-
Boxster	WP0ZZZ 98ZDK1 00061-
Boxster (US)	WP0CA2 A8*DS1 10061-
Boxster (US)	WP0CA2 A8*DK1 10061-
Boxster (CH)	WP0CA2 98*DS1 10061-
Boxster (CH)	WP0CA2 98*DK1 10061-
Boxster S	WP0ZZZ 98ZDS1 20061-
Boxster S	WP0ZZZ 98ZDK1 20061-
Boxster S (US)	WP0CB2 A8*DS1 30061-
Boxster S (US)	WP0CB2 A8*DK1 30061-
Boxster S (CH)	WP0CB2 98*DS1 30061-
Boxster S (CH)	WP0CB2 98*DK1 30061-

Note: The 'US' entry includes Canada, while the 'CH' entry includes China, Korea, Mexico and Brazil. The * in the code is a check digit, either replaced by a number from 0 to 9, or the letter X.

E-Serie models

2014 MY	
Boxster	WP0ZZZ 98ZES1 10061-
Boxster	WP0ZZZ 98ZEK1 10061-
Boxster (US)	WP0CA2 A8*ES1 20061-
Boxster (US)	WP0CA2 A8*EK1 20061-
Boxster (CH)	WP0CA2 98*ES1 20061-
Boxster (CH)	WP0CA2 98*EK1 20061-
Boxster S	WP0ZZZ 98ZES1 30061-
Boxster S	WP0ZZZ 98ZEK1 30061-
Boxster S (US)	WP0CB2 A8*ES1 40061-
Boxster S (US)	WP0CB2 A8*EK1 40061-
Boxster S (CH)	WP0CB2 98*ES1 40061-
Boxster S (CH)	WP0CB2 98*EK1 40061-
Cayman	WP0ZZZ 98ZES1 00061-
Cayman	WP0ZZZ 98ZEK1 00061-
Cayman (US)	WP0AA2 A8*ES1 10061-
Cayman (US)	WP0AA2 A8*EK1 10061-
Cayman (CH)	WP0AA2 98*ES1 10061-
Cayman (CH)	WP0AA2 98*EK1 10061-

Cayman S	WP0ZZZ 98ZES1 20061-
Cayman S	WP0ZZZ 98ZEK1 20061-
Cayman S (US)	WP0AB2 A8*ES1 30061-
Cayman S (US)	WP0AB2 A8*EK1 30061-
Cayman S (CH)	WP0AB2 98*ES1 30061-
Cayman S (CH)	WP0AB2 98*EK1 30061-

F-Serie models

2015 MY

Boxster	WP0ZZZ 98ZFS1 10061-
Boxster	WP0ZZZ 98ZFK1 10061-
Boxster (US)	WP0CA2 A8*FS1 30061-
Boxster (US)	WP0CA2 A8*FK1 30061-
Boxster (CH)	WP0CA2 98*FS1 10061-
Boxster (CH)	WP0CA2 98*FK1 10061-
Boxster S	WP0ZZZ 98ZFS1 30061-
Boxster S	WP0ZZZ 98ZFK1 30061-
Boxster S (US)	WP0CB2 A8*FS1 30061-
Boxster S (US)	WP0CB2 A8*FK1 30061-
Boxster S (CH)	WP0CB2 98*FS1 30061-
Boxster S (CH)	WP0CB2 98*FK1 30061-
Cayman	WP0ZZZ 98ZFS1 60061-
Cayman	WP0ZZZ 98ZFK1 60061-
Cayman (US)	WP0AA2 A8*FS1 60061-
Cayman (US)	WP0AA2 A8*FK1 60061-
Cayman (CH)	WP0AA2 98*FS1 60061-
Cayman (CH)	WP0AA2 98*FK1 60061-
Cayman S	WP0ZZZ 98ZFS1 80061-
Cayman S	WP0ZZZ 98ZFK1 80061-
Cayman S (US)	WP0AB2 A8*FS1 80061-
Cayman S (US)	WP0AB2 A8*FK1 80061-
Cayman S (CH)	WP0AB2 98*FS1 80061-
Cayman S (CH)	WP0AB2 98*FK1 80061-
Cayman GT4	WP0ZZZ 98ZFK1 95061-
Cayman GT4 (US)	WP0AC2 A8*FK1 95061-
Cayman GT4 (CH)	WP0AC2 98*FK1 95061-

G-Serie models

2016 MY

Boxster	WP0ZZZ 98ZGS1 10061-
Boxster (US)	WP0CA2 A8*GS1 20061-
Boxster (CH)	WP0CA2 98*GS1 20061-
Boxster S	WP0ZZZ 98ZGS1 30061-
Boxster S (US)	WP0CB2 A8*GS1 40061-
Boxster S (CH)	WP0CB2 98*GS1 40061-
Boxster Spyder	WP0ZZZ 98ZGS1 50061-
Boxster Spyder (US)	WP0CC2 A8*GS1 52061-
Boxster Spyder (CN)	WP0CC2 98*GS1 52061-
Cayman	WP0ZZZ 98ZGK1 60061-
Cayman (US)	WP0AA2 A8*GK1 70061-
Cayman (CH)	WP0AA2 98*GK1 60061-
Cayman S	WP0ZZZ 98ZGK1 80061-
Cayman S (US)	WP0AB2 A8*GK1 85061-
Cayman S (CH)	WP0AB2 98*GK1 80061-
Cayman GT4	WP0ZZZ 98ZGK1 95061-
Cayman GT4 (US)	WP0AC2 A8*GK1 95061-
Cayman GT4 (CH)	WP0AC2 98*GK1 97061-

Note: The GTS employed regular S chassis numbers, with the I011 option code establishing it as a special version. The strict S grade carried the I009 code, incidentally, with I008 used on the base models. Also, one needs to be aware that a second batch of GT4s was built using a limited range of lower numbers in the final year; these started with 88061- in the ZZZ series, 91061- for North America, and 91051- for the China, Korea, Mexico and Brazil grouping.

Appendix IV

Sales & production figures

It is unfortunate that the factory no longer releases annual production figures as a matter of policy, leaving us to rely on those published by the VDA. Careful study of this data (taking launch dates into consideration and going back and forth to eliminate certain rogue entries) and the fact that the figures become more and more accurate mid-run, gives us a reasonable idea of the build numbers at least. Perhaps we will be able to confirm things in a few years, when the 981s become old classics – let's hope so …

Boxster sales figures

This section covers cars dispatched to distributors by the works. Actual yearly sales (CY) may be slightly different, as a vehicle may be sold awaiting delivery or in stock from the end of one year to early the next. There will have been a fair few 987s in the early export figures, and 982s in the 2016 export entry, although the domestic numbers are thought to be accurate; no sales were recorded in 2017. Even though the GTS and Spyder are included in the S column, at least the table gives a good idea of the model mix and the balance between home sales and exports.

Boxster production figures

Please note that these annual (CY) figures do not include rebuilt chassis, unless they have been allocated a new number within an existing batch. Due to a new policy at the factory, the author is unable to split production between the two factories, as both are located in Germany, and this is all that matters to the VDA (it only separates cars produced outside Germany). Please see the note after this set of figures, as a second set provides us with another perspective.

	Boxster		Boxster S		
	Germany	Export	Germany	Export	CY total
2012	559	5287	508	4436	10,790
2013	1297	6989	1383	5393	15,062
2014	1274	7472	1435	2730	12,911
2015	1037	6766	1328	1415	10,546
2016	114	753	738	128	1733

	Boxster	Boxster S	CY Total
2012	5384	5036	10,420
2013	8481	6740	15,221
2014	6933	5764	12,697
2015	6320	5119	11,439
2016	344	2016	2360
Total number of Boxsters built (2012-2016)			27,462
Total number of Boxster Ss built (2012-2016)			24,675
Total number of cars built (2012-2016)			**52,137**

The GTS grade is included in the regular S column, incidentally. One was left to presume that the Spyder, of which about 2500 were built, was also included in the S figures; normally the VDA splits models by engine size (as it did with the Cayman GT4), but there was no clear separation in the Boxster line, only between the strict and S grades, and getting raw data out of the factory in Stuttgart is like getting blood from a stone nowadays. Thankfully, though, Porsche released some total production figures for the Type 981 Boxsters in its 25th anniversary press pack, and we can see that the Spyders appear to have slipped through VDA's net. These are the official totals for all of the 981 Boxsters:

Boxster	28,511
Boxster S	18,297
Boxster GTS	5077
Boxster Spyder	2489
Total 981 models	**54,374**

Cayman sales figures

The same basic notes in the Boxster sales section apply. Again, there will doubtless be a few 987s in the early export figures, and 982s in

the 2016 export entry, although the domestic numbers are thought to be accurate; apart from a handful of GT4s, no other 981 sales were recorded in 2017.

| | Cayman | | Cayman S | | Cayman GT4 | | |
	Germany	Export	Germany	Export	Germany	Export	CY total
2013	509	6714	480	5576	-	-	13,279
2014	493	6776	613	2505	-	-	10,387
2015	330	5460	411	1649	469	2258	10,577
2016	135	2062	146	372	713	3274	6702
2017	-	-	-	-	-	31	31

Cayman production figures

The same things apply on rebuilt chassis and the factory split (or lack of one, to be perfectly correct) as noted in the equivalent Boxster section. Please note that the vast majority of the 2012 figure will be the last of the 987 Caymans, which were all built in Stuttgart, although the other entries show 981 models only. While the GT4 is listed separately, the GTS grade is included in the regular S column.

	Cayman	Cayman S	Cayman GT4	CY Total
2012	511	242	-	753
2013	7385	6627	-	14,012
2014	5471	4942	-	10,413
2015	4167	3552	2797	10,516
2016	1238	1333	4072	6643
Total number of Caymans built (2012-2016)				18,772
Total number of Cayman Ss built (2012-2016)				16,696
Total number of Cayman GT4s built (2012-2016)				6869
Total number of cars built (2012-2016)				**42,337**

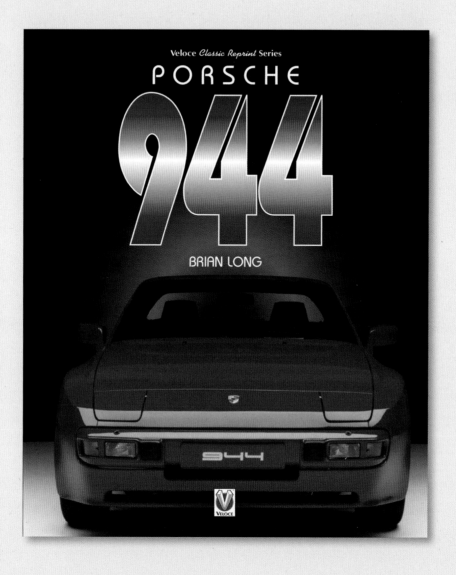

The definitive history of the 944 by an acknowledged expert. The 944 was introduced in time for the 1982 model year to fill the gap between the 924 and 928, and quickly became the fastest-selling Porsche of all time. Production of the 944 series ended in mid-1991, when the 968 took the model's place in the Porsche line-up.

ISBN: 978-1-787111-35-6
Paperback • 25x20.7cm • 192 pages • 190 colour pictures

For more information and price details, visit our website at
www.veloce.co.uk • email: info@veloce.co.uk Tel: +44(0)1305 260068

PORSCHE

Boxster & Cayman

THE 987 SERIES 2004 TO 2013

BRIAN LONG

The definitive history of the Porsche 987 series Boxster and Cayman lines, including an overview of all the models sold in each of the world's major markets. Packed full of information and contemporary illustrations sourced from the factory, it provides the perfect guide for enthusiasts, historians and those looking for authenticity.

ISBN: 978-1-787110-81-6
Hardback • 25x25cm • 180 pages • 288 colour and b&w pictures

For more information and price details, visit our website at
www.veloce.co.uk • email: info@veloce.co.uk • Tel: +44(0)1305 260068

Having these books in your pocket is just like having a real marque expert by your side. Benefit from the authors' years of real ownership experience, learn how to spot a bad car quickly, and how to assess a promising one like a professional. Get the right car at the right price!

The **Essential** Buyer's Guide

COPIES SOLD 200,000 THIS SERIES

Porsche

987 BOXSTER & CAYMAN

1st Generation. Model years 2005 to 2009
Boxster, Boxster S, Boxster Spyder, Cayman & Cayman S

Your marque expert: Adrian Streather

ISBN: 978-1-845844-24-0
Paperback • 19.5x13.9cm
• 64 pages • 112 pictures

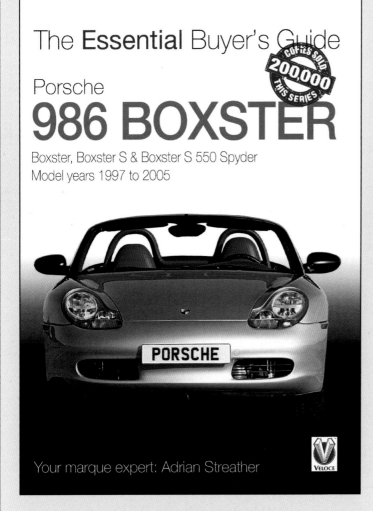

The **Essential** Buyer's Guide

COPIES SOLD 200,000 THIS SERIES

Porsche

986 BOXSTER

Boxster, Boxster S & Boxster S 550 Spyder
Model years 1997 to 2005

PORSCHE

Your marque expert: Adrian Streather

ISBN: 978-1-787116-54-2
Paperback • 19.5x13.9cm
• 64 pages • 110 pictures

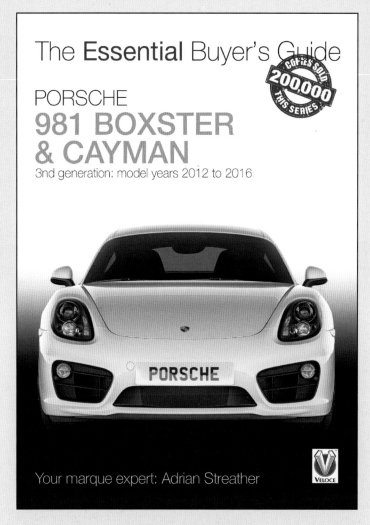

Index

Alfa Romeo 21, 138
AMG 57
Audi 9, 13, 39, 46, 168
Auto Express 124, 135, 170
Auto Motor und Sport 52, 98
Autocar 20, 40, 52, 57, 85, 113, 170
Autodromo do Algave 90, 152
Automobile 52, 60, 127
Autoweek 52, 98

BBC 170
Beijing (Peking) Show 118, 119, 178
Bentley 46
Blume, Oliver 168
BMW 8, 21, 46, 57
Bohn, Arno 7
Bugatti 46
Burgess, Scott 123
Burn, Jonathan 135

Cackett, Nic 53
Cadillac 98
Car 138, 164
Car & Driver 52, 60, 90, 99, 153, 169, 170
Car Graphic 136
Catchpole, Henry 124
Citroën 51
Conway, Gavin 151, 153
Costello, Mike 135

Detroit Show 7, 13, 39
Dodge 98
Drive 135
Dürheimer, Wolfgang 46

Edig, Thomas 46
Esquire 60
Evo 90, 124

Ferrari 127
FIA 172
Fiat 21, 46
Ford 169
Frankel, Andrew 113
Frankfurt Show 9, 11, 15, 168

General Motors 21
Geneva Show 8, 47, 99, 119, 138, 178
Gomez, Carlos 177

Haerter, Holger 46
Hatz, Wolfgang 46
Honda 21

ItalDesign 46

Jurnecka, Rory 99

Kable, Greg 52, 53
Karmann 45, 46
Kaya, M M 177

Lagaay, Harm 7, 13
Laguna Seca 127
Lamborghini 46
Lanchester, F W 21
Land Rover 90
Larson, Grant 7, 13
Le Mans 175
Leimgruber, Wolfgang 46
Lethmate, Ronny 177
Los Angeles Show 17, 18, 82, 84, 90, 116, 172
Lotus 57

Macht, Michael 46
Magna Steyr 45
Mauer, Michael 21, 23
Mazda 8, 18, 21, 29, 59
Meaden, Dickie 90
Mercedes-Benz 8, 21, 22, 57, 59, 90, 175
Merkel, Angela 168
Mezger, Hans 46
Miller, Ben 164
Mortara, Scott 127
Motor Authority 112
Motor Trend 98, 99, 123, 127, 169
MotorSport 113
Müller, Matthias 46, 82, 168

Nakagawa, Tadashi 21
Neubauer, Alfred 22
New York Show 59, 138
Nürburgring 90, 117, 125, 139, 176-178

Opel 46

Paris Salon 9, 11, 15, 99
Piana, Gabriele 177
Porsche, Ferry 10

Porsche Museum 7, 24, 27, 29, 87, 120, 121, 142, 152
Potsch, Hans-Dieter 46
Preuninger, Andreas 143
Probst, Randy 99

Qatar Holding LLC 46

Road & Track 60, 112, 143, 169
Robinson, Hugh 21, 23
Röhrl, Walter 152
Roth, Jan 21, 119

San Jose Show 26
Scania 46
Schwab, Fred 7
SEAT 46
Sherman, Don 60
Skoda 46
Subaru 98
Sunday Times, The 151
Sutcliffe, Steve 91, 170
Suzuki 136

Tokyo Show 116
Top Gear 170
Toyota 21, 175

Valmet 10, 11, 15, 45
Volkswagen 9, 15, 28, 39, 46, 139, 168, 175
Von Platen, Detlev 59, 168, 170

Watson, Mat 124
Weckbach, Stefan 119
Wheels 90, 113, 170
Wiedeking, Wendelin 7, 8, 46
Winterkorn, Martin 45, 46, 168
World Car Awards 59, 98

Zellmer, Klaus 170
ZF 9, 38

The Porsche company is mentioned throughout this book, along with its products and subsidiaries.